BUILDING BLOCS

My Life in Dialogue and Development in Russia

John S. Reuther

DartFrog

301 S. McDowell St.
Suite 125-1625
Charlotte, NC 28204
www.DartFrogBooks.com

Table of Contents

Prologue

Late June, 1968

In the first weeks of summer 1968, my father hosted a delegation from the Soviet Union at our DC home. I was newly back from the California Democratic presidential primary in Los Angeles, and I was at loose ends. I was dejected, dispirited, and still reeling from the shock of Robert Kennedy's assassination. Nevertheless, I attended the gathering that my father had arranged.

Among the guests were individuals affiliated with Soviet trade unions. Dad was fully aware that their unions weren't like ours—they were part of the government. They didn't necessarily prioritize the workers' best interests, but my father, who at the time was the director of international relations for the United Auto Workers, believed in talking to everybody, so he invited them to our home for dinner.

There were maybe three or four guests that evening, including Harry Givorgian, a New York-based correspondent for *Trud*, the Soviet trade union journal. I peppered them with questions all night long, especially Harry. Harry had been to the house before—he'd been with us in April, just a few months earlier, when Martin Luther King was shot. We'd watched together from a rooftop as parts of DC went up in flames. That now seemed like a lifetime ago.

Harry already knew that my postgraduate studies focused on US-Soviet relations, and after responding to my barrage of questions as patiently as possible, he finally shook his head and sighed. "John, sitting here in Washington and reading books can only get you so far. It is a beginning, but it is only a beginning. If you want to become a Soviet specialist, you need firsthand experience. Come to Moscow. Learn the language, the history, the culture. Get to know the people."

I was still nodding in agreement when he added, "I can make that happen." Harry offered to arrange a year studying at Moscow State University. The council of trade unions would be my sponsor.

A year in Moscow sounded really appealing. To work on Bobby Kennedy's campaign, I had taken a leave of absence from my job at the Office of Economic Opportunity. After the assassination, I didn't know what I wanted to do, but I knew that I had no desire to go back to working for my government—not when it was diverting money from the War on Poverty and using it instead for the war in Vietnam.

After discussing Harry's offer at great length with my father, I decided to accept it. The decision to study in Moscow set the stage for everything that followed. It was the key that opened the door to the rest of my life.

CHAPTER 1

1943-1953

Roots

I come from a family of labor organizers who fought for social and economic justice for the working class and for civil rights, both here in the United States and around the world. My father was one of the Reuther brothers, influential leaders of the United Auto Workers (UAW) over many decades. Beginning in the 1930s, they made national headlines for taking on the American automobile industry—and winning. Always persistent, often stubborn, and sometimes hardnosed when fighting for workers' rights, they won a series of victories over the automakers that resulted in better working conditions and a higher standard of living for UAW members. They won not only higher wages but also safer working conditions, pension programs, cost of living increases, nondiscrimination policies, and healthcare coverage. These victories set the standard for other industries, improving the lives of blue-collar workers across the country.

(L to R: Uncle Roy, Uncle Walter and my father Victor Reuther, circa 1950s. Photo credit: Walter P. Reuther Library, Archives of Labor and Urban Affairs, Wayne State University)

From my father, Victor Reuther, I learned that my paternal great-grandfather was a Christian Socialist who left his native Germany in 1892. Fed up with centuries of wars, the church's tolerance of these wars, and the clergy's greater concern for the afterlife of their parishioners than for the miserable conditions they endured on earth, he immigrated with his family to the United States.

My grandfather, Valentine Reuther, settled in West Virginia and first found work in the iron and steel mills. He would eventually drive a horse-drawn beer wagon for a living, but his time in the mills led him to become a union organizer in the brewery that employed him. Having inherited his father's socialist views, Valentine was a union leader by the age of twenty-three. He also became a staunch supporter of Eugene V.

Debs and backed his quadrennial presidential campaigns from 1900 through 1920, the last of which Debs conducted while incarcerated. My father was six years old when Grandfather Valentine took him to visit Debs in the Moundsville, West Virginia penitentiary.

Child labor in West Virginia's coal mines was common practice at the time, and Valentine was most outspoken in his opposition. The Lutheran pastor in his hometown of Wheeling was staunchly and vocally anti-union. Grandfather Valentine found that unacceptable. My dad told me that one Sunday, he watched in astonishment as his father stood up beside him in church and called out the minister for his anti-labor views. That kind of direct confrontation with a man of the cloth never happened, certainly not during the Sunday sermon, and it scared Dad a lot. He feared that the roof would open, and that the entire pew full of Reuthers would be zapped by a bolt of God's vengeful lightning.

The incident ended the family's affiliation with the Lutheran Church. Grandfather Valentine resigned their membership and began holding weekly religious services at home. Like his father before him, he believed in the linkage between sacred and secular, so Sunday services were always accompanied by vigorous debates on the political and social issues of the day.

Those conversations were not just among the adults. Grandfather Valentine and his wife Anna had four sons—my father Victor (so-named because Victor was Eugene Debs' middle name), and my uncles Walter, Roy, and Theodore (Ted). The last Reuther offspring, daughter Christine, came along in 1923. She did not participate in these discussions, not because of her gender, but because she was too young. During the week, Grandfather assigned each of the boys a debate topic to discuss at the regular Sunday gathering. On Sunday morning, however, he often switched assignments—if my father had prepared to argue against child labor, he would now be instructed to advocate for it instead. In this way, the brothers gained insight into the pros and cons of a wide range of social, political, and religious issues, and it proved to be excellent training. As adults, when they did take a stand, not only were they effective in presenting and defending their point of view, they did so with an understanding of why others might disagree.

(L to R: Ted, Roy, Christine, Victor, and Walter in front of their home in Wheeling, WV in 1926. Photo credit: Walter P. Reuther Library, Archives of Labor and Urban Affairs, Wayne State University)

The Depression hit West Viriginia hard. Lured by Henry Ford's promise of $5 a day on the assembly lines—an unprecedented wage for unskilled work at the time—all of the brothers except Ted left Wheeling for Detroit in the late 1920s and early 1930s. As the oldest, Ted stayed behind to support their parents. He ultimately became a middle-management employee with Wheeling Steel, thus ensuring his place as the perpetual brunt of endless good-natured family jokes about being the only "white sheep" in the family.

True to family tradition, Walter, Roy, and Victor became very active in the Socialist Party once they got to Detroit. They began organizing workers, first in their own plant, and then on an industrywide basis. Of the three brothers, Walter became the best known and perhaps the most influential. The website of the Walter P. Reuther Library of Labor and Urban Affairs at Wayne State University in Detroit summarizes his impact well:

> *Reuther believed that the labor movement was a social movement, that unions had the power to improve the lives of all working-class Americans, and the potential to change the world for the betterment of all. As president of the UAW, Reuther supported the civil rights movement, environmental causes, public housing projects, and health care improvements. He also promoted international relations and political reform at the local, state and federal levels.*

When Walter was elected UAW president in 1947, my father and uncle were right by his side. Each brother had a specific sphere of responsibility. Walter was the leader and public face of the union. Uncle Roy played a key role in political, legislative, and civil rights action. My father specialized in international trade unionism, forging personal connections with labor movements overseas.

Dad also headed up the UAW's worker education efforts, speaking up for what were at the time radical points of view, including the idea of promoting women and minorities into union leadership. These were part of the bedrock principles and philosophy of life he had inherited from his own parents. In *The Brothers Reuther*, his memoir, Dad wrote that at the 1947 UAW national convention, Uncle Walter described Grandfather Valentine as a man "who indoctrinated his boys when they were pretty young and told them that the most important thing in the world to fight for was the other guy, the brotherhood of man, and the Golden Rule."

Dad continued this tradition in our own family, but my brother, sister and I received it less as indoctrination and more as firm but gentle guidance. We were raised to believe that our society should be inclusive, that our strength comes from exploring new ideas and cultures different from our own, and that we are only as strong and secure in life as the weakest among us.

We learned at least as much from watching our parents as we did from anything we were taught directly. Those observations included sitting between Mom and Dad at the dinner table as colorful, and at times heated, words flew between them. These fights were not about family matters, but about how to keep the UAW moving forward. My parents were mostly in agreement about what they were trying to achieve but argued about which strategies would work best to obtain the desired result.

At times it was like watching a tennis match, and my mother always held her own. Her maiden name was Sophie Goodlavich, and her parents had come to the US as teenagers from an area of Poland that later became Lithuania. Mom grew up in East Braintree, Massachusetts, working at shoe factories and other manual jobs, but education was always a priority. In her twenties, she enrolled in a Harvard extension program and took a train into Boston to attend class after her factory workday was over. She was quite progressive and raised money to support shipyard workers who were striking for better working conditions. Her activism caught the attention of a clergyman who had ties to Socialist party leader Norman Thomas. Thomas was so impressed that he arranged for Sophie to attend Brookwood Labor College in Katonah, New York.

At that time, Mom was running the bakery department at the local A&P market. When she told her supervisor that she was leaving to study at Brookwood, he warned her not to go, saying, "That's a Communist school."

Mom didn't know what a Communist was and asked him to explain. To do so, he gave her an analogy: "Under Communism, if you have a toothbrush and your friend doesn't, then you have to share your toothbrush with him." Mother decided to attend Brookwood anyway but packed two toothbrushes when she left home. She hid the one she used in a drawer under some clothing. The other she displayed prominently in a glass on top of her dresser—for the Communists.

She met Victor when he and his brothers were lecturing at Brookwood in 1936. They were married in July of that year. My sister Carole was born in 1939. My brother Eric was born in 1942. I came along in December of 1943.

(Victor and Sophie in their first apartment in 1937. Photo credit: Walter P. Reuther Library, Archives of Labor and Urban Affairs, Wayne State University)

(Dad, mom, Carole, me and Eric. Photo credit: Walter P. Reuther Library, Archives of Labor and Urban Affairs, Wayne State University)

The Dangers of Being a Reuther

When he became UAW president, Uncle Walter surely had rivals within the union hierarchy, but his most dangerous adversaries sat across from him at the bargaining table. The auto companies, desperate to keep the UAW out of their factories, hired professional union-busting thugs, and no tactics were off-limits.

Including murder. On Tuesday, April 20, 1948, Uncle Walter returned home after dark. He usually parked behind his modest house on Detroit's west side, but on this particular evening he parked in front. That random decision saved his life.

Someone with a shotgun was lying in wait in his backyard and surely would have killed him had he parked back there. Even so, it was a close call. Walter's wife, May, was also in the house when the would-be assassin fired through the kitchen window just as Walter was opening the refrigerator. Several slugs went into the refrigerator door; the rest struck him in the torso and biceps, shattering his right arm above the elbow. One shot was a through-and-through, entering his back and exiting his stomach. Uncle Walter survived, but his arm was permanently damaged, and he needed weeks of rehab before he could resume his leadership responsibilities.

A little over a year later, it happened again—except this time, my father was the target. On May 24, 1949, he was sitting in his easy chair reading a newspaper when someone fired a double-barreled shotgun through our living room window. Most of the ammo whizzed just over Dad's head, making a crater in the wall along the stairs, but the rest hit him in the chest and face, breaking his collarbone and taking out his right eye.

My sister Carole, then ten, was awakened by the noise, and ran downstairs to find Dad lying on the floor in a pool of blood. Mother ran out into the street, screaming for help, and one of our neighbors called the police and an ambulance. This neighbor then comforted Carole, who was badly shaken by what she had seen, and took her back to their home, where she stayed the night. Mom went to the hospital to be with Dad, and another neighbor came to remain with Eric and me overnight.

Both of us slept through the entire incident. We only learned of it when Mom and the neighbor woke us the next morning. Eric and I dressed quickly and went downstairs to find plainclothes detectives swarming over our living room. There was a large bloodstain on the carpet near where Dad had been sitting. "Look, John. Blood!" Eric exclaimed.

"Oh no," one of the detectives responded. "That's red wine that was spilled."

Even at age seven, Eric wasn't having it. "You can't fool us," he replied quickly. "We know that's blood."

There is strong reason to believe that the hitman had been hired by the automakers, and that members of the Detroit PD were paid to look the other way. No suspects were questioned or arrested. After one of our neighbors told police he could describe the shooter, he began getting threatening phone calls, telling him to shut up or else.

Realizing that the police were making no effort to solve the crime, the union tried to bring in the FBI. As Dad described it in *The Brothers Reuther*:

> *A number of congressmen and cabinet members urged the FBI to enter the case. UAW lawyers Irving Levy and Joseph L. Rauh Jr. were instructed to approach Attorney General Tom Clark to seek his help in involving the FBI. Clark was most sympathetic and said he would talk with J. Edgar Hoover and let them know the next day. Joe Rauh remembers Clark's exact words: "Fellows, Edgar says no. He says he's not going to send the FBI in every time some nigger woman gets raped."*

There was a lot of press coverage about the shooting, but Mom did her best to shield us kids from reporters whenever we visited Dad in the hospital. My father recovered, but he lost his right eye and carried bullet fragments and shards of glass in his head from his shattered eyeglasses for the rest of his life.

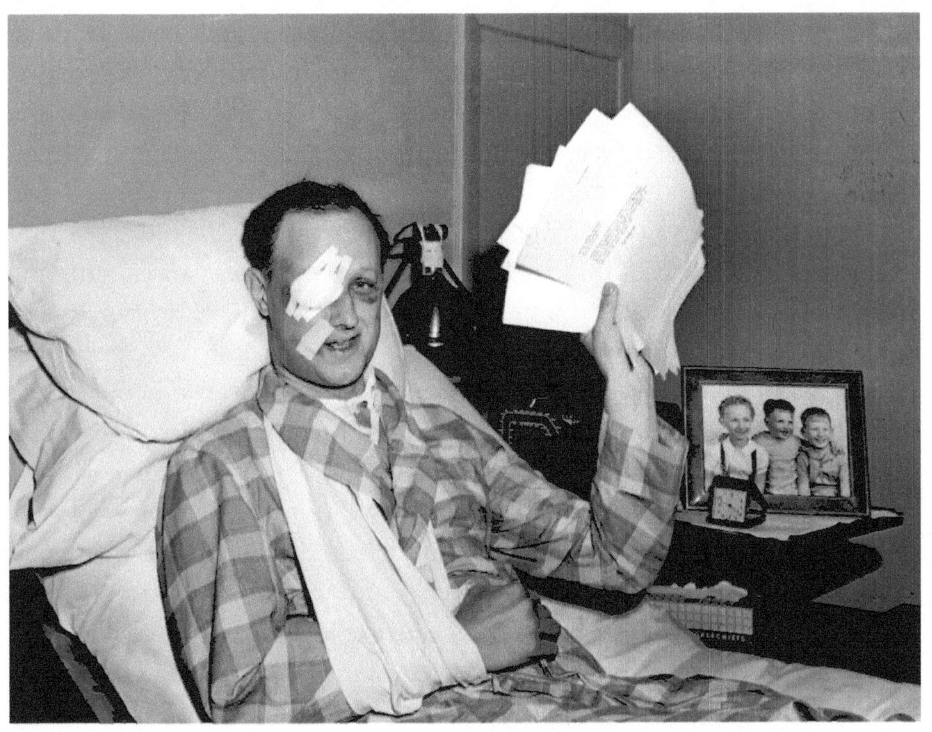

*(Dad in the hospital holding up letters from well-wishers, with a photo
of us by his side. Photo credit: Walter P. Reuther Library, Archives
of Labor and Urban Affairs, Wayne State University)*

Daily life changed dramatically after the attack. There were physical
modifications to the house: thick bulletproof glass on the ground floor
windows, and bulletproof steel venetian blinds on the windows that
looked out on the two streets of our corner home. We got a boxer as a
guard dog, and a tall wire fence was installed around our yard.

No family member was ever alone. Three bodyguards were on duty
around the clock. They even picked up Carole, Eric and me at school.
These men were dedicated and trusted UAW associates, not hired professional security personnel. Whether at home or in public, Dad was
always armed—he wore a .38 in a shoulder holster under his arm. Mom
was packing, too. She tucked her own .38 into her apron pocket when
she took out the trash.

She wasn't happy about it. Mom became increasingly stressed about living in what felt like a maximum-security prison—something had to give.

The UAW came up with a solution. Through its membership in the Congress of Industrial Organizations (CIO), it actively encouraged participation in the newly formed International Confederation of Free Trade Unions (ICFTU) in postwar Europe. When Dad was offered the position of director of the CIO office in Paris, he accepted. It was an exciting job opportunity, but it was also a chance for our family to leave our security-constrained life behind.

In May of 1951, we left Detroit for New York, where we boarded the French passenger liner SS *Liberté* and set sail for Le Havre. Newly promoted from guard dog to family pet, Taffy the boxer made the trip with us.

Brother Eric was nine and I was seven, and we became great explorers during our five-day Atlantic crossing. Freed from bodyguards and chaperones, we regularly snuck out of third class and up into first class. On one escapade, we went in search of Taffy's kennel. Another adventure yielded an unexpected celebrity sighting. We were standing on the first-class deck one brisk and breezy evening when the cabin-area doors swung open and out walked Humphrey Bogart and Lauren Bacall. Never one to be shy, Eric walked right up to Bogart and asked for his autograph. He gladly complied, as did Ms. Bacall. All too soon, however, the wind coming off the Atlantic got the better of them. "Let's go back inside," Bogie said to his wife. "It's cold out here!"

Cold? *Cold*?? Whether it was because we were so excited to be there or because we were at that age when your lips could be blue but you didn't feel a thing, Eric and I were completely unfazed by the weather. Nevertheless, the two Hollywood superstars quickly retreated back inside, taking with them my image of Bogart as the invincible rugged hero.

Life in France

We rented a house in Enghien-les-Bains, a town about eight miles outside of Paris. The "Bains" in the name refers to a well-known resort spa built atop the town's natural hot springs; there was also a popular casino and a beautiful lake where Eric and I caught frogs. In our first year, all three of us kids took intensive language instruction together. The second year we split up and went to our separate grade levels at the Lycée Claude-Bernard, a regular public school. All classes there were taught in French, but that wasn't the only adjustment. In Detroit, we had written in pencil and printed each word. At the lycée, students wrote in cursive and in ink, even for math, dipping our pens into the inkwells that were recessed in a hole on each desk.

(At school in France)

Fitting in socially wasn't easy; in fact, I never did. I was the classic outsider, and my best friend was another foreign student whose family lived in a very modest house that lacked running water. At the time, I thought that he was Russian, but from his name, Fedorenko, I now believe he was probably from Ukraine. The two of us bonded over our struggles with French. Whenever we made mistakes in class, which was often, the punishment was physical. Our teacher struck our palms with a cubic ruler, which resembled a long, square rod. Because Fedorenko's errors were more frequent and more grievous than mine, she took to lifting the pant leg of his shorts and striking him with the ruler on his exposed derrière.

Somewhere I still have my report cards, and my teacher's comments were all variations on the same disappointed theme: "John is not doing well. I hope for improvement next time." I think she was quite pleased and more than a little relieved when she learned I would be returning to the States. On my last report card, she wrote a conciliatory note to my parents and added that at long last I was doing much better in French. In a way, it was her going-away present to me.

Perhaps the greatest gift of living in Enghien-les-Bains was that it taught me how to love travel. As a family, we took car trips all over France. Some of our adventures were comic. We were hopelessly lost in the French countryside when Dad spotted a policeman and asked him for directions. He and my mother listened very carefully to his response, but apparently their French was not much better than mine. As Dad drove away, he looked at Mom and asked, "Did you understand what he said?"

"Didn't he have the most beautiful brown eyes!" she responded.

On a Christmas trip to Algiers, we took a side trip to a town called Bou Saada. Our trade union hosts had invited my father to a nightclub and seemed surprised when he showed up with his wife and kids. The evening's entertainment consisted of some very covered-up women performing a rather boring sword dance, and I've always suspected that both their costumes and their choreography would have been a lot more risqué if Dad had left the rest of us back at the hotel.

On a more serious trip, we went to Germany, where we toured the Dachau concentration camp. Our guide was a US military officer who had helped liberate the camp. He showed us the ovens and said that some of the prisoners were not yet dead when they were cremated. Eric brought home a brochure called "Lest We Forget." Once you've been there, the memory of what you've seen stays with you. Forgetting is not possible.

Many of our trips were connected to Dad's work forging relationships with labor leaders in various European countries. We visited South Wales and stayed with Aneurin "Nye" Bevan, a Labour Party member of Parliament who had been minister of health under Clement Atlee. It was Bevan who spearheaded the campaign to establish the UK's National Health Service, which still provides medical care for all British citizens. Jennie Lee, Nye's wife, was a Labour Party leader and activist in her own right. After his death, she became minister of the arts in Harold Wilson's cabinet.

It was only much later that I understood that Aneurin Bevan and Jennie Lee were people of great integrity and accomplishment. At the time, I saw them through a kid's eyes—to me they were just Nye and Jennie on their farm in South Wales.

CHAPTER 2

1953-1958

Returning Stateside

We left France in August of 1953, but we didn't return to Detroit. We moved to Washington, DC instead, where Dad was to become the UAW's director of international affairs. While looking for a home there, we initially stayed at the home of our close family friend and labor attorney, Arthur Goldberg. Arthur eventually became secretary of labor under JFK, then was named to the Supreme Court, and finally became LBJ's UN ambassador.

Mom and Dad bought a three-story brick home in the Cleveland Park area of northwest DC, just a few blocks from Phoebe Hearst School, where I started fifth grade. Missing two years of schooling in the US left me way behind my classmates in spelling and grammar, but my teacher, Mrs. Webb, understood the learning gaps I faced.

(At home in Cleveland Park)

My sixth-grade teacher, Mrs. Dodge, lacked Mrs. Webb's warmth and compassion. She had very little patience with me, probably because of my slowness in class, but it's also possible that she was not a fan of labor unions or liberal Democrats. I was especially terrible at spelling, and it seemed to me that she took special delight in pointing out my mistakes to the rest of the class.

One day, I brought her a note from Dad, asking that I be excused early to join him at a gathering with President Eisenhower. My teacher read the note to herself, and then announced to the entire class, "Even his father can't spell. He misspelled President Eisenhower's name!"

Eric and I often played in the woods near our house. We built forts and shot our BB guns at birds and other targets. This expansive wooded area was adjacent to a large, stately home. We didn't know who lived there, but we knew enough to stay away from the house.

One snowy day, we brought some small firecrackers with us into the woods. We made snowballs, inserted the firecrackers, lit them, and threw them as far as we could. When our arms got tired, we headed for home. As we were leaving, a man in a suit stepped in front of us and opened his jacket. He then removed a handgun and pointed at us. "Hold it right there!" he said sternly. "Where is your gun?!"

Eric sheepishly reached into his pockets, took out the last of the firecrackers, and held them out in front of him for the man to inspect. Seeing what they were, he holstered his weapon and ordered us to follow him.

He marched us to Wisconsin Avenue, up the driveway of the old stone house, and into a basement office. After interrogating us closely, he explained that we had been setting off firecrackers on the property of the "very important person" who lived there. As a member of the man's security detail, he had thought the explosions were gunshots. Without identifying the VIP, he took our names, address, and phone number, and called our parents. Once he verified who we were, he let us go. Only after we got home did Dad tell us that the man who lived in the house was CIA Director Allen Dulles, brother of Secretary of State John Foster Dulles.

As UAW director of international affairs, Dad was away more than he was home, which meant that Mom was functionally a single parent for much of our childhood. We missed Dad a lot, but he always tried to make up for his absences in some way. On a return flight from Europe in 1956, he was delighted to find that his seatmate was the popular comedian and movie star Danny Kaye. They talked their way across the Atlantic, and when Kaye appeared in concert in DC soon thereafter, he left us house seats for the performance and made a special point of acknowledging us in the audience. I was delighted to meet him backstage after the show.

Among our closest friends in Washington were Joe Rauh and his wife Olie. They lived close by, and Eric and I often swam in their pool on summer Sundays. Joe had been one of the lawyers who tried to get the FBI to investigate the assassination attempt in Detroit—but like Nye Bevan, I knew him as a family friend without being aware of how brilliant and well connected he was. Magna cum laude in economics as a Harvard undergrad and first in his class at Harvard Law, Joe had clerked at the Supreme Court for both Benjamin Cardozo and Felix Frankfurter and had become one of the preeminent attorneys in Washington.

When playwright Arthur Miller was subpoenaed by the infamous House Un-American Activities Committee (HUAC), he retained Joe to represent him. On the day Miller testified before the committee in June of 1956, Joe was with him, of course, but he was also accompanied by his fiancée, Marilyn Monroe. The couple got married eight days later, and although Eric and I never met either of them face-to-face, we knew they had stayed with Joe and Olie while they were in DC. That next Sunday, Eric and I made every effort to ascertain exactly where Marilyn Monroe had sat on the edge of Joe's pool. Then we took turns sitting in that same spot, hoping some of the glamor and mystique would transfer from her backside to ours.

When school started up again after the summer, it was time to select a foreign language to study. My unpleasant memories of struggling with French were so strong that I chose Latin instead. It was a mistake. I was at least a "C" student in most subjects, but I flunked Latin. After belatedly switching to French, my self-esteem got a boost when I was quickly promoted into Honors French. At the lycée in Enghien-les-Bains, my French had been deemed mediocre or worse, but here at home I was considered far more advanced than most of my fellow students.

Both my interest in my studies and my GPA improved dramatically when I took biology. My teacher was a woman I'd known since elementary school. She'd been the den mother of a sister troop of Girl Scouts—my Boy Scout troop often had joint functions with them. She was a kind and friendly human being; more than anyone else, she was the person responsible for my finally becoming a strong student. With her encouragement, I always chose the most difficult questions on the bio oral exams. I wanted to excel because she had mastered the ability to both challenge me and, at the same time, reassure me that I could do it.

I was doing so well and feeling so fulfilled by my studies that I thought I'd found my calling. I announced to my parents that I was going to become a career scientist and convinced them to let me install a chemistry lab in the basement. We'd already done the classic electrolysis experiment in school, running an electric current through a beaker of water (H_2O) to separate it into its two components, hydrogen (H) and oxygen (O). I thought I'd try a similar experiment at home, but with a different substance—table salt ($NaCl$).

I created a small brick oven where I thought I'd be able to heat the salt to a high enough temperature that it would liquefy. The plan was to pass an electrical current through the molten salt to separate the sodium (Na) from the chlorine (Cl). To heat the salt, I created an electric arc by attaching electrical cords to carbon rods from flashlight batteries, all of this plugged into a 110-volt outlet! I touched the rods together, then separated them slightly to produce an arc of current, but it wasn't hot enough to melt the salt. The first time I tried it, I wore sunglasses to protect my eyes during the experiment, but when I repeated it for a friend, I gave him the glasses and watched without any protection.

That night I awoke with searing pain in my eyes. Mom got me to the hospital. I had pretty much fried my corneas. To treat my corneal flash burns, the doctors applied antibiotic ointment to both eyes, then covered them with gauze bandages. Still more gauze was wound around my head to hold the bandages in place. It wasn't Halloween, but I was well on my way to looking like a mummy that belonged in the local haunted house.

I couldn't see a thing, and I had to stay that way for about three days. Dad had been away when it happened, but I was still bandaged up when he returned home. Seeing me like that was triggering. He'd lost an eye during the assassination attempt, and his father, Grandfather Valentine, had lost an eye when a warm bottle of ginger ale exploded while he was lifting it into the icebox. Dad feared that there was some kind of Reuther family curse that had been visited on me. Fortunately, when the bandages were removed a few days later, my eyeballs were intact, and I regained full sight with no limitations or further pain.

After that, my parents reinforced the need for us to think carefully about the consequences our actions might have on our physical health, but most of their teaching involved ethics and moral integrity. Eric, Carole, and I were taught to do the right thing—even if it was difficult, even if we stood alone, even if no one ever said thank you—and the expectation from Mom and Dad was that each of us would follow suit.

Not that we always did. My brother Eric was recruited to join Pi Delta, an exclusive high school fraternity whose members included football players and other popular guys at Wilson High. Mom and Dad were not happy about his membership—fraternities had a long history of prejudice, discrimination, and exclusion—but they also knew it was important for Eric to have close friends and a sense of belonging.

Periodically, the Pi Delts would have joint fraternity-sorority parties. Drinking was often involved. One party took place at the home of a girl whose father was a sitting congressman. Some of the guys got drunk, went into the garage, opened a bag of fertilizer/cow manure and dumped it into the congressman's fancy car. Not surprisingly, he became irate and shut down the party. He also demanded that the fraternity pay for the damage. By this time, Eric was president of the frat, and the members voted to have him reimburse the congressman, but to do so in pennies. And he did.

The incident had several repercussions, including a formal debate at Wilson High about whether to continue to allow fraternities and sororities at school. Eric was chosen to speak in favor; the senior class president spoke against. Both were then invited to repeat this debate on *Teen Talk,* a local TV show. As soon as Eric got home from the studio, Mom and Dad sat him down to discuss it. The bottom line was that they were horrified. So were many of their progressive friends and colleagues.

When I started at Wilson in 1959, my parents were adamant that I stay away from fraternities, especially Pi Delta. This was a problem, since I already knew a bunch of the brothers. Eric and I were only two years apart in age, so I'd hung out with them when he was a member. He'd already graduated and gone on to college when I was invited to join. My parents told me it was out of the question, but I secretly pledged anyway. I don't know how I could have so blatantly disobeyed them. I must have rationalized that these were my close friends and teammates and succumbed to peer pressure.

Pi Delta meetings were held on Friday nights and we convened at a different member's home each week. I always was honest with my parents in telling them in advance where I would be; I just neglected to mention that I'd be attending a fraternity meeting. One Friday afternoon, Mom ran into the mother of one of my friends. During the conversation, my friend's mother mentioned that their two sons would be seeing each other at Russell's house that evening for the Pi Delta meeting. Mom quickly replied that she must be mistaken, since I was not a member. My friend's mother shook her head. I was surely a member of Pi Delta, she said, and she knew this because I'd attended frat meetings in her own home.

Busted.

When Mom confronted me, I confessed, admitting that not only was I a member, but that I'd also been elected vice president.

What happened next says a great deal about the values my parents lived by and imparted to us at every opportunity. Almost any other parent would have pulled me out of the fraternity, both for joining it in the first place and also for lying about it. Not Sophie Goodlavich Reuther. For her, this was a teaching moment. She decided that we were going to change Pi Delta into a force for good—and we did. To raise money for a local orphanage, the fraternity began sponsoring bake sales at Wilson High, and even our beefy Pi Delta football players became willing participants.

CHAPTER 3

1958-1962

Teen Summers

A key part of our family education was learning how to earn a living, and that started with getting a summer job. I was fourteen in 1958 when I spent my first summer working at the Pottstown Community Boys and Girls camp in Reading, Pennsylvania, about an hour northwest of Philadelphia. I showed up expecting to spend the summer washing dishes in the camp kitchen, but when one of their counselors was a no-show, I was promoted from scullery duty to fill the position.

Each counselor lived in a cabin with six to eight campers. Since working with the youngest campers required more experience than I had, I was assigned to the cabin with the oldest boys, some of whom were older than I was. It was a great Tom Sawyer-like first summer job. We swam and fished a lot in a local river, and while there, I earned Red Cross Advanced Swimmer and Lifeguard certificates.

Later that fall, Eric and I both achieved Pioneer status in a local scuba diving club. To get our certificates, we trained in flooded stone quarries in Maryland, but our first introduction to underwater diving had taken place when we were living in France. On a vacation trip to Corsica, we had donned masks, snorkels and flippers for the first time. I loved it instantly, and it was the beginning of my lifelong interest in marine biology.

(Eric and me with our catch after fishing in Lake Michigan)

I was sixteen in the summer of 1960 when a colleague of Dad's got me a job in the Poconos. I was a waiter at Kutay's Riverside Resort, a group of twelve rustic cabins along the Delaware River near Bushkill, Pennsylvania. The clients of the resort were elderly Jewish couples who had been coming there every summer for years. Since there were only two of us waiting tables, we didn't have any days off, but we were allowed to swim in the river during whatever free time we had.

One day after lunch, I was snorkeling with my mask and flippers. Across the river was a summer camp that offered water skiing lessons, and because sound really travels underwater, I hadn't realized that a speedboat towing a skier had swerved into Kutay's swimming area. Desperate for air after a long period underwater, I surfaced right in front of the boat. The bow struck my head, shoving me back underwater, and the propeller made slices in my left arm as I sank.

I lost consciousness briefly, and as I came to, I realized I was headed straight for the bottom of the river. I distinctly remember thinking, "My God, if I don't do something, I'm going to die!" My legs started kicking, and I rose to the surface.

The driver had felt the bump and had already circled back to see what he'd hit. Apparently, he was relieved that it wasn't a rock—I heard him call out to the skier behind him, who was now in the water, "It's only a swimmer! It's okay!"

Except I wasn't okay, not in the slightest. Blood was gushing from my forehead and from the deep gashes in my left arm. I must have been in shock, because I set off barefoot for the shore across a shallow area that was full of shells and sharp stones. It should have been painful, but my feet didn't feel a thing.

I was still dripping wet as one of the resort guests helped me into his car to drive me to the nearby hospital. Elderly Mrs. Kutay got in the back seat with me and soon offered to take off her dress and cover me with it to keep me warm, an offer I politely declined. We were met at the emergency room door by a nurse with a wheelchair; I was to be taken straight into surgery. Mrs. Kutay walked beside me all the way down the corridor, and kept repeating, "Now remember, John, if the doctor asks you, your day off is Thursday." If I'd somehow let it slip that I didn't have any days off, it would have been a violation of Pennsylvania law, and that would have caused problems for her business.

The surgeon put eight stitches in my arm and twenty-one in my head. He also sewed up the torn artery that was gushing just beneath my scalp. The issue of days off never came up, but he did tell me that this was the third time he'd operated on a patient who'd been struck by a boat. "You're the first one to survive!" he said proudly.

This accident happened in July 1960, and Mom and Dad were traveling abroad for international labor meetings. I didn't want to worry them while they were overseas, so I deliberately omitted this news from the letters I sent them. I suppose I should have known that my injury was too big a secret to keep. After someone from the UAW got a message to them while they were in Israel, they put through an urgent, international call to Kutay's Resort to speak with me. At that time, international calls were a rarity, and very expensive. You can imagine the reaction of our Jewish guests during lunch when an international call came through to the dining room—from Israel—and it was for me, the *goyishe* waiter!

Early Political Involvement

I was born into a political family and a political household. From the time we got back from France, Washington leaders and elected officials—almost all of them Democrats—were frequent visitors and callers to our home. In spring of 1961, a lot of the buzz had to do with the disastrous Bay of Pigs invasion. This military operation had been planned in the waning days of the Eisenhower administration. When put into action, it was a colossal failure on every level. About 1,200 members of the invading force, many of them Cuban exiles, had been captured and were now being held in Castro's jails.

President Kennedy, who'd only been in office for three months at the time, regretted having greenlighted the operation. Taking responsibility for his error in judgment, he called Uncle Walter and asked him to help organize a group that became known as the Tractors for Freedom Committee. The purpose of the committee was to raise money to buy agricultural machinery. The plan was to ransom the POWs with tractors, plows, and combines that would be sent to Cuba in exchange for the imprisoned men.

Former First Lady Eleanor Roosevelt and Dr. Milton Eisenhower, President Eisenhower's brother, were among the committee leaders. When Uncle Walter called Dad to ask for his participation, I answered the phone and stayed on the line to listen as he discussed the details of his conversation with JFK. I knew that Kennedy had insisted that his involvement remain a secret, at least at the outset.

With Dad and Mom's encouragement, I organized a chapter of Tractors for Freedom at Wilson High, and we started raising money. I probably should have expected that there would be considerable pushback at school about doing anything that would benefit Fidel Castro. The school administration became so concerned that banning us was a real possibility, but as soon as Kennedy went public with his support, they permitted us to continue. As it turned out, the organization itself was short-lived. The committee disbanded when it was determined that Castro's demands were more like extortion than ransom. At Wilson, we returned any individual donations we could trace by name and donated everything else to local charities.

(Counting the Tractors for Freedom donations)

Shocking Family News

After he graduated from Wilson High, Eric began his college studies at Wesleyan University in Middletown, Connecticut. It was January of 1961, and he'd just returned there after Christmas break, when I was awakened in the middle of the night by the insistent ringing of the doorbell, followed by a lot of pounding on the front door. It was really cold, so I grabbed what I thought was my robe and went down to see who was at the door at this ungodly hour.

It was Eric. "What are you doing back from college?" I asked.

"John," he replied, "what are you doing with a pair of pants around your shoulders?"

My issue was much easier to deal with than his. Toni House, Eric's girlfriend, had also graduated from Wilson High and was now a student at Hollins University, a women's college in Roanoke, Virginia. She'd just told Eric that she was pregnant, and that they would have to get married.

Eric knew he had to tell Mom and Dad as soon as possible, but this was not the kind of news you break over the phone. He'd come back to DC to do it in person. Standing in the foyer, it took a minute for me to wrap my brains around the situation—my brother was going to be a father, and I was going to be an uncle—then the two of us went upstairs to wake our parents and have the conversation.

Mom and Dad got up and we all went downstairs, made coffee, and held a family conference around the dining room table. We continued our discussion at breakfast, with Mom turning to me in conclusion and saying, "By God, John, when you go to college, we're going to put a lock on your fly!"

Summer and the Sterns

To line up a job for me for the summer of 1961, Mom and Dad invited one of their friends—Mrs. Helen B. "Leni" Stern—to our home. Mrs. Stern was looking for a babysitter/camp counselor to live with her large family and several additional kids at their summer home on Martha's Vineyard. As Mom left her to talk with me in the living room, the very beautiful Mrs. Stern, who reminded me of Doris Day, kicked off her shoes, folded her legs under her on the couch, and proceeded to tell me what would be expected of me if I took the job.

The plan was for me to drive three of their four children—Henry, Michael, and Holly—in the family VW Microbus from their home in Alexandria, Virginia to Woods Hole, Massachusetts. From there, we'd take the ferry to Vineyard Haven on the island.

For me, it was a dream job. I'd have my own living quarters in a suite above their stand-alone garage and spend my days keeping the kids occupied with swimming, games, and excursions. Since there was a cook/housekeeper on premises, as well as a nanny for their youngest son, David, I'd have evenings and Sundays free.

Leni's husband, Philip M. Stern, was an affluent liberal Democratic Party activist, philanthropist, and author. He'd been born into great wealth—his grandfather, Julius Rosenwald, was a man whose business acumen catapulted a little dry goods store into a retail behemoth called Sears, Roebuck.

The family fortune didn't make him conservative—far from it. Phil Stern and Dad were close colleagues in the fight for social and economic justice. Phil was also one of the owners and the editor of the *Arlington Sun* and would go on to write a number of very powerful books warning against the insidious power of private money in politics.

At the time Leni offered me the job, Phil was the deputy assistant secretary of state for public affairs in the Kennedy administration. During the summer, he spent Monday through Friday in DC before joining his family on Martha's Vineyard every weekend. He would often commute to Massachusetts with JFK himself, who flew as often as he could to the Kennedy compound at Hyannis Port on Cape Cod. Because there was regular ferry service from Hyannis to the Vineyard, getting to Lambert's Cove, where the Stern summer home was located, was easy.

It was a Friday evening late in the school year when Phil and Leni invited me to their home in the DC suburb of Alexandria, Virginia to meet their children and to familiarize myself with their VW Microbus. I got along great with the kids, but I had to somewhat awkwardly confess that driving the VW might be a bit of a challenge. At seventeen, I'd had my license for a year, but I had no experience whatsoever with a stick shift.

"No problem," said Phil as he tossed me the keys. My assignment was to drive the VW home to Cleveland Park and practice over the weekend. It was a true baptism by fire. The VW and I both survived but learning to drive a stick-shift vehicle while navigating DC's brutal rush-hour traffic is not an experience I recommend.

The daylong drive from DC to Woods Hole was quite the road trip. For starters, it was noisy—in addition to the Stern children, I was chauffeuring several of their friends, as well. Once we settled in, the Sterns encouraged me to use my imagination in thinking up activities for the kids and their playmates. I had permission to use their open account at the local general store to purchase anything I needed to develop recreational and educational activities for the kids. Phil was interested in underwater diving and knew I had a diving certificate, so we did some scuba diving in the waters in front of their house. He was delighted with my spearfishing in nearby Lake Tashmoo, which was accessible to us by their speedboat from the Vineyard Sound, and I was proud to bring home some large striped bass for dinner.

They wanted their kids to be kids during the summer and didn't mind at all when I bought some lumber, rope, and plastic sheeting to make an enormous, waterproof kite that could be pulled behind their speedboat, allowing us to soar a bit above the water while water skiing. They didn't even object to my taking evening dates by speedboat to a local bar across the Vineyard Sound, and sometimes for nighttime swimming in Lake Tashmoo. However, Phil was not at all pleased when he arrived one weekend to discover that I had used a chainsaw purchased at the local hardware store to cut down a number of trees on their large property to build a log cabin fort for the kids to play in. He didn't mind the expense or the idea of a fort, but he quickly made me understand that cutting down trees on the property was not allowed.

The only other time I got in trouble was when I took the kids to swim in Lake Tashmoo. We usually went by boat, but this time we took the VW bus, which meant I had to find a road or driveway that would lead us to the shore. I found one, but it was marked "Private Road. No Public Access."

Probably because the area looked so isolated, I ignored it and was soon parked alongside a pier where a large sailboat was docked. I didn't see anyone around, so I walked past the boat to the end of the pier with the Stern kids and several of their playmates, all laughing and screaming with delight as they jumped into the water. I stood next to what I learned later was the *Mary Ann*, a forty-three-foot motorless Chesapeake Bay bugeye ketch, keeping my eyes on the kids and calling out to them if they got too far from the pier.

All too soon we were not the only ones there. Legendary actor James Cagney emerged from the cabin of the *Mary Ann*, walked right up to me, and said to me in a voice that anyone would have recognized from one of his gangster movies, "You didn't see the sign?"

"Well, yes, I-I-I did," I stammered.

"Didn't mean a thing to you, did it?"

Remembering the many scenes of Cagney pulling out a pistol and filling people full of slugs, I got the kids out of the water and into the VW as fast as I could.

With my growing interest in biology and my fascination with underwater diving, there was no way I was going to spend the summer on Martha's Vineyard and not visit the Woods Hole Oceanographic Institution, which was just a short ferry ride from Vineyard Haven. Leni decided to join me with the kids on the visit, and as we were standing on the deck enjoying the view, she handed me David, her youngest son, to hold for a while.

The timing couldn't have been worse. I'd just made eye contact with a beautiful blonde named Gayle Pope. We struck up a conversation, but it was clear that she assumed the infant in my arms was my own, handed to me by my wife. As soon as I told Leni about this missed opportunity, she took David from my arms and sent me off to go find her.

I located Gayle at the bow of the boat and lost no time explaining to her that Leni was not my wife and that David was not my child—and that this was my summer job. We struck up a friendship, exchanging addresses and phone numbers, which led to Gayle inviting me to spend a weekend at her family's home in Wellesley later that summer. When summer ended, Gayle came to visit me at our family home in Washington, during which time my father—who was an excellent amateur photographer—took some great photos of her. In 1962, Gayle used those photos to enter the Miss Massachusetts beauty pageant, which she won. It was the beginning of her highly successful modeling career. She appeared on the covers of *Vogue*, *Cosmopolitan*, and other magazines.

I spent the summers of both '61 and '62 on Martha's Vineyard taking care of the Stern children. It always felt more like vacation than work, and I became very close to the kids and to both Phil and Leni, who always made me feel like a member of their family.

I still have the notes they wrote me, one in June of 1961 and the other in August of 1962. Together they bookend the time I spent working for them, one of the happiest times of my life.

The first one was apparently typed by Phil on the eve of my first trip in the Microbus from DC to the Vineyard.

> *Dear John—*
>
> *This is just a quick note to wish you well on your trip tomorrow, and to tell you how very happy we are that you will be a part of our family this summer... If you should have any difficulties or problems of any sort, please feel that you can take either or both of us into your confidence. We will be as responsive and as understanding as we possibly can. Above all else, please know that we have great faith in you, and that we look forward to the summer with you as one of the star roles! Children are precious possessions, and we believe that you will give to them some of your own good values. This is something which makes us happy and grateful.*
>
> *Fondly,*
> *The Sterns*

The second was handwritten by Leni and given to me at the end of my second summer with them.

> *Dear John—*
>
> *It's hard to put into words what your being with us for another summer has meant to the whole family. You have, in a way, become a very real member of our family, and we shall miss you in a million different ways. Our blessings go with you, and we wish you luck in whatever you undertake to achieve in this wonderful world. We believe in you, and we love you very much! Bon Voyage!*
>
> *With great affection and thanks,*
> *Leni and Phil Stern*

I couldn't think of a better, more uplifting way to set off for the next chapter of my life: college.

CHAPTER 4

1962-1964

Freshman Year at Cornell

I had really struggled academically in high school at first, but I began to excel in my junior and senior years. I was also active in student government—president of our sophomore class—and I played football. With my grades and my extracurricular activities, I had several really good options when it came to attending college. One was Wesleyan University, where Eric was studying. Another was Dartmouth—their football scouts had watched one of our high school games and saw me intercept a pass for a touchdown. I was tempted, but Jon Stanat, my best friend and fellow science buddy, planned to attend Cornell. I applied there and was accepted into their School of Agriculture.

Why agriculture? Primarily because that's where I could major in marine biology, but another huge advantage was financial. Cornell is a private, Ivy League university, which means it's pricey, but tuition at the School of Agriculture was underwritten in part by the state of New York.

An intensive, science-oriented first semester had me starting to reconsider whether a love of scuba diving was a good enough reason to major in marine biology, and the October 1962 Cuban missile crisis increased my uncertainty. It intensified my already strong interest in politics and world affairs, as well as my feelings of patriotism—so much so that I considered dropping out of college and enlisting in the Marines.

With my interest and career goals shifting away from marine biology, it seemed to me that my best option was to transfer within Cornell to the College of Liberal Arts & Sciences. I checked in with my parents, who were understandably concerned about being able to afford the extra tuition that would come with the transfer. I also spoke with an English professor, who told me that the value of undergraduate studies was not in what subject matter you studied, but in learning how to think criti-cally, and how to express yourself. Specialization in a particular area of academic interest, he said, would come in grad school.

My parents were already paying for Eric's tuition at Wesleyan in addi-tion to my own, and they'd already paid for my sister's Carole's college education. Not wanting to burden them further, instead of transferring to the College of Liberal Arts & Sciences, I transferred instead to Cornell's School of Industrial & Labor Relations (ILR), which, like the College of Agriculture, was state supported. Making the switch at the beginning of my sophomore year was easy—because of my last name, the university already expected that I'd have a deep interest in the labor movement. In addition to ILR courses, I was able to add language study, history, and comparative world economics. My course work looked a lot like the lib-eral arts education I was seeking, but at a much lower tuition rate.

(Family portrait at home in Washington)

That first year, Jon Stanat and I roomed together in the freshman dorm, and we both played freshman football. We looked up to the varsity players, many of whom were members of Delta Upsilon fraternity (DU). One was Cornell quarterback Gary Wood. Another was Hungarian-born Pete Gogolak, the first soccer-style placekicker in college football. After setting the NCAA distance record for field goals—fifty yards, which is a chip shot today—he went on to play professionally, first for the Buffalo Bills and then for the New York Giants. Wood, Gogolak and their teammates were the guys I wanted to hang out with. I was all too aware that my parents disapproved of fraternities, but when both Jon and I were invited to pledge DU, we accepted. My mother's idea of making fraternities a force for the greater good—a seed planted at Pi Delta in high school—did follow me to DU. I was instrumental in convincing my fraternity brothers to financially "adopt" an overseas orphan through monthly contributions to an American charitable organization.

Two memorable events at ILR both involved guest lecturers who were prominent in the labor movement. The first was Teamsters Union President Jimmy Hoffa. My friends and I attended Hoffa's speech not expecting much—his loose (or maybe not so loose) association with organized crime was already well known. We sat there expecting the stereotype, thinking he would sound like someone out of a gangster movie, but instead he spoke articulately and with few notes, and we all came away quite impressed. After his speech, I met him in person at a reception at the prestigious and rather snooty Telluride House. Hoffa knew Uncle Walter, of course, but he also knew about my father and Uncle Roy, who was then UAW's national legislative director. I was taken aback when Hoffa told me that although many people thought that my father was the intellectual in the family, the real intellectual was Roy.

When I learned that Uncle Walter himself would also be speaking at Cornell, I quickly arranged a reception for him at DU—I wanted to beat the stuck-up guys at Telluride to the punch. I was proud that my brothers were able to meet and interact with him, even though I was fairly certain that most of them were far more politically conservative than anyone in the Reuther family.

Summer, 1963—Adventures in Las Vegas

By the late spring of 1963, brother Eric and his wife Toni knew that their marriage wasn't going to work out, and they decided to split up. Getting a divorce in DC at that time—even an amicable, uncontested one—took a full calendar year, and neither Eric nor Toni wanted to wait that long.

The plan was for Eric and me to drive to Las Vegas when the school year ended so he could establish Nevada residency. Six weeks later, he'd have satisfied the eligibility requirement for an immediate divorce. Of course, we wouldn't be able to afford to just hang out in Vegas for a month and a half. We'd need jobs to support ourselves.

Family friend Joe Rauh had an associate—a guy who knew somebody who knew somebody—at the Sands, then one of the prestige hotels on the Strip. (It was where the Venetian is now.) Rauh arranged for a letter of introduction, which would include a request that we be hired as waiters.

Eric and I took off for the five-day drive from DC to Las Vegas in the air-cooled Saab that Dad had purchased from a close friend—the labor attaché at the Swedish Embassy—who was completing his tour of duty and heading back to Stockholm. We stayed overnight with friends or relatives most of the way across the country, but there was nobody we knew west of Colorado, and we ended up camping out in Utah—not the pine forested, ski resort part of Utah, but the scorching desert part of Utah.

It was too hot for the Saab's air-cooled engine, which breathed its last in the middle of nowhere, leaving us stranded in Utah about two hundred miles from Vegas. We hitched a ride to the nearest town, Cedar City, and had the car towed to a repair shop there. The mechanic soon told us that the engine was toast. The only way to make the Saab drivable was to put in a new motor, which would have to be trucked in from Chicago.

We left the Saab in Cedar City and took a bus to Las Vegas. We went directly to the Sands to present our letter of introduction to the casino manager. As far as we knew, we were all set up—we'd be waiting tables by breakfast time, if not sooner. The casino manager directed us to the bell captain, who read our letter, then frowned. Eric recalled his words precisely: "If you don't get the fuck out of here, I'm going to kick your ass."

It was our introduction to the fact that everything in Vegas works a little differently from how it works elsewhere. Joe Rauh's connections in DC were impeccable, but in Vegas they meant nothing. Someone had to explain to us that if you wanted to work as a waiter in a hotel/casino on the Strip, you had to go through Culinary Workers Union Local 226.

Eric and I left the Sands on foot. After paying to have the Saab towed, we'd had to pay bus fare to get to Las Vegas. Now we needed a place to stay for six weeks, and we were short on cash. With what little money we had, we paid in advance for a week in an unairconditioned hotel room. The common bathroom was down the hall. The room came with a small refrigerator, which is where we stashed the peanut butter, jelly, and bread that we bought with the last of our cash.

The next day, we went to the Culinary Workers union hall, registered to become waiters, and discovered that we were in for another rude awakening. Nobody, we were told, starts out as a waiter. Everyone begins as a busboy and works their way up. The union put us on the waitlist for busboy jobs, but we checked back every day and didn't seem to be moving up the list at all. I resorted to searching the help-wanted postings in the local paper. I responded to one ad for a babysitting job, but I didn't even get an interview. Worst of all, we were running out of peanut butter.

It was time to call for backup. We phoned home, and Dad agreed to use his connections to help us get work. He called Paul Schrade, then California regional director for the UAW, who called the California head of the Culinary Workers, who in turn called his counterpart at Local 226 in Vegas.

Soon enough, Eric and I were told to report back to the union office, and to be wearing white shirts and black pants—they had jobs for us. We were sent to the Tallyho Hotel, where we were hired as busboys working in the small restaurant near the pool. Located on the site now occupied by Planet Hollywood, the Tallyho was unique on the Strip because it had no casino and no slot machines—no gambling at all. At most times of the year, it was a family vacation spot, but for the upcoming July 22 World Heavyweight title fight—a much anticipated rematch between Sonny Liston and Floyd Patterson—the Tallyho had been designated as official press headquarters. Instead of families, it was swarming with top sports journalists and other notables.

A few days before the fight, Eric and I were the only two busboys working our shift. I emerged from the kitchen carrying a heavy tray and saw Eric seated at one of the tables, just like a guest. He was engaged in earnest conversation with a customer: Norman Mailer.

My brother had always been an avid reader, and the author he loved most in high school was Norman Mailer. His favorite book was *The Naked and the Dead*, Mailer's breakout novel about men on the front lines during World War II. (It was a favorite of mine, too.)

Mailer, a true boxing fan, was in Las Vegas to cover the Liston-Patterson fight. As Eric explained it, as soon as he saw Mailer ordering breakfast, he simply had to tell his favorite author how much he admired his writing. Mailer, who had no patience for phonies but loved sincere, well-informed praise, invited Eric to take a seat and talk about it.

Sitting with a customer, especially someone as famous as Mailer, raised eyebrows with hotel management, so when they needed to promote one of the busboys to the dinner shift in the main dining room, Eric was passed over and I got the job. This meant we had totally different work hours—back at the motel, we were like ships passing in the night. The only time we got to spend time together was when one of us had a day off, and sometimes not even then. Eric had to use one of his days off to take the bus back to Cedar City and pick up the Saab that Dad had paid to have repaired.

One evening was particularly hectic—every table in the main dining room was full. Out of the corner of my eye, I watched as two men came in. They really stood out from the hotel guests—lots of muscle, no neck. After speaking with some of the other staff, they confronted me, demanding to know what my status was with Culinary Workers Union Local 226. I told them what I'd been told at the union hall when Eric and I were first sent to the Tallyho—that a union rep would meet with us after we'd been on the job for a bit.

Apparently, that wasn't the right answer. "We'll take care of that right now," one of them said. The two tough guys then insisted that I follow them into an adjoining room.

I shook my head and attempted to ignore the less-than-subtle touch of menace in his voice. Being alone in a room with those two thugs struck me as a very bad idea. "Not now," I replied in a voice I hoped was not shaking. "As you can see, we're much too busy. I'll go down to the union hall first thing in the morning."

That wasn't the right answer, either, and the two guys did a slow burn as I tried to explain that— given my family history—there was no way I would even think of trying to avoid joining the union. They were so angry when they left that I was listening for footsteps and looking over my shoulder all the way back to the motel.

I did go to the union hall the next morning, just as I said I would, but the way I was treated by these union bullies left a bad taste in my mouth that never went away. I was raised in a union family with sensitive and caring individuals who respected and fought for the rights of other human beings, and this goon squad represented a brand of unionism I neither understood nor condoned.

As always, however, even bad experiences teach us something. From this interaction, I learned how much personal contacts and experiences matter in the formation of our opinions. I also learned that it takes only a few minutes to sway you in one direction or another.

As Labor Day approached, I flew back to DC and then left for Cornell for early football practice. Eric stayed behind in Vegas, where he completed the divorce soon after he had been there long enough to qualify as a Nevada resident. Even after the divorce, we remained close with Toni, and she continued to allow Valerie, their daughter, to spend lots of time with my parents.

National Politics—Assassination and Young Citizens for Johnson

I was a Cornell sophomore in November of 1963, when President Kennedy was assassinated. Like everyone else, I remember exactly where I was when I found out. I was shopping in downtown Ithaca and went past a shop that sold televisions. Back then it was commonplace for appliance stores to have a working TV in the window to get the attention of passersby. A small crowd had gathered on the sidewalk in front of the shop window. They were in tears, and they were staring at Walter Cronkite, who'd just announced that Kennedy was dead.

I knew I wanted to be with my family for the memorial service, so that night I stuck out my thumb to hitchhike home. A trucker in an 18-wheeler picked me up; he even got me something to eat at a truck stop along the way.

Despite his family wealth, Kennedy was not an elitist. To the contrary, he was a true friend of the labor movement, both here and overseas, and Uncle Walter was one of many national and international leaders who came to DC for the funeral. My father and I were with him in his hotel room when we were joined by Willy Brandt. At the time, Brandt was still mayor of West Berlin; six years later, he'd be elected chancellor of West Germany. Harold Wilson, then leader of Britain's Labour Party, arrived as well. He'd become prime minister the following year. All three of them—Willy Brandt, Harold Wilson, and Uncle Walter—walked in the funeral procession behind the cortege.

Once again, as a member of the Reuther family, it was my privilege to meet men of stature and accomplishment—and yes, at the time, almost all of them were men. Being around them stimulated and reinforced my growing interest in politics and world affairs, but as had been the case many years earlier when I met Nye Bevan, I got to interact with them on a personal basis, as human beings.

Through Dad's congressional contacts, I was invited to work in DC during the summer of 1964. I was to be a student intern at the Democratic Study Group (DSG) in the House of Representatives. Before my summer internship even started, however, I was called to Washington to participate in a very important press conference—one that needed someone youthful with the last name "Reuther" in attendance.

Lyndon Johnson had become president upon the death of JFK. He was completing Kennedy's term, but now he was running for election in his own right. The problem was that, unlike JFK, there was a distinct lack of enthusiasm among young people for his candidacy. In an effort to appeal to the youth vote, a program called Young Citizens for Johnson (YCJ) was enlisting prominent young political leaders, actors, musicians, athletes, and other famous folk from all walks of life to serve on the YCJ national steering committee.

The initial press conference was held on Friday, June 5. Senator Birch Bayh of Indiana, who at age thirty-six was one of the youngest members of the Senate, led the YCJ and kicked off the press conference. He began by making introductions. In addition to LBJ's daughters, Lynda Bird and Luci Baines, those present included: pitcher Don Drysdale of the Los Angeles Dodgers; Peter Duchin, son of the late bandleader, Eddie Duchin; Bobby Mitchell of the Washington Redskins (now the Washington Commanders); and Charlotte Ford, daughter of automaker Henry Ford II.

In a way, Charlotte Ford was why I was there. With Charlotte signaling support for President Johnson from the younger generation of the Ford family, YCJ wanted a young Reuther to represent the United Auto Workers family—for "balance."

(With Charlotte Ford at the YCJ press conference)

The launch generated a great deal of publicity, much of it focused on the idea of labor and management uniting behind Lyndon Johnson. That meant there were lots of photos of Charlotte Ford and me together. Reporters had already spoken with Charlotte before the press conference. When they told her that I would be serving with her on the steering committee, it was reported in *The Boston Globe* that she said, "That's great, I'll be anxious to meet him." The *Globe* noted that "Reuther could not be reached for comment. His mother said, 'He's hitchhiking to Washington from school—wouldn't even take a bus.'"

Hitchhiking was actually my preferred way of traveling between Ithaca and DC. It was faster than taking the bus, since there was no direct route between the two cities. It also had the further advantage of being free. In the *Akron Beacon Journal*, James Robinson wrote that Charlotte "flew in Friday morning from her mother's Fifth Avenue home in New York City. Reuther came in a day earlier after an all-night hitchhiking trip from Cornell University, in Ithaca, N.Y." Robinson then quoted me as saying "I can't afford a car, you know... That's my father's influence."

Lady Bird Johnson wrote about the launch of YCJ in her book, *A White House Diary*:

> *Senator Birch Bayh of Indiana and his wife, Marvella, were the spark-plugs of a standing-room [only] rally in the Senate caucus room yesterday for the formation of the Young Citizens for Johnson... Beautiful Charlotte Ford, the daughter of Henry Ford II, sat across the table from John Reuther (nice counterpoint this was), son of labor leader Victor Reuther... Luci and Lynda were on hand to show their appreciation for the Young Citizens."*

I was fortunate to be seated next to star running back/wide receiver and eventual Hall of Famer Bobby Mitchell. Mitchell was the first African American to play for the Redskins (the last pro team to integrate its roster) and was ultimately named to three Pro Bowls. When Senator Bayh told reporters that after the press conference each of us on the national steering committee would have the opportunity to share our personal press releases with our local news outlets, Bobby leaned over to say that this was going to be a problem, since he really didn't come prepared with anything like that. "Don't worry," I told him. "Thanks to the UAW, I have a very long press release. It's twenty-four pages, and I'd be happy to give you half of it!" The laugh we shared was the beginning of a great friendship.

When the press conference ended, Senator Bayh explained how the rest of the day would go, but the room was so noisy that I didn't hear the details of the schedule. Lynda Bird Johnson was standing nearby and encouraged me to ask Senator Bayh to repeat what he'd said. The plan was for us to pay our respects at the JFK gravesite at Arlington National Cemetery, then go to the White House for a special tour.

Lynda Bird and I only spoke briefly before we all left for the buses, but when I got home that evening, Mom handed me an envelope as soon as I walked in the door. She said it had just been hand-delivered from the White House. Lynda Bird had invited me for drinks and dancing after the state dinner for the guest of honor, Danish Prime Minister Jens Otto Krag, that next Monday. I was thrilled, but there was one obstacle I'd have to overcome: The invitation clearly stated that the dress code for the evening was black tie. I was between my sophomore and junior years at Cornell—I didn't own a tuxedo, and my family was not about to buy or even rent one.

It was time to improvise. The next morning, Mom took me to a local department store, where we found an off-white dinner jacket on sale for $4.95. That would do for the top half, but I still needed formal trousers—the ones with the black satin stripe running down the seam. Mom bought a spool of black silk ribbon and sewed the stripes onto a pair of black dress pants that were already in my closet. Dad had a white tux shirt that fit me, as well as a black bowtie, but when I told Mom that I needed a cummerbund for my waist, she drew the line. "Just keep your jacket buttoned," she said, "and no one will notice you don't have a cummerbund."

On the night of the event, I got dressed and went downstairs for my final inspection. As I turned around to show Mom how I looked, she noticed a hole in my black sock over my right heel, and it was big enough that she could see my skin. Since I was already running late, instead of sending me back upstairs to change my socks, Mom got out some black shoe polish and applied it to my heel. As I looked at myself in the mirror, about to go to the White House in my bargain basement dinner jacket, makeshift formal pants, and my painted heel, my self-esteem nosedived. Mom watched me deflate before her very eyes, then said something I've never forgotten: "You can go anywhere you want, dressed any way you want, and hold your head up high because your name is Reuther!"

With that rousing sendoff, I got into Dad's black Chevy Corvair—the same car that Ralph Nader would write about as *Unsafe at Any Speed*—and drove myself to the White House. I showed my invitation to the guards at the designated gate and after checking my name against the guest list, they waved me through. I was directed to the White House guest parking area, where I nestled the Corvair among the surrounding limousines, most of which were still occupied by their chauffeurs.

Lynda Bird greeted me at the South Portico, and I soon realized that not all the YCJ steering committee members had been invited. In fact, the only other YCJ member I recognized was Peter Duchin, and he was there in his official capacity as bandleader and pianist. Just as it dawned on me that possibly I was there as her date for the evening, the enormous doors from the dining room swung open and the dinner guests flowed into the ballroom. I was mortified—all the other men were wearing black tuxedos except one, Prime Minister Krag. President Johnson excused himself and went upstairs. When he returned, he too was wearing a white jacket—now there were three of us. Not every president would have done that. LBJ had a reputation for being uncouth and rough around the edges, but he had a knack for making his guests feel comfortable and at ease.

What happened next was a bit awkward—which is to say that *I* was awkward. I was not only somewhat shy and self-conscious, I was also not much of a dancer. Lynda Bird finally took my hand and led me out onto the dance floor. I'm sure it was obvious to her, and to everyone, for that matter, that dancing was not my strong suit. It was, however, the start of a friendship that continued through the summer presidential campaign season.

I saw Lynda Bird again in mid-August, when I flew to New York to attend a barbecue celebration for LBJ at Gracie Mansion, the official residence of the mayor. It was a Young Citizens for Johnson event—the invitations had been issued in the names of Charlotte Ford and the mayor's son, Robert F. Wagner Jr. Lynda Bird was the guest of honor at this barbecue for about 2,000 people.

Following the event, I grabbed a taxi back to the airport and was lucky to get one of the seats up front on the next shuttle back to DC. I'd just buckled my seatbelt for takeoff when I was approached by a man who identified himself as a Secret Service agent. "Miss Lynda Bird Johnson would like you to join her further back in the plane," he said. He walked me to the seat he had freed up next to Lynda Bird, and she and I spent the flight making small talk about the campaign and about life in general.

I liked Lynda Bird, and I thought she was very bright. We were friends but not romantically involved. The next time I saw her was when I was invited to a masquerade ball she was hosting at the White House. Guests were to come dressed as characters from American history. My plus-one was a young woman I'd met on Martha's Vineyard when I was working for Phil and Leni Stern a few years earlier. She essentially had the same job I did; she was the nanny for the children of another family that was summering on the island.

The two of us decided to be Arthur Dimmesdale and Hester Prynne from *The Scarlet Letter* and dressed as Puritans. Lynda Bird, on the other hand, looked stunning in a gorgeous, pale yellow ball gown covered in yellow roses—she was every inch the Yellow Rose of Texas.

At one point during the ball, President Johnson approached me and asked if he could have the next dance with "Hester Prynne." Naturally, I said yes. Seeing them on the dance floor stirred such a great sense of confidence in me that I walked over to the high-ranking general who was speaking with Lady Bird Johnson and asked if he would permit me to have the next dance with her. Feeling completely self-assured, I took her hand and proceeded to dance and chat with the First Lady—in that moment, the dance lessons I'd been taking paid off.

Later that evening, I drove my date back to her Washington apartment. As soon as she unlocked the door, she immediately ran for the phone. She couldn't wait to call her parents to tell them that she'd danced with the President of the United States. When a young man takes a young lady out on a date, he is always hopeful that he will find some way to impress her. I don't remember anything ever topping this, at least not for me.

The 1964 Democratic National Convention was held in late August in Atlantic City. President Johnson had chosen Senator Hubert Humphrey (D-Minnesota) as his running mate. On the last day of the convention, the Young Citizens for Johnson held a rally with about 15,000 young people and some incredible speakers and entertainers. Among those performing was a young vocalist named Barbra Streisand.

Gene Theroux, then a Georgetown Law student, was the associate director of Young Citizens for Johnson. He had arranged for some of the members of the YCJ national steering committee to be given official roles for our rally at the convention, and my assignment was to host Barbra Streisand. In the context of this event, "hosting" meant it was my job to make sure that Barbra knew where the rehearsal would be held, did what I could to make sure she was there on time, and ultimately, escorted her onto the stage to perform "People," the show-stopper song from the Tony award-winning Broadway musical *Funny Girl*.

I became a bit concerned when she was late for rehearsal. One of my colleagues pointed out two gentlemen sitting in the first row and indicated that one of them was Barbra Streisand's husband. I walked up to him and put my foot squarely in my mouth: "Excuse me, Mr. Streisand, but do you know how much longer it will be before your wife will be here?" The man sitting next to Barbra's husband guffawed loudly—he was Marty Erlichman, Barbra's manager. He was laughing because I'd failed to recognize Elliott Gould, a Broadway star in his own right. He and Barbra had met when they both were cast in the musical *I Can Get It for You Wholesale*.

Barbra eventually made it to rehearsal, and I later managed to keep my feet on the ground as I escorted her to the stage at the convention hall to sing "People." After the song, Barbra told me she had a pressing problem. *Funny Girl* was still running on Broadway, she was still in it, and she had a performance that evening. Barbra urgently needed a ride if she was going to make it back to the Winter Garden in time for the opening curtain. My job was to find her that ride! I soon found myself asking a favor of the best driver in Atlantic City: Paul Newman. He'd been our emcee for the rally, and one of his hobbies was racing sports cars. For this occasion, however, he had a driver of his own, and Barbra rode with him back to Manhattan.

Although much of my time and energy during the summer of 1964 was spent with the Young Citizens for Johnson, I was also an intern with the Democratic Study Group (DSG) in the House of Representatives. A *Baltimore Sun* reporter called the DSG "the heart and brains of the liberal Democratic bloc." During the debate over LBJ's signature piece of legislation, the Civil Rights Act of 1964, the DSG played a key role in thwarting the Dixiecrats, who were all too ready to do whatever they could to scuttle the bill. My assignment had been to assist with research and legislative updates and distribute that information to House members and to the press. I also helped mobilize the whip system among congressional staff. In the days before cellphones, the whip system was a phone tree that had been set up to expedite contact with staffers of congressional supporters of the bill. Its purpose was to ensure that members of Congress made it to the House floor in time for the vote. The bill passed, and I was proud to have played even a small role in the victory.

I was fortunate to have a great relationship with the leadership and full-time staff of the DSG. When I finished my work there in late August before returning to Cornell, all of them signed my farewell limerick:

There was a young man from Cornell.
With all pretty girls he played hell.
His POVERTY work
He never did shirk
He liked the poor girls just as well.

CHAPTER 5

1964-1967

Junior Year

In late 1964, just prior to Cornell's winter break, Dad and Mom went off on a long trip overseas, leaving me with their car, which I drove up to Ithaca. Since they would still be gone for Christmas, I was invited to spend the holidays in Michigan with Uncle Walter's family.

Uncle Walter had just undergone surgery for removal of a growth in his lungs, and he was recuperating at home with Aunt May and their two daughters, Linda and Lisa. The weather in the Detroit area was unusually warm for that time of year, which meant there was a lot of melting snow, and even more fog. This was especially true on the day we'd planned to visit Uncle Roy and Aunt Fania. I was very much looking forward to seeing them—it had been much too long, and I missed them a lot.

We set off for their house, which was not far from where Walter and May lived, but as we drove, the fog kept getting thicker and thicker. Eventually we found ourselves pretty much driving blind. We could barely make out the highway a few feet ahead of us, and a number of cars had already driven off the road. Aunt May insisted that we return to their home—it was much too dangerous, she said, to continue. From a safety standpoint she was right, I suppose, but I second-guessed the decision to turn back for a long time after that. Why? Because I never saw Uncle Roy again.

I returned to Washington shortly after Christmas. While I was there, the DSG invited me to attend an early January 1965 cocktail reception on Capitol Hill for our newly elected Democratic members of Congress. One of them was Michigan Representative Billie S. Farnum. I hadn't seen him since I was in elementary school, but back then, I'd seen him every day. Billie and his brother Bob had been two of the guys who served as UAW bodyguards for us after the assassination attempt on Dad.

I was also invited to attend one of President Johnson's Inaugural Balls. My guest, Polly Pierce, was a fellow Cornell student whose father had brought her to the Delta Upsilon house for a tour. Polly was very beautiful, and I had an immediate crush on her.

Summer of 1965

Gene Theroux, with whom I'd worked on the Young Citizens for Johnson campaign, contacted me at Cornell in early 1965. He'd since become director of the Independent Research Service, and he told me that he was putting together a representative group of "real American" young people for a trip abroad. The purpose of this group was to counterbalance another group of young people—Gene called them very naïve—who would be attending the Communist-organized World Youth Festival in Algeria that summer. Gene and the Independent Research Service felt that these kids were so green and impressionable that they'd be easy marks for Marxists, and they would also leave people with a very skewed impression of what young Americans were all about.

Before saying yes, I spoke with my father about participating and mentioned that the trip would be fully financed by Gene's organization. Although Dad had some reservations, he did not forbid me from going. He did give me one clear warning, however. He said it was crucial that before heading off to Algeria, I had to make it clear—in writing—to both the FBI and the State Department that I was not one of the gullible ones. To the contrary, I needed to explicitly declare that I was attending the festival as a member of the group whose purpose was to give the correct impression of American young people.

I wrote letters to FBI Director J. Edgar Hoover and to Secretary of State Dean Rusk, stating my reasons for traveling with Gene's group and asking both the FBI and the State Department to make note of this in any records they had on me. I still have a copy of J. Edgar Hoover's personal signed letter of response, in which he confirmed that, "Your letter of June 26th, with enclosures, has been received, and you may be assured this material will be made a matter of record in this Bureau."

That summer, Dad and Uncle Walter were planning a trip to Europe to participate in international labor meetings. Since those meetings would take place before the youth festival, I thought I'd be able to join them. I told Gene that I'd attend the festival only if I could first accompany my father and uncle, then arrive separately in Algiers. He had no problem with that arrangement, so I traveled across Europe with a small Reuther entourage that included Dad, Uncle Walter, Aunt May, their daughter Lisa, Walter's top aide Irv Bluestone, and Irv's wife Zelda. We toured France, Switzerland, and Belgium; visited relatives in Germany; and attended the International Confederation of Free Trade Unions (ICFTU) meetings in Amsterdam. I also got to see my then-girlfriend Polly from Cornell, with whom I had attended the LBJ inaugural ball that past January. She was working in the Amsterdam Hilton hotel as part of her training program through the Cornell School of Hotel Administration.

(With Aunt May, Uncle Walter and Dad in Germany)

(In the Swiss Alps)

I also had a chance to return to Enghien-les-Bains, where we had lived in France when we first left Detroit. I reconnected with our neighbors from across the street, who took me to a Paris nightclub where a very young Mireille Mathieu was performing.

We were already in Europe when the planned World Youth Festival was suddenly canceled. Algerian President Ahmed Ben Bella was overthrown in a bloodless coup led by his defense minister, Houari Boumédiène. Ben Bella had established close ties with Cuba's Fidel Castro and with other African leaders, including Gamal Abdel Nasser of Egypt and Kwame Nkrumah of Ghana. He also was connected with the USSR and had been named a "Hero of the Soviet Union" in April 1964. If there was going to be a coup, I guess I have to be glad that it happened before I got to Algiers, not during the time I would have been there. Several years later, rumors circulated that the Independent Research Service might have been financed by the CIA, but I certainly was not aware of it at the time.

Senior Year

As I began my senior year at Cornell, American involvement in Vietnam was escalating significantly. Congress had passed the Gulf of Tonkin resolution in August of 1964. Operation Rolling Thunder had begun, and we were bombing targets not just in South Vietnam, but in the north as well. None of our efforts seemed to be doing any good. As a Reuther, progressive politics was in my blood, and it was not long before I began to have serious misgivings about our role in Southeast Asia. This put me at odds with most of my fraternity brothers. Like the rest of the country, they were still very much in favor of the war.

During lunch at the frat house, another DU member rose to say that later that afternoon, Cornell's president would stand in review of a parade by students participating in our Reserve Officers Training Corps (ROTC) program. Antiwar demonstrators were expected to try to disrupt the march, he said, and he encouraged the rest of us to join him there. The idea was to show our solidarity with ROTC students and our support for the war itself. He said that we should be prepared to interact with the demonstrators and indicated that DU brothers should not wear our fraternity jackets or carry our Cornell IDs. "Interact with demonstrators" was a bit of code. Without saying so overtly, he was strongly suggesting that we should be prepared to confront the protestors, and that it would be wise to leave our IDs at home in case it got physical.

I stood up and mildly took exception to his remarks. Those who were demonstrating against the war would most likely be carrying their IDs, I said, because they believed strongly in their cause. If my brothers felt equally strongly about supporting the war, I contended, they should be equally willing to be personally identified with their position. My remarks were met with laughter and derision, after which I was pelted with food items from around the lunchroom. From that point on, my brothers jokingly referred to me as the house Communist.

I didn't realize it until later, but I was in the vanguard of what would soon start happening everywhere. As the Vietnam War dragged on, and as more and more body bags started coming home, cracks in relationships opened that would never be healed—not just between friends and frat brothers on campus, but also between family members at dinner tables around the country.

Christmas with Eric in Venezuela, 1965

After his Vegas divorce from Toni in 1963, Eric had moved to California, where he worked the night shift at GM's Buick/Oldsmobile/Pontiac manufacturing plant in Fremont. It wasn't meant to be a permanent position. Eric had applied to serve in the Peace Corps, but his acceptance was on hold because he had been married and had a dependent child. He became a member of UAW Local 1364, where he signed checks during a brief strike, and where, after some time, he was nominated to run for shop steward. He declined the nomination, since his acceptance into the Peace Corps had just come through.

He trained in Berkeley for several months before joining a team of Peace Corps volunteers headed to Venezuela in November 1964. They were assigned to work in Cumaná, a city on the Caribbean coast about 250 miles east of Caracas. They were there to help build subsidized housing for about 3,000 low-income local residents.

My 1965 Christmas present from Mom and Dad was a trip to Venezuela to visit Eric. I arrived to find him living in a rudimentary one-room house made of concrete blocks. There was no glass in the windows, and his bed was a hammock slung in the corner. And yet… he was happy. Eric loved the Peace Corps, and he loved the work he was doing.

December 22 was my twenty-second birthday, so Eric and his Peace Corps friends took me out to celebrate in nearby Puerto La Cruz. Because it was a refinery town and a major port for US oil companies, it had a lot of upscale bars where equally upscale ladies of the evening plied their trade.

As I sat at the bar sipping a cocktail, one of the ladies eased herself into the seat next to me and began talking to me in Spanish. I, of course, didn't understand a word, so she left briefly and returned with a couple of picture books in Spanish. We started playing a very grown-up version of See 'N Say—she pointed at objects in the books, said their name aloud, and asked me to repeat it.

The first couple of times she invited me to leave with her, I blushingly declined, but meanwhile, the cocktails kept coming, and I finally nodded my head "yes." As we walked toward her room, Eric and his Peace Corps compadres broke out in song: "Happy birthday to you! Happy birthday to you! Happy birthday dear John… "

I was quite shy growing up. I'd had girlfriends in high school and college, but we'd never gone all the way. On my twenty-second birthday, I was still a virgin. And now, despite all the alcohol, or perhaps because of it, I was flustered. I tried to get undressed, but there was a stubborn knot in the laces of one of my tennis shoes, and it took what seemed like forever to get that shoe off my foot.

Apparently, we made love, or at least I think that's what we did. As I was getting dressed, I knew I was supposed to leave her money, but I had only Venezuelan currency, and I had no idea what the going rate for her services was supposed to be. I gave her all the cash I had, and when she accepted it, she somehow made me understand that she didn't want me to tell my brother and his friends how much I'd paid her. I thought that meant I'd given her too much, but the opposite was true. When I talked with Eric later that night, he was astonished at how little I'd paid.

Finishing My Senior Year

I moved into a small rooming house just off campus at the beginning of senior year—after getting food thrown at me in the frat house, I no longer wanted to live there. Three foreign students lived on my floor. We each had our own room, but we shared a small bathroom. I liked living there, especially getting to know my Malaysian neighbor, Abu Bakar Bin Mahmud, and my Burmese neighbor, a professor from Rangoon (now Yangon).

These friendships solidified my growing interest in international relations.

In the second semester I took a course that compared the economic systems of the United States and the Soviet Union. I was intrigued by the syllabus materials and by professor Mills Gardner Clark. Prof. Clark had traveled often to the Soviet Union, and his lectures brought back fond childhood memories. At bedtime, Dad used to tell us stories about his adventures with Uncle Walter bicycling through Europe in the 1930s, and about the three years they had spent building cars in the Soviet Union.

(Dad and Uncle Walter on their bicycle trip through Europe in the 1930s. Photo credit: Walter P. Reuther Library, Archives of Labor and Urban Affairs, Wayne State University)

When Ford stopped producing the Model A, Henry Ford sold all the manufacturing equipment to the Soviets, who then set up an auto plant in the city of Gorky (now Nizhny Novgorod). Dad and Walter had been blacklisted in Michigan because of their union activities and were unable to find work in the auto industry, so they worked their way across the Atlantic on a freighter and bicycled around Europe, using the home of German relatives as their base. When they heard there was a shortage of experienced autoworkers in Gorky, they got work visas and headed east. I grew up hearing stories of how they had lived and worked there. When I was a little older, they also shared some of the early terrors of the Stalin period, including the loss of friends to prison camps and executions.

One of the many things I inherited from my father was his wanderlust—a yearning to see the world and experience other cultures and lifestyles. During the time we lived in Enghien-les-Bains, he took us on a lot of family trips, and I loved it. That's when I knew for sure I'd been bitten by the Reuther family travel bug. I had already developed a great interest in Russia, thanks to Dad's stories, but now as a senior at Cornell, I had a thirst to learn more.

One of the ILR courses during senior year was scheduled to be taught by a UAW colleague of Uncle Walter's. When there was a change in teachers, I lost all interest and rarely attended class. In short, I blew it off, and flunking was the all-too-predictable result. Once I'd failed the course, I didn't have enough credits to graduate, so during the summer of 1966, I took intensive Russian 101 at Georgetown University in DC.

1967 Internship with Birch Bayh, AU School of International Service

Learning the Russian language, or at least beginning to learn it, added to my growing fascination with the Soviet Union. Once I'd completed the requirements for my bachelor's degree, I thought back to the wise advice I'd received from my English professor as a freshman—that the purpose of undergraduate work was to learn how to think, and that grad school was for diving into a specific area of interest. I enrolled in the master's program at the School of International Service at American University (AU) in Washington. My area of concentration would be US-Soviet Studies.

While at AU, I worked briefly as an intern in the DC office of Indiana Senator Birch Bayh, who remembered me from the Young Citizens for Johnson campaign. I performed the usual intern tasks, including drafting responses to constituent mail. Senator Bayh had started receiving a lot of letters about a possible nationwide rail strike. Since I was from the Reuther family and now possessed a newly minted bachelor's degree from Cornell's School of Industrial & Labor Relations, I was assigned to look at the issue and make a preliminary determination about what position the senator should take.

From the volume of mail we received, I was already aware that many of Senator Bayh's conservative Indiana constituents favored federal intervention to prevent a work stoppage. Before making any recommendation to the senator, however, I wanted to discuss the prospective walkout with my father. Dad explained that the situation was a slippery slope and said that if LBJ intervened to forbid a strike, it wouldn't end there. The federal government would then have to assume responsibility for addressing worker grievances in some other way, which might entail government-imposed prices and wages.

I knew that the senator's constituents, although they staunchly opposed a national rail strike, would balk at that level of government intervention in the free market. I prepared a draft response reflecting this position for Senator Bayh's review. To my surprise, he called me into his office and told me that my analysis had won the day. He would have to come down against federal action to prevent a nationwide rail strike. That may have been the only time I impacted the senator's thinking while I was an intern, but it was gratifying, nevertheless.

Shortly thereafter, Jack Conway, Uncle Walter's former administrative assistant, arranged a full-time position for me at the Office of Economic Opportunity (OEO), where he was the director of the Community Action Program (CAP). This meant I had little or no free time, as I was still working toward my master's degree by taking night courses at American University.

I became a congressional liaison for the Job Corps. As originally envisioned, the Job Corps was intended to be a key program in LBJ's War on Poverty. Its training offered a leg up toward gainful employment for disadvantaged kids who lacked basic education and job skills. By 1968, however, the program was scrambling to fulfill its original purpose. Its funding was being siphoned off to pay for Vietnam even as the rationale for Job Corps training had come under suspicion. Rumors about a secret agenda were not unfounded. To satisfy the Pentagon's demand for more ground troops for the war, Johnson had actively considered using the Job Corps to train young men of draft age to prepare for enlistment.

Those of us in OEO Congressional Relations spent most of our time helping congressional offices craft responses to angry constituents. They had been promised job training, they wrote, but it now sounded like they were going to be handed an M16 instead.

CHAPTER 6

1968

Roy and MLK

The new year started tragically for our family. Uncle Roy suffered a heart attack and died on January 11. He was only fifty-eight years old. As family members gathered in Michigan for his memorial service, we were joined by national political and union figures. I eavesdropped as Bobby Kennedy spoke with my grandmother, Anna Reuther, Roy's mom. She told him she knew he shared the pain of losing a family member so early and unexpectedly in life. She also talked to him about how it's not right for a mother to have to bury her son. One great strength of our family, however, was that in spite of the deep sadness and tragedy that brought us together, we were able to celebrate the full life Uncle Roy had lived and talk about our memories of the happy times we'd shared with him.

The year got worse from there. On April 4, Dr. Martin Luther King Jr. was assassinated in Memphis, Tennessee. It is said that anger is grief's bodyguard, and the nationwide reaction to King's death was both angry and violent. There were protests and rioting in all of our major cities, including, of course, DC.

Out of concern for our safety, OEO sent us all home early. At this point, home for me was a small apartment in southwest Washington within walking distance of the Capitol. To get there from the office, I deliberately chose a route that would take me through one of the major areas of unrest. I don't think it occurred to me that this was an unwise decision, or that I might be in physical danger. Uncle Walter was very close to Dr. King, and we all shared his values. Our entire family had been so much a part of the struggle for civil rights and social justice for so long that I felt no fear walking through this predominantly Black neighborhood.

I was not far from an appliance store when I saw a woman carrying a small TV. Before long, four guys in an expensive car soon pulled up and parked. When they emerged from the vehicle, they were wearing bandanas over their faces, like you'd see in a cowboy movie. As soon as they saw people *without* masks making off with TVs and small refrigerators, however, they seemed embarrassed. I assumed they felt overdressed in a way, because they sheepishly pulled off their face coverings and joined the others. Once they'd loaded up their car, they drove away from the curb, only to stop at the traffic signal on the corner. The idea of breaking the law by brazenly looting a store then obeying it by stopping for a red light struck me as both bizarre and, in a strange way, humorous.

I went into a nearby bar while this was going on. Since I was the only White person around, someone asked if I was with the press. I shook my head and explained that I was just a person who had grown up in Washington, heard what was going on, and wanted to see it for myself. I walked out just as police cars arrived and blocked the intersection. The officers, who were White, called for everyone who had gathered there to drop the items they were carrying and leave the area. They were polite and courteous as they spoke, but they were also holding their service revolvers in plain sight. As they were speaking, a guy who had been raiding the liquor store backed out carrying a case of booze. He had no idea the cops were there until he turned around. He put the box down as soon as an officer asked him to do so, then joined the rest of the crowd walking slowly from the scene.

That night I took the streetcar to my parents' house. They were having dinner with Harry Givorgian, a journalist from the Soviet trade union newspaper *Trud*. Givorgian was based in New York, but he often covered the UAW and had become a friend of my father's. I told them what I had seen, and after dinner we all walked to a nearby apartment building. As kids, we'd learned how to access the building elevator. We always took it all the way to the top because there was a panoramic view of the city from the roof. As the four of us looked around, my eyes were immediately drawn to the general area where I'd been that afternoon.

There was an eerie red glow and smoke rising from the vicinity, and I could only assume that the neighborhood was on fire.

I returned to the intersection days later. It was unrecognizable. The liquor store, the appliance store, and the bar had all burned to the ground. So had an entire city block of apartments and townhouses—the very homes where people had brought their looted treasures.

It was yet another confirmation that MLK's assassination and its aftermath was a tragedy many times over. What I'd witnessed early in the day was by turns comedic, hopeful and promising—as far as I could tell, the police didn't arrest anyone, and they didn't want to. Their goal had been to end the looting and convince people to go home, and that's what they accomplished. But that brief victory didn't last. When the sun went down, looting turned to arson, and everything went up in flames.

Ironically, the only thing I could think of in the moment was a quote from Dr. King himself: "The old law of 'an eye for an eye' leaves everybody blind."

RFK

By 1968, Vietnam had become a quagmire. We had sent in more than 450,000 men, but there was nothing even remotely like victory on the horizon. Across the street from the White House, growing throngs of angry demonstrators chanted antiwar slogans night and day: "Hey, hey, LBJ, how many kids did you kill today?" was a particular favorite. They were loud enough for the president to hear inside the Oval Office.

The year 1968 was an election year, and with Johnson's favorability at 36 percent, Senator Eugene McCarthy of Minnesota announced his own candidacy for the Democratic nomination. On March 12, Johnson defeated him in the New Hampshire primary, but just barely. His slim 48 percent to 42 percent margin stood in stark contrast to his resounding win there in the 1964 general election.

Bobby Kennedy and Lyndon Johnson were never close, to put it mildly. In 1960, Bobby had strenuously opposed his brother's selection of Johnson as his vice-presidential running mate. Losing his brother to assassination, then watching LBJ take his place in the Oval Office, increased his resentment. In 1964, Bobby had stepped down as Attorney General to run for the Senate from New York. Once there, his opposition to the Vietnam War and Johnson's escalation of it created further tension between them.

With McCarthy's near-miss in New Hampshire, whatever had prevented Bobby from overtly challenging Johnson fell away. Four days later, Robert Kennedy announced his candidacy for the presidency. Always the astute politician, LBJ knew his prospects for reelection were dimming. On March 31, he announced a partial halt to the US bombing of Vietnam, then dropped a bombshell of his own: "I shall not seek, and I will not accept, the nomination of my party for another term as your president."

Vice President Hubert Humphrey of Minnesota immediately became Johnson's heir apparent, but he, of course, was saddled with accountability for the mess in Vietnam. He also lacked Bobby's charisma.

Uncle Walter wanted the UAW to remain neutral. Humphrey had been a longtime friend of labor, and he was Walter's personal friend as well. My mother and I were constrained by no such ties, and broke ranks to support RFK. In the May 7 DC Democratic primary, she ran as a delegate pledged to Bobby Kennedy and won.

The UAW national convention was to be held in Atlantic City just days later. Knowing that both Kennedy and Humphrey would be there, I asked Dad to get me in, and I let the Kennedy campaign know that I would do anything I could to help.

Hubert Humphrey was the first to speak. Even though Walter had warned convention delegates in advance that there would be no demonstrations of support for either speaker, the pro-Humphrey faction came prepared. During his speech, there were *Humphrey for President* posters and banners everywhere.

Game on.

Kennedy was to speak on May 9, so I got on the phone with Kennedy headquarters in Washington and asked them to send posters to Atlantic City. Unfortunately, they sent them by Greyhound bus, so they arrived too late for Bobby's speech. Nevertheless, several other Kennedy supporters had the same idea and came prepared, so we still were able to put on a good show of support.

Knowing that Walter was trying to remain neutral, Bobby took advantage of the fact that Mom had won a Kennedy delegate seat in the DC primary. He mentioned her victory and thanked her by name during his speech. With those words, Bobby made sure that the UAW convention understood that he had support from the Reuther family. Before the convention ended, Dad, Mom and I had photos taken with him.

It wasn't long before I took a leave of absence from my job at OEO to help Bobby Kennedy get elected. The timing was good—I'd finished all my master's course requirements and exams at AU and all that remained was to write my thesis.

The campaign sent me to California. They wanted to capture the state's big block of delegate votes for the Democratic National Convention that would take place in Chicago in August. My work involved liaison and coordination with the United Farm Workers (UFW). The head of the UFW was Cesar Chavez, who had been a family friend for years, but that didn't get me any special benefits—when it came to work assignments, I was just another volunteer. Much of my time was spent delivering flyers and campaign literature and learning to drive an enormous truck.

June 4, 1968, was primary day in California, and I was in the lobby of the Ambassador Hotel when Bobby returned from giving a series of last-minute morning speeches. As we shook hands, I mentioned that I was working with his campaign and that I was the son of Sophie Reuther, one of his pledged delegates. He smiled that famous Kennedy smile.

Paul Schrade was with him. Paul was the UAW's West Coast regional director and a dear family friend. When Eric and I needed help getting jobs in Las Vegas, Dad had called Paul. He was now Bobby's labor coordinator, much to the chagrin of Uncle Walter, who was still trying to keep UAW leadership neutral. That evening, Paul brought me up to the Kennedy suite in the Ambassador to watch the returns on TV. It was still early, but it was already clear that Bobby had won, and Bobby asked Paul to reach out to Walter by phone. The plan was for me to initiate a conversation with my uncle, then pass the phone to Bobby so he could ask for Walter's endorsement. It was a clever idea, but it didn't work. We knew that Walter was staying in San Francisco with Linda, his daughter, but nobody was answering the phone at her home.

It was almost midnight as we watched a live TV interview with Frank Mankiewicz, Bobby's press secretary. Mankiewicz told the on-air reporter that the senator would be coming down shortly to make his victory speech. "If Frank said I'm coming down," Bobby announced, "let's go down."

Almost everyone in the suite headed for the elevator. Some of us, including me, realized that we wouldn't all fit, so we took the stairs instead. As it turned out, we got to the first floor before Bobby and his top staff. I headed for the rear stage area where Bobby would enter, but a security guard refused to let me through. Luckily for me, Roger Mudd of CBS News was there. He remembered me from a number of years earlier, when he had interviewed me as a high school student about the "Tractors for Freedom" program, and he convinced the guard to let me pass.

I walked onto the stage where Bobby would give his victory speech and discovered I was the only one there. Feeling too conspicuous by myself, I stepped off the stage into the front row of the standing audience. I watched most of Bobby's speech from there, but as he was thanking his many volunteers, I realized there would be no easy way for me to rejoin the group onstage. To be readmitted into the Kennedy suite upstairs, I had to leave before he was done.

Bobby was still speaking when I got to the room. Ted Sorensen, who had been Jack Kennedy's advisor and speechwriter, was sitting at the foot of one of the beds, and I plunked myself down next to him. When the shocking announcement came that Bobby had been shot, Sorensen buried his head in his arms and doubled over. "Oh God!" he cried. "Not again!" At the time, we didn't know how gravely he'd been wounded, but even so, I was shocked at the turn of events.

Hours later, we learned that Paul Schrade had also been shot as he walked with Bobby through the hotel kitchen. The bullet hit Paul in the forehead, fracturing his skull. Miraculously, it did not enter his brain. It was not until much later that I had time to reflect on what might have been. If I had stayed with the rest of our group and remained on stage, I would have exited with Bobby and everyone else through the kitchen. I would have been in the midst of the group when the gunman opened fire.

After the shooting, I was given a key to the Kennedy hotel suite so that I could help Kennedy family and friends gain access. Later that day, we were told that if we wanted to return to Washington, our only option was the campaign staff plane, which would be departing that evening. It was going to be a redeye flight that would land in DC in the early morning.

Bobby was still alive when we took off from LAX. The mood on the plane was upbeat—we even had a pillow fight somewhere over Kansas. Yes, Bobby had been injured, but we all assumed he'd survive and recover.

Smiling as we deplaned at dawn in Washington National Airport (now Ronald Reagan Washington National Airport), we were met at the gate by grieving, tearful staffers who delivered the somber news.

Some days later, I realized that I still had the key to the Kennedy suite at the Ambassador. I have it to this day.

CHAPTER 7

1968-1969

Bobby's assassination hit me hard. I was depressed and demoralized, both for myself and for my country. I was also at loose ends. I didn't have it in me to go back to work for a government program whose budget was being gutted to pay for the Vietnam War.

As director of international relations for the UAW in Washington, my father often hosted visiting foreign trade union delegations and labor party groups at our home. Shortly after Bobby was killed, I was there when Dad's guests were from the Soviet Union. I peppered them with questions all night long, especially New York-based correspondent Harry Givorgian, the same journalist who had been with us after Martin Luther King was shot. He already knew that my postgraduate studies focused on US-Soviet relations, and after responding to my many questions, he finally told me that reading books while sitting in DC wasn't going to be enough. If I wanted to become a true specialist, he said, I had to spend time in the Soviet Union. He told me to come to Moscow, learn the language, and get an in-depth personal understanding of Russian people, Russian history, and Russian culture. And Harry said he could make it happen. He offered to arrange a year in Moscow for me through the All-Union Central Council of Trade Unions (AUCCTU), which would sponsor me as a student.

A year in Moscow sounded really appealing, especially since I had already finished all my course work and exams at American University. To complete my master's degree, all I had left to do was to write my thesis. I discussed Harry's offer at great length with my father. He explained that the Soviet trade union organization that would sponsor me was actually a government organization, and that its chairman, Alexander Shelepin, was the former head of the KGB. He wanted me to know that Soviet trade unions were not part of what he called the "free trade union movement," and did not represent what he respected in that movement. I was not particularly concerned about any relationship between the KGB and the AUCCTU because I just assumed the KGB had a relationship with all Soviet organizations at that time, since all such organizations were governmental. Despite my father's cautionary advice, I decided to accept the invitation. My year in Moscow would entail six months of language study at Moscow State University (MGU) followed by six months of thesis research, after which I would return to the States to write it up.

There was one looming problem: my draft status. Deferments for graduate students were being phased out and I had been reclassified 1A, which meant that I was eligible to be drafted and sent to Vietnam.

Except that if I got drafted, I wouldn't go. At the time of the Cuban missile crisis in 1962, I'd actively contemplated dropping out of Cornell and enlisting in the Marines, but that now seemed like a lifetime ago. My opposition to the Vietnam War was so deep-seated that I was fully prepared to refuse induction.

I considered declaring myself a conscientious objector and took a look at the form I'd have to complete to qualify. It posed a series of hypothetical situations and asked how I would react in each one. One involved what I would do if invading troops were on US soil and were about to kill my mother. The question they wanted me to answer was whether I would fire a weapon at the enemy to save her life.

The questionnaire was designed to winnow out young men like me, who were opposed to this particular war, from men who were opposed to any and all wars and would not bear arms under any circumstances. Although refusing to go to Vietnam was a matter of principle for me, I realized that I did not qualify as a conscientious objector, at least not the way the US military was defining it. I was not active in the antiwar movement. I was just a person with an unwavering belief that what my country was doing in Vietnam was wrong, and with an equally resolute determination not to participate. I also knew I was unwilling to avoid the draft by leaving the country to take refuge in Canada or some other noncombatant nation.

That left me just one option. If called up to enlist, I would simply refuse to step forward at my induction, which was a felony. Muhammed Ali had been convicted of the same crime a year earlier. I was looking at three to five years in prison.

I had already passed the physical exam for the draft. I now took the mental exam, which was meant to determine whether I had any specialized knowledge or skills that could be put to use by the military. It was a multiple-choice exam, with five possible answers for each question. If I remember correctly, I answered the questions I knew and guessed the rest. Within a few weeks, I began getting phone calls from the Army, then the Navy, and then the Air Force, all asking me to please consider serving in their specific branch. I finally asked one of these recruiters why I was getting all these calls. It's very rare, he told me, when a potential draftee answers all of the mental exam questions correctly.

And then the notice came in the mail. I'd been formally called up. I put on a jacket and tie for my appearance before the local draft board. I fully intended to declare that I would not serve and that I was ready to go to jail—I had already discussed this with my parents, and they respected my decision. They too were very much opposed to the war in Vietnam, and I assume they understood that if I fled to Canada, I might never be able to come back to the United States. I was the only son they had to worry about. Eric was classified 4F. When he was much younger, he'd somehow injured his index finger—his trigger finger—so he was not draftable.

Sitting at the table at the draft board was a sweet-looking, grandmotherly woman who was visibly shaken when I told her what I was about to do. She asked whether I'd considered continuing my education and I responded that before I'd been called up, I had planned to do exactly that. I told her that I'd intended to continue my graduate education in Moscow, but that I doubted whether the Selective Service System would accept this as an alternative to being drafted. "Let's try!" she said.

The dean of the School of International Service at American University wrote to the draft board on my behalf and confirmed that I was about to begin a year of graduate language study and thesis research in Moscow. He explained that it was an initial step toward earning a Ph.D. in U.S.-Soviet Relations. It worked, and I was granted a totally unexpected deferment.

First Year in Moscow

The Soviet trade unions were still working to secure my visa when I left for Europe on August 19, 1968. The plan was for me to go to Denmark, visit some of Dad's friends, then travel to Sweden, where I would pick up my visa from the Soviet Embassy in Stockholm. I loved Copenhagen, especially Tivoli Gardens, but the most memorable event of my time there was being awakened by my host very early on the morning of August 21. He woke me up with startling news: 250,000 troops and 2,000 tanks—primarily from the Soviet Union but also from Warsaw Pact members Poland, Bulgaria, and Hungary—had marched into Czechoslovakia. The invasion set off a major diplomatic confrontation between East and West. I immediately realized that this might prevent me from studying in Moscow.

In Stockholm I was a guest at the home of Arne Geijer, who had been president of the International Confederation of Free Trade Unions and was also chairman of the Swedish Trade Union Confederation. The Reuther and Geijer families were close; Arne's daughter had lived with us for some time in Washington.

When I contacted the Soviet Embassy, they had no word about my visa. All of their communications channels were apparently jammed up with messages regarding the events in Czechoslovakia. A week later there was still nothing, and it seemed likely that my visa, and thus my year in Moscow, had been collateral damage from the Czech invasion. After talking it over with the Geijers and calling my parents, I took out an application to study at the university in Stockholm. At the same time, however, my father sent an urgent telex to the All-Union Central Council of Trade Unions in Moscow, explaining that if I did not receive the visa within the next few days, I would cancel my plans to come to the USSR. Apparently, that galvanized them into action. The Soviet Embassy called the next day and said that my visa was ready.

I flew to Moscow on September 1st and was met at the airport by Harold Shetinin, a staff member of the All-Union Central Council of Trade Unions, my sponsors. I then lived for a week at the AUCCTU-owned and operated Sputnik hotel. The hotel was busy while I was there; other guests included a large Czech military delegation that had been brought in to show support for the invasion of their country.

I moved into a dorm room at MGU and was enrolled in a program designed to provide foreign students with a full year of intensive Russian language study. The goal was to make us fluent enough to take advanced coursework in our fields of specialization—coursework that would be taught exclusively in Russian. Included in my small study group were six other students: two Canadian women, a Danish woman, a man from Iraq, and two other women—one from Afghanistan, one from Turkey—whose fathers were military attachés in their respective embassies.

Since the seven of us had no language in common, all lessons were taught in Russian. We started with books that were similar to elementary level study guides. An illustration of a family sitting at home watching TV had arrows connected to the word for each object in Russian: television, table, father, mother, child, cat, dog, etc.

Many other students in the program were North Vietnamese, and it didn't take long for word to spread that one of their fellow students was an American. Whenever we had a break from class, we walked around the halls, many of which had been decorated with North Vietnamese propaganda posters. One showed Vietnamese peasants making farm implements out of metal scraps from a downed US warplane—the twentieth century depiction of "swords into plowshares" from the Old Testament book of Isaiah. In the center of the poster was an image of Robert McNamara.

As I was looking at it, one of the Vietnamese students came to stand beside me. He looked at me, smiled, then pointed at McNamara and pronounced one of the Russian words we had learned that day: dog. I had to let it slide. My opinion of Bob McNamara was scarcely better than his, but my Russian was not yet good enough to tell him that McNamara was no longer secretary of defense and was instead now president of the World Bank.

Staying in contact with my parents required some ingenuity. Letters sent by conventional mail took about a month to arrive, and that generated a lot of anxiety back home. Dad eventually contacted friends at the State Department and they pulled some strings to allow us to use the embassy diplomatic pouch for our correspondence. I'd brought a portable cassette recorder with me to Moscow and would often tape short update letters to them instead of painstakingly writing them out. The cassettes went swiftly to DC via the pouch, and then on to my parents. Dad re-recorded my letters onto reel-to-reel tapes, then reused my cassettes to send letters from him and Mom back to Moscow.

He saved these reel-to-reel tapes, which eventually were quite helpful in jogging my memory about what life was like for me at MGU. Even so, I can't imagine what my parents might have thought as they listened to them. Vodka was one of the four basic food groups at MGU, and after imbibing at an evening party, I would sometimes return to my room a tad inebriated. Because getting tipsy tends to loosen the tongue, I would often reach for my cassette recorder and relate all the latest jokes and anecdotes to Mom and Dad. Neither one of them was fluent in Russian, so I would recite the jokes in English with a Russian accent. Listening to myself many years later, I cringed a little—I sounded like Boris Badenov, the Russian spy cartoon character from *Rocky & Bullwinkle*.

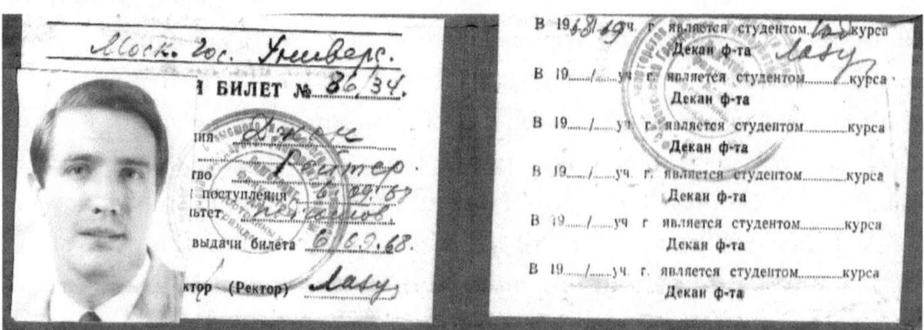

(MGU student ID)

(My first winter in Moscow)

There was a notice in my passport that US citizens who planned to stay for an extended time in certain countries, including the Soviet Union, should go in person to the embassy and provide information about where they could be reached in an emergency. The embassy staffer I met with was quite surprised to learn that I was a privately-sponsored student at MGU—virtually all other American students in Russia were part of the official governmental exchange program. There was also considerable interest in the fact that I was Walter Reuther's nephew.

Clearly this information made its way up the embassy hierarchy, because I was soon invited to embassy parties and social gatherings. I later discovered that almost as soon as I landed in Moscow, I had become the object of considerable interest among our diplomats. On October 11, 1968, barely six weeks after I arrived, an official Airgram in the name of Ambassador Llewellyn Thompson had been sent to the State Department. Marked "Limited Official Use," the subject line was "Moscow University Student John Reuther."

The upper lefthand corner carried a three-column chart indicating all the government agencies that were to receive Thompson's message, including the number of copies distributed to each one. Six went to the Department of Labor, three to the Army, and five to the Navy, and then it got interesting. Ten copies went to the United States Information Agency (USIA), three to the National Security Agency (NSA), and *eleven* to the CIA.

I can only assume that some friend of Dad's who worked in a government agency—and that could have been any number of people—got a copy of this message and passed it along to him. He shared it with me years later, once I was back in the States.

The Airgram began by noting that I was attending Moscow State University as a privately sponsored student. It was further noted that I had told embassy officers about the circumstances under which I'd come to Moscow, including the details about my initial conversation with *Trud* correspondent Harry Givorgian at my parents' home when the idea was first raised about my studying in Russia. "Reuther said he has never been under any illusion about the nature of the Soviets' interest in him," the note stated, "which he said is clearly the result of a determination on their part that the United Auto Workers, and his uncle in particular, constitute a progressive, militant force in the United States worthy of every encouragement."

The note added that the lectures I was attending in my Russian language studies have "heavy ideological content" and that "the length of the preparatory instruction would preclude his taking any substantive courses, unless he remains for a second year, which he is seriously considering." They wrote, "He is not overly disturbed by this development, however, and feels that a knowledge of Russian will in any event be a useful thing and that, in the process, he will learn a good deal about the USSR and the Soviet people." The note was accurate about the "heavy ideological content" of the course work. Our language courses soon became specifically designated as history courses, and history was taught from the Soviet Cold War point of view.

The final paragraphs reflect how I was perceived at that time by embassy officials:

It is apparent that Reuther derives considerable enjoyment from discussions with Soviet students and others about the United States and American labor, discussions which he says are surely disappointing to those who expected his views to be more compatible with Communist doctrine. He said he is at pains to explain to Soviet acquaintances the fundamental differences between American and Soviet labor unions, and he describes the latter as essentially an instrument for labor control and discipline. He said the subject of Czechoslovakia often enters into such conversations, and that he is quick to point out on such occasions that the occupation of that country did little to enhance respect for the Soviet Union among American workers. Reuther said he had recently written a letter to his father, transmitting to him the resolutions of Soviet workers' groups on Czechoslovakia, which he said illustrate the gulf separating Soviet and American labor.

John Reuther is a tall, dark-haired, handsome young man in his early twenties. He has an outgoing personality, a sense of humor, and great composure and self-assurance. He has made friends with American exchange students at Moscow University and, unlike some privately sponsored American students here, apparently has no desire to avoid the American Embassy.

Vitaly was my roommate in the MGU dorm, and I believe it was no accident that he was paired with me. Vitaly was majoring in English literature, which meant that he had more than a little knowledge of English, so even in the early stages of my Russian language study, we could understand each other. We each had our own narrow sleeping room with a twin bed, desk, closet, shelves, and a window. Our shared bathroom facilities included a shower, toilet and sink, all of which were accessible from the common entrance to our suite from the hall. Vitaly and I got along well and kidded each other a lot. He sometimes called me a capitalist, especially after I bought a large German reel-to-reel tape recorder.

I still have the photo that shows me sitting on my bed in the dorm. My guess is that Vitaly took it using the camera that I'd bought at one of the hard currency shops. The wall above my pillow was decorated with a large map of the USA and a Bobby Kennedy poster—one of the batch that hadn't arrived in Atlantic City in time for his speech at the UAW convention in May. That had only been six months earlier, but so much had happened since. (Early in 1969, after Richard Nixon was sworn in as President, I went to the embassy, picked up a free poster of the new president, and taped it to the wall over the toilet.)

Harold Shetinin of the AUCCTU, the man who had met me at the airport when I first arrived, continued to see to it that I felt very welcome in Moscow. He frequently got me tickets to the Bolshoi, which I loved not just for the beauty of the dance but because my brain needed the rest. Our classroom sessions at MGU were like a full-time job and then some—nine to five Monday through Friday and till noon on Saturday. At the Bolshoi, I could sit there and enjoy the ballet and the music without having to think in Russian.

For the grand November 7 celebration of the 1917 October Revolution—the Soviet equivalent of the Fourth of July—Harold provided me with special access to Red Square. I was in the bleachers right next to Lenin's Mausoleum, which meant I was not far from Leonid Brezhnev himself as he stood on the VIP viewing platform above the tomb's entrance while troops and military hardware paraded past him.

Mom and Dad saved all my correspondence from Moscow, and in one of those early letters, I started a paragraph saying, "Let me tell you all about my sex life…" The rest of the page was blank, but that was about to change. The only phone number I had in Moscow, which I gave to Harold and the US Embassy and anyone else who wanted it, was the house phone on my floor of the dorm. It was strategically placed on a desk by the elevator, and when a call came in, the student on phone duty would buzz the appropriate room. I was on duty when a call came in from a young woman asking in Russian whether I was John Reuther, the American student living on that floor. She said her name was Lena, then asked me to meet her in the courtyard as soon as my phone shift ended.

I didn't know anyone named Lena, but she had a nice voice, and… there was the matter of that blank page. Before leaving for my rendezvous in the courtyard, I told Vitaly what had happened. "If I don't come back tonight," I said, "call the American Embassy!"

Lena was as beautiful as her voice, and she took me to her quarters in an adjacent dorm wing—she had a completely private room all to herself. That was unusual, but she explained that because she was doing graduate work, she was entitled to it. We talked about life in general and about our backgrounds. A few rounds of vodka later, my limited Russian was no longer an impediment. We had progressed to entirely nonverbal communication, and my page was no longer blank. It was the beginning of a long, sporadic relationship that lasted for the duration of my studies in Russia.

Just as my being paired with Vitaly as my roommate was not a coincidence, it's hard to avoid the conclusion that Lena's sudden appearance in my life had been orchestrated as well. I have little doubt that she'd been asked to approach me by Soviet authorities, perhaps by the KGB. I also believe that we were genuinely attracted to each other, so I don't think for her it was *just* work. Even so, she did test me from time to time with invitations to attend prohibited activities, including meeting up with known Soviet dissidents. I always declined. I assumed that if I had gone, it could have been used against me in some way, possibly to coerce me into doing something for the KGB.

When I left DC for the Soviet Union, the plan had been to spend only a semester studying Russian before starting research for my thesis, but as soon as I began, I realized how much I had to learn. With the endorsement of the draft board, I decided to extend my visa. I would spend the entire 1968-1969 school year learning Russian, and the following year working with an MGU professor gathering materials for my thesis. This bought me a little extra time to decide what my thesis subject would be—when I arrived in Moscow, I had no idea.

Toward that end I got a little help from an unexpected source. The ambassador's residence was a stunning Neoclassical Revival mansion called Spaso House. Both Ambassador Llewellyn Thompson and his successor, Jacob Beam, invited American students to the house for parties, movies, and for holiday dinners like Thanksgiving. Robert Peck was the embassy officer who oversaw the house and managed the staff. Over several visits to Spaso House, the two of us became friendly enough that he invited me to join him on a trip to Finland—at the time, our diplomats never traveled solo in the USSR.

We took the overnight train to Helsinki so he could pick up a car he had purchased for his personal use. On the fifteen-hour drive back to Moscow, we discussed my thesis, and Bob convinced me that the subject matter should be the history of the Soviet trade union system. He contended that my access to Soviet trade unions, coupled with the VIP treatment they were already providing, gave me a unique research opportunity. It would be a shame, he said, not to take advantage of it. Once the topic had been settled, it was determined that my scientific advisor would be MGU history professor Vladimir Drobizhev, who specialized in modern Russian history from the beginning of communism to the present day.

Kazakhstan—Summer of 1969

My work with Professor Drobizhev would not start until September, so I had to make plans for the summer. Harold and the AUCCTU suggested I join a detachment of student construction volunteers who would be building a schoolhouse in a logging region north of Moscow. Professor Drobizhev discouraged me from going. He knew that there were already foreign students scheduled to work with this detachment, which meant I would be speaking a lot of English instead of improving my Russian. He urged me to join a different construction detachment instead, one comprised entirely of Russian students.

Pursuing this question with Harold, I reminded him that his boss, former KGB head Alexander Shelepin, had told me when I first arrived in Moscow that if I ever needed his assistance, I should feel free to get in touch with him. This was sheer namedropping on my part. I got the feeling that Harold didn't like the idea of my being so far away for a summer, so I invoked Shelepin's name in an effort to persuade him. It worked. I was soon accepted into a summer work detachment comprised of students from the MGU physics department.

Our destination was a state farm on the steppes of Kazakhstan. On the day of our departure, we gathered for photographs in front of the university. We were all wearing our uniforms—a khaki military-style jacket with a patch on the sleeve indicating we were members of MGU Physics Department Detachment No. 2, and matching pants. As this was my first such experience, I didn't know how casual these groups were, so I also wore a tie, generating much laughter from the rest of the detachment.

(At the train station in Moscow, ready to depart for Kazakhstan. The commander of our detachment, Kolya, is next to me in the hat.)

Getting to Kazakhstan was an adventure, starting with a three-day, 1,700-mile train trip in the company of hundreds of other students. Three days on the train was enough for me to become friends with the commander of our detachment, Nikolai Bezezichniy, known to one and all as Kolya. Kolya was a fourth-year physics student who was highly respected and admired by everyone in the group. On the train, he took me under his wing and appointed me as one of his discipline agents.

With my red ID bandana on my arm, the two of us patrolled the cabins of our detachment making sure everyone abided by the rules, which included no alcohol and no gambling—for the entire summer.

Leaving the train at Tselinograd (now Astana), Kazakhstan's capital city, we went by truck to a state farm in the village of Astrakhanka, about two hours northwest. We all lived together, thirty-two boys and ten girls, in a large one-room schoolhouse that had been built by a previous student detachment. Since school was out for the summer, it was our dorm, with long rows of bunk beds on either side of the room. Washing and toilet facilities were outside. We ate our meals in the farm's dining room, not far from the schoolhouse.

We lined up each morning to hear Kolya tell us the plans for the day, then dispersed to work on our assigned projects, which included a reinforced concrete hospital, a barn, and a trench silo where the farm would store silage to feed sheep and cattle over the winter. We worked ten hours on weekdays and six hours a day on weekends. It was hard, physical labor. I carried heavy rocks, placed them on the walls we were building, then mortared them into place. My whole adult life I have suffered from back problems, and I think it all started that summer. Even so, I loved what I was doing. On one of the cassettes I sent back to my parents, I talked about the value of the experience I had in Kazakhstan, and how much it meant to me.

> *[It was] one of the greatest experiences I've had, and it paved the way for many more opportunities that I've had here with young people... There's nothing better than living with and working beside someone under kind of rough conditions to open up a person to different viewpoints, a different way of life, a different way of thinking, and this work experience has broken through a lot of walls that might have been between us, official walls, and so I'm looking forward to doing this type of work again.*

(Lined up to hear the plans for the day)

(At work with the detachment)

After dinner, we usually sat around a campfire singing songs. Many were about lovers tragically separated during the Stalin years; others were patriotic songs from World War II, which the Soviets called the Great Patriotic War. It was from my detachment friends that I learned that the USSR suffered far heavier losses, both civilian and military, than any other country—26 million deaths.

We also listened to the Voice of America (VOA) on my shortwave radio, which broadcast the July 1969 Apollo 11 mission and the first landing on the moon. Russian language VOA "propaganda" broadcasts were jammed by the Soviets with a loud buzzing noise, but the English broadcasts came through clearly. As physics students, my new friends were extremely interested—twelve of them stayed up all night with me when the spacecraft landed, and we listened together as Neil Armstrong said, "That's one small step for a man, one giant leap for mankind." By this time, my Russian was good enough to translate all the major key moments and words, so my friends understood it.

While I was there, we had a carnival of sorts that included all the students working in that part of Kazakhstan. We played competitive sports, including basketball. I was on our Physics-2 detachment team and was the high scorer in our win, after which my teammates tossed me up in the air as we celebrated our victory. All of us also put on a show for residents of the local village. A fellow student and I sang a duet of the 1960 ballad "Green Fields," which had been a big hit by The Brothers Four. When we were introduced, it was mentioned that one of us was an American, and, since my colleague was wearing a tie, local villagers who came up to us after the show assumed that he was the one from the USA.

I learned later that beyond entertainment, there was usually another, more ideological bent to these local gatherings. It was customary for student detachments working in remote rural areas to give speeches on cultural events and current affairs. These lectures were more like sermons and had a clear sociopolitical component that was meant to reinforce Communist dogma. Subject matter included topics such as the positive impact the presence of Soviet troops was having on Czechoslovakia. Kolya didn't include such discussions in our gatherings with the local villagers, I suspect because of my presence, and was later greatly criticized for it.

Sochi—Summer of 1969

Although my fellow students would stay on in Kazakhstan for the whole summer, Harold Shetinin and the AUCCTU arranged a vacation for me before MGU classes resumed in the fall. After a month with the Physics-2 detachment, I returned briefly to Moscow before traveling to

Sochi, a resort city on the Black Sea. (Sochi would eventually become the host city for the XXII Winter Olympics.)

Prior to leaving for Sochi, I was invited to a party at the embassy, at which I related the details of my work in Kazakhstan. Years later, I found in files my father saved for me a copy of a second Airgram. This one had been sent from the embassy to DC on August 7, 1969, shortly after the party. Like the first Airgram a year earlier, it too had an extensive distribution list: six copies to the Department of Labor, three copies to the Army, five to the Air Force, five to the Navy, ten to the USIA, three to the NSA, and *twenty* to the CIA. (I can only conclude that for the CIA, eleven copies the first time wasn't enough.)

Unlike the initial Airgram, however, this time I could tell how my father had ended up with it. One of his friends at USIA had forwarded a copy to him—the words "Official Business" on the envelope had been crossed out with a ballpoint pen. Whomever I had spoken with at the embassy party had either recorded the conversation or had a near photographic memory.

The Airgram began with background information on me and my family, my studies in Russia, and my decision to remain for a second year after getting the okay from my draft board. It mentioned that to get permission to join the Physics-2 detachment going to Kazakhstan, I had invoked the name of A.N. Shelepin, Politburo member and trade union boss, who had assured me of his assistance if I ever needed it.

The next section related details about our construction detachment, specifically that Kolya had boasted to me that I'd been assigned to it because of his experience leading similar excursions over previous summers. I was quoted as saying that most of the volunteers were doing such work for their second, third, or fourth year in a volunteer detachment, and that "they seemed to be the Russian equivalent of 'Big Men on Campus' (pre-SDS version), active in sports and organized activities during the school year, now out to enjoy a summer extension of university fellowship." This last comment was a bit of gratuitous editorializing by whomever prepared the memo—I'm quite sure I never would have mentioned the Students for a Democratic Society at all.

It then described the living conditions of our detachment, with considerable detail about what we ate and what kinds of food shortages we experienced. I was quoted as saying "no one complained much, and there was always enough starch to fill up on." It also observed that I'd lost a considerable amount of weight.

There was also a paragraph on "Attitudes toward Americans," saying that "Few of the local people had ever seen an American before, but their spontaneous reaction was positive, warm, even admiring... often sounded the theme that 'peoples get along, it is just governments that disagree.'"

There was a very positive paragraph about the reaction of the local people and the students to the Apollo 11 moon landing. "The direct and open coverage (which had been shown locally on TV the following day) impressed everyone," it said, "particularly the students, many of whom commented on the contrast presented by the secrecy of their own space shots."

A key paragraph entitled "Detachment Attacked for Not Propagandizing" followed. It noted that "After about three weeks on the job, the detachment was visited by a regional supervisor... an older, professional party man of some sort... who attacked the detachment for its inactivity... the worst detachment in the region... for not having organized a lecture program... for the local people... concentrating on scientific subjects they knew well, but for a starter... a lecture explaining Soviet assistance to Czechoslovakia." The final notation said, "When Reuther left a week later, the lecture on Czechoslovakia was only a few days off. For their first scientific presentation, the students were offering an explanation of the Apollo 11 mission."

This regional supervisor believed I had been a bad influence on my fellow members of the detachment. It is likely that this was also the beginning of the end of Kolya's good reputation among the authorities, as he later suffered greatly for his close relationship to me.

In comparison with the rather spartan conditions in Kazakhstan, I was completely spoiled at the all-inclusive trade union resort in Sochi. I had everything I could eat and more, as well as endless opportunities to swim in the Black Sea. I walked around the beautiful town, toured surrounding areas, and spent time with the other guests, including some very attractive young women from France.

I wasn't the only one who was aware of their presence. A couple of vacationing male students from Moscow took to swimming around the barrier that separated our resort from the public beach in order to fraternize with the mademoiselles. On their last day in Sochi, the guys threw themselves a farewell bash, to which we were all invited. Everybody pitched in, but my ostensibly modest contribution turned out to be surprisingly valuable: two Sears Roebuck permanent press shirts that my mother had bought me for about $4.95 each. What we Americans thought of as everyday consumer goods were still in extremely short supply in Russia, and the boys made a bundle by selling those shirts on the black market. As a result, we were able to enjoy a great night at an outdoor Georgian restaurant in the hills with a panoramic view of both Sochi and the Black Sea, an open fire pit, live music, and free-flowing food and beverage.

CHAPTER 8

1969-1970

Second Year of Studies in Moscow

When the fall semester began in 1969, I had a new roommate. After graduating, Vitaly had been called up to serve with the Soviet armed forces that were stationed in Egypt. Soviet military personnel were advising the Egyptian army on how to defend their positions near the Suez Canal against repeated Israeli airstrikes. While Vitaly was home on leave, we got together for drinks. When I asked him whether there had been any Soviet casualties in Egypt, he told me that the military transport that flew him back to Moscow also carried a number of body bags.

I tried to keep a poker face and not reveal the alarm I was feeling, but I was fairly certain that it was not public knowledge that there had been Soviet casualties. I felt obligated to share this information with the American Embassy; I was concerned about possible retaliation by the USSR against Israel, and the potential this might have to draw the United States into the conflict.

As soon as I got to the embassy and began to explain why I was there, I was escorted to a room within a room—a clear plastic bubble. I could hear air circulating within what I think were double-paned walls. The circulating air sounded more like a vacuum than an AC system, and I assumed the white noise was intended to prevent electronic eavesdropping. I sat at the table and told the story of my conversation with Vitaly, but I don't recall being approached further on the subject.

While Vitaly was in Moscow on home leave, he bought an enormous number of rolls of East German film. I asked him why, and he told me that film was much more expensive in Egypt—he planned to sell them there and make a big profit. Vitaly, apparently, had become what he'd accused me of being a year earlier: a capitalist.

Although I got along well enough with my new roommate, who was a historian, my best friends at MGU were still my Physics-2 detachment workmates. We gathered regularly for evening parties of drinking, singing, and sharing stories about life. I took a certain pride in wearing my student construction detachment uniform—it was regarded as a badge of honor in Russia. I was wearing it one day when I went to the American Embassy to pick up my mail. Not surprisingly, the Russian security guards on the street refused to let me onto embassy grounds until I showed them my US passport and the official Russian travel permit that had allowed me to go to Kazakhstan. They looked amazed, and from then on, always let me in with a smile.

(Gathered with my Physics-2 workmates)

When I first started my studies in Moscow, I realized that the monthly stipend I was getting through the university was more than I needed. This apparently was a problem I shared with other American students at MGU. The rubles I received were not convertible currency—I couldn't exchange them for dollars or pounds or francs or deutschmarks. The only thing I could do with them was spend them in the shops in Moscow. The problem was that there wasn't much that I wanted or needed to buy, and now the rubles were starting to pile up. When I asked some of the other American students what they did with their extra rubles, they told me that they bought vintage books and sent them back to the States—not just any books, but collections of classic literature by Russian authors.

I followed their example and began buying the works of writers such as Tolstoy, Pushkin, Lermontov, and others. I started by purchasing individual volumes one or two at a time at used bookstores. As I tried to put together full sets, however, I discovered that I could buy books published after World War II, but I couldn't find the prewar volumes I needed to complete my sets. Prewar books were hard to find, and very expensive compared to post war books. When I mentioned this to the other Americans, they connected me with a Russian book collector and dealer.

I went to his apartment, which was packed with books from wall to wall and floor to ceiling. These were Russian language anthologies— sometimes over thirty volumes in a set—collections of the lifetime works of Russia's greatest writers. For the right price, or sometimes in exchange for consumer items he needed, the dealer sold me both individual volumes and entire sets of books that I was collecting.

Once or twice a week, the library at the US Embassy gave American students individual copies of American classic literature by writers such as Steinbeck, Hemingway, and Fitzgerald. Leaving the embassy, we hid these books under our coats or jackets. No one wanted to attract unwanted attention by openly distributing American literature—students had been expelled for this kind of activity. Most of us gave them to our Russian friends or traded them to our book dealer. I gave mine to Vitaly, who knew more about American literature than I did, but generally I read them first.

As I dove into my thesis research, I became quite close to my advisor, Professor Drobizhev. As he suggested, I began my research on the history of the Soviet trade unions in the stacks of the Lenin Library, where I read through old trade union journals from the early 1900s, before the Revolution. My goal was to gather information on the initial concepts of trade union organizing from that period. Professor Drobizhev and I would then get together in the late afternoon at his apartment in downtown Moscow to discuss what I'd found.

Even after I stopped going to the library, however, we kept meeting at his apartment. We drank cognac until his wife came home from work, then we would have a bite to eat or just open another bottle for the three of us. More often than not, we talked about recent US history—the part of it I had lived through or witnessed, including my family's experiences in the American labor movement, my work on the War on Poverty and in the civil rights movement, my work in the Bobby Kennedy campaign, and the presidency of John F. Kennedy. One evening I brought a film projector from the American Embassy to his apartment so we could screen the very impressive USIA-produced film, *John F. Kennedy: Years of Lightning, Day of Drums*, narrated by Gregory Peck.

Senator Birch Bayh at MGU

The American Embassy had a huge library of films, which our diplomats took to their apartments together for viewing—this was before VCRs came on the market. In the fall of 1969, another USIA film became available: it showed the Apollo 11 moon landing and had been dubbed into Russian with an American jazz soundtrack. I made arrangements with the embassy to get a copy of the film and a projector. My plan was to show it at the university.

My friend Kolya had a lot of influence at MGU, and he was able to get permission to use an auditorium in the dorm to screen the film. Coincidentally, Indiana Senator Birch Bayh was in Moscow with a delegation of US legislators. He remembered me from when I'd interned in his office two years earlier and agreed to forgo an official dinner at Spaso House with Ambassador Beam in order to attend the showing of the Apollo 11 film.

To bring a guest—any guest—into the dorms, it was always necessary to go to the foreign student office and pick up a written "permit slip." I didn't want to make a big deal with security, or possibly with the KGB, by informing the university that I was bringing a US Senator into our dorm, so I simply had the permit slip made out for my guest, Mr. Birch Bayh.

Even so, getting into the screening wasn't easy. I picked up the senator at Spaso House in an embassy car, but by the time we arrived at MGU, hundreds of students had already packed the two-story auditorium. Many more were clustered at the entrance—they had even broken out the glass panels in the doors so they could stick their heads in and see the screen! Kolya had saved two seats for us down front, but there was no way to get to them; the crowd at the door was too thick. He got up onstage to announce that the screening could not begin until the guest of honor, Senator Bayh, and the fellow student who made the film available could enter the hall and take their seats. Nobody moved. Senator Bayh and I took the elevator up one floor, entered the auditorium via the balcony, and then came downstairs, picking our way around the students who had packed the steps to watch the film.

It was a memorable event for all of us—even Senator Bayh had not yet seen the moon landing. As a second feature, I was also able to get the film of Game 7 of the 1969 NBA Finals between the Lakers and the Celtics—everyone in Russia loves basketball. Word about the Apollo 11 film spread quickly through MGU, so Kolya showed it eight more times the following evening.

As riveting as those films were, for me the real highlight of the evening happened after the screening was over. I brought Senator Bayh to a small gathering of friends from the Physics-2 detachment. About ten of us crammed ourselves into a dorm room and MGU students did what we always did—we got out the guitars and the vodka, which we drank from Erlenmeyer flasks they'd "borrowed" from chem lab.

As the initial toast was being made to welcome Senator Bayh to the university, he looked at me with concern, as he was a nondrinker, then leaned over and whispered in my ear. He wanted to know whether he was expected to drain his amply filled flask to the bottom. I whispered back that everyone else would, but added that if he felt strongly that he should not, I would be happy to explain his position to the students, and said they would understand. The toast that Kolya made was incredibly moving, a sincere message of hope that America and the Soviet Union would come together in peace. As the toast ended, Senator Bayh turned to me, nodded, and said, "Well, John, for God and Country," then chug-a-lugged his vodka just like the rest of us. What followed was a frank and honest discussion of international relations in general and American foreign policy in particular.

As the music began, one of the students sang a song that he had written in support of the North Vietnamese people. Several of the other students, whom I had told of Birch Bayh's growing public opposition to the war, were uneasy as I translated the Russian lyrics into English for him. After the song ended, Kolya asked me to apologize to Senator Bayh, and to explain the embarrassment in the context of support that they all felt for the Vietnamese. He was afraid that the lyrics to the song were somewhat anti-American, and he didn't want to offend the senator.

Without comment, Senator Bayh asked me to hand him the guitar. I did but warned him that this was a seven-string Russian gypsy guitar. "Not a problem," he replied, and proceeded to drop one string, then retune the instrument as he would a classical guitar. He then turned to me and asked, "John, do you know the words to 'Blowing in the Wind?'" As Senator Bayh started to play and the two of us began to serenade the group together, the students already knew it was a song of peace, a song against war, and they all joined in. It was a remarkable moment.

It was 1 a.m. when we walked Senator Bayh to the embassy car that was waiting for us in the courtyard. Feeling the spirit (and "spirits") of the evening, we linked arms and began singing "We Shall Overcome" as we walked. As the senator and I were riding back to his hotel, he suggested I come to work for him following my scheduled return to the States in the summer of 1970. He wanted me to work with him on the push for a Constitutional amendment—the 26th—that would give eighteen-year-olds the right to vote. To be adopted, it would require ratification by three-quarters of all state legislatures. I told him I looked forward to joining the team.

Senator McCarthy and Other Visitors to Moscow

Senator Bayh was not the only senator who came to Moscow. In early January of 1970, I learned from the embassy that Eugene McCarthy had arrived. We had first arranged for him to meet with a group of students at MGU, much as Birch Bayh had done, but after that plan fell through, we instead scheduled a gathering in his suite in the Hotel National. That meant our group would be much smaller—only four close friends from the construction detachment, including Kolya, came with me.

As we began, I told Senator McCarthy that, although my Russian wasn't perfect, I would be translating his remarks to the students and their comments and questions back to him. He responded by opening the door to the next room and inviting his official Soviet interpreter to join us.

I doubt whether Senator McCarthy grasped the implication of what he had done. My student friends were already reluctant to speak frankly; they clearly understood that an elegant suite in the National had probably been bugged by the KGB. Now, however, the presence of an official government translator left no doubt that whatever they said would be reported back to the authorities. When McCarthy asked the young Russians what they thought about the Communist system, the responses they gave were cookie-cutter rah-rah supportive. The senator may have been surprised, but I surely was not.

Sometime later, I was sitting with Kolya when he asked whether I ever got homesick. I responded that I often did, and he confessed that he did as well. He said he was planning to go home to see his wife and daughter, who lived in the city of Tolyatti, and invited me to go with him. Tolyatti is Russia's Motown, the location of the VAZ auto plant, largest in the Soviet Union. When I told him that I'd have to get a special internal visa to go with him, he told me not to worry and bought plane tickets to Kuybyshev (now Samara) for both of us, slightly changing the spelling of my last name on the ticket to reflect a more common, Jewish name in Russian.

Kuybyshev was home to the large Zhiguli dam and hydroelectric power station. It was also an industrial center for Russian defense and aerospace industries. As such, it was closed to foreigners. Both Kolya and I wore our student volunteer detachment uniforms for the flight to Kuybyshev, then took a bus to Tolyatti. We stayed at Kolya's apartment with his wife and daughter, and went fishing along the banks of the Volga, not far from the power station.

Shortly after we returned to Moscow, Mom and Dad came to visit. Harold from the trade union office got a car and was riding with us as I showed my parents around Moscow. While we were driving, I made a terrible slip of the tongue. I told my folks about the trip with Kolya to Kuybyshev and Tolyatti. My unauthorized travel to a forbidden area of the country had been orchestrated by Kolya, and it significantly affected his life. It was only in hindsight that I realized what a dreadful mistake I had made.

Hard Currency

After Mom and Dad departed, I took some of the dollars they had given me and went to the National Hotel, where we had met with Senator McCarthy. The National had a small, hard-currency-only shop just off the lobby where I was hoping to find a zoom lens for my Soviet-made Zenit camera. In the USSR, there were often shortages, but for foreigners, most consumer goods not available in regular shops could be purchased in hard-currency, or "D coupon," shops. D coupons were diplomatic coupons available to foreign envoys and journalists. Since Russian citizens were not allowed to have hard currency or D coupons, these hard-currency shops were usually found in tourist hotels, and they were strictly off limits for locals.

I spoke Russian with the salesclerk in the National shop, and she told me that although they didn't carry the lens I wanted, I would be able to get it from the hard-currency shop in the gigantic Rossiya Hotel on the other side of Red Square. After buying some East German film with the dollars my parents had given me, I left the shop and noticed that a man who had been leaning against a column in the shop now appeared to be following me. To get to Red Square from the National, you had to cross some major streets, which was only possible via a long, underground pedestrian passageway. I was well into the tunnel when I was grabbed by the shoulder from behind and told in strong language to stop in place.

It was, of course, the man I'd seen, and he now said I was under arrest and that he was taking me to headquarters. When I asked what I had done wrong, he showed me his official ID and told me that I had illegally used hard currency in the National shop. As soon as I showed him my US passport and MGU student ID, his face turned as red as the Soviet flag. "Excuse me," he sputtered as he walked away. Continuing on toward the hard currency shop at the Rossiya, where I did buy my zoom lens, I was more than a little proud of myself. "Amazing!" I thought. "I was almost arrested because this government agent thought I was Russian!"

Travel Abroad

In late December of 1969, a delegation of American family friends and colleagues arrived in Moscow. The group included friends from the UAW and Americans for Democratic Action (ADA), the progressive political group that Uncle Walter had helped found. These friends came bearing gifts from Mom and Dad, including a most welcome twenty-two-pound box of apples and oranges. Fresh produce was often hard to come by, especially in winter.

With the help of Harold and other contacts at the AUCCTU, I arranged for the group to tour a Moscow auto plant, then meet with the leadership of the Russian auto workers union. On Christmas night, we all went to the Bolshoi, where I saw my seventh performance of *Swan Lake.*

In the theater, my family friends were to my right and on my left were two vacationing young American schoolteachers who taught at an American military base in West Germany. I introduced them to my friends, and after the show, we all crossed the street to the Metropol hotel, where the teachers were staying. The Metropol had a very interesting bar that featured live *balalaika* music. This was unusual—Moscow tourist hotels usually played American and British rock 'n roll. After my family friends went back to their hotel, the teachers invited me up to their room. By the time I thought about returning to the dorm, the subway had shut down for the night, so I ended up staying till morning… and that was the beginning of my relationship with Patsy.

A few months later, she invited me to meet her at the Army base in Augsburg, about an hour west of Munich, and then go with her and some friends to an Italian ski resort in Selva, in the Dolomite Mountains. As it turned out, Dad was going to be in Europe at the same time. I wired ahead to his hotel in Brussels to say that I would meet up with him in Stockholm, but he never got the message—there had been a fire in the hotel shortly before he was due to arrive in Belgium and he ended up staying someplace else.

I landed in Stockholm the morning he was to meet with Arne Geijer and grabbed a taxi straight from the airport to Arne's office. I arrived a few minutes before 9:00 and found my father pacing back and forth on the sidewalk, waiting to go upstairs at 9 on the dot.

I asked Dad whether he had any holes in his schedule that day so we could spend some time together. He told me that he was meeting with Swedish Prime Minister Olof Palme later in the afternoon, and that I was welcome to come along. Palme had studied in the States in the late 1940s and had written his senior thesis on the United Auto Workers union. After graduating, he had interviewed his hero, Uncle Walter, in Detroit. That afternoon, Dad and I met alone with the prime minister, who said he hoped to see us soon at the opening ceremonies for the UAW Family Education Center in northern Michigan.

I had a great time with Patsy and her friends in the Italian Alps, and when we returned to her apartment on the base in Augsburg, she let me "borrow" her access to the PX. I purchased some consumer goods on behalf of my bookdealer friend, including a Samsonite suitcase and some stereo equipment. When I got to Moscow, I traded them for pre-war volumes of Russian literature to add to my growing collection.

Soon thereafter, Olof Palme arrived in Moscow for an official visit. Veteran diplomat Gunnar Jarring, then Sweden's ambassador to the Soviet Union, hosted a reception for him at his home, and I was invited. Why was I there? Because of the ambassador's daughter. During my studies in Moscow, I had met Eva Jarring at a diplomatic social function. We dated periodically after that.

During the reception Ambassador Jarring's wife took me aside into a private adjoining office, where I was introduced to Soviet Prime Minister Alexei Kosygin, his personal translator, and three or four other guests. As I introduced myself to Prime Minister Kosygin, I listened as his translator told him a great deal of information about Uncle Walter and the UAW. When my embassy friends learned that I had spoken personally with the Russian leader, they were quite impressed. At the time, the Cold War was at its frostiest, and even high-ranking American diplomats were not afforded that kind of opportunity.

A Death in the Family

The scheduled opening of the UAW Family Education Center in northern Michigan did not take place as planned, and for the most tragic of reasons. On Sunday, May 10, 1970, I received a call at the dorm from close friends at the American Embassy. They passed along the sad news they had just heard: Uncle Walter and Aunt May had been killed in a plane crash the previous day. They'd been headed for the UAW Family Education Center in northern Michigan, which was nearing completion, and their chartered Learjet went down while trying to land in dense fog. All on board had been killed, including the two pilots, a nephew of May's who was one of Walter's bodyguards, and our close family friend, Oskar Stonorov, the architect who had designed the Black Lake Family Education Center. My friends added that there was a possibility that my father had also been on the plane and invited me to come immediately to the embassy. As soon as I arrived, they placed an international call to our home in Washington. I was relieved beyond words when Dad answered the phone.

Dad and I made plans for me to fly home for the memorial service, which was to be held in Detroit. Harold Shetinin saw me off, and on our way to the airport, I confided in him that I was bringing with me a very heavy suitcase full of prewar volumes of Russian literature. These books could only leave the Soviet Union after being reviewed and cleared with an official stamp from the Lenin Library, which I had not yet done. Harold reassured me that he would take care of everything, but I became concerned when a Soviet airport customs officer demanded to look inside the suitcase. Harold stepped in immediately and pulled rank as an official of the AUCCTU to insist that it not be opened. The suitcase was checked onto the flight to Dulles, but when we landed in DC, the bag didn't come off the plane. None of my luggage did. About a week later, it all showed up and everything was in place, including not just the books but also many reel-to-reel audio tapes I had recorded during my year and a half in Russia.

On the morning of the memorial service for Uncle Walter and Aunt May, auto workers around the country observed three minutes of silence in his honor. The service itself was both moving and comforting at the same time. The entire extended Reuther family was there, of course, but many people from the labor movement and from progressive politics attended as well, including Cesar Chavez, Hubert Humphrey, Whitney Young, Ted Kennedy, and Coretta Scott King. Mrs. King spoke to the solidarity that Uncle Walter fostered between the labor movement and the civil rights movement, a solidarity he proved with his physical presence, over and over. "He was there in person when the storm clouds were thick," she declared, "at Montgomery, Birmingham, Selma, Jackson, Washington, and Memphis."

*(With my arm around Dad at Walter and May's memorial service
in Detroit. Photo credit: Walter P. Reuther Library, Archives of
Labor and Urban Affairs, Wayne State University)*

Prior to the service, our extended family gathered in a Detroit hotel. I was in the lobby when I saw Ted Kennedy. As I escorted him to our suite, he asked me what I was doing. After I told him about my studies in Moscow, he asked what I planned to do when I returned to the States. When I mentioned that Senator Bayh had offered me a job, he suggested that I put that off for a bit and come to Massachusetts to work on his reelection campaign. I told him I would like that very much.

I saw him again a week later at the National Cathedral in DC, where he was among several thousand people who attended a second memorial service for Uncle Walter and Aunt May. The service was led by the Very Reverend Francis B. Sayre Jr., dean of the Cathedral and a family friend. I was the speaker on behalf of our family, and I was in distinguished company, sharing the honors with former Supreme Court Chief Justice Earl Warren; Sam Brown from the National Vietnam Moratorium;

former Swedish Prime Minister Tage Erlander; former Secretary of Labor Willard Wirtz; Clarence Mitchell of the Leadership Conference on Civil Rights; Anna Roosevelt Halsted, daughter of Franklin and Eleanor Roosevelt; James Jordan of the Sanitation Workers Local in Memphis, Tennessee; and Jack Conway, Walter's former assistant, the man who had arranged for my position at the OEO.

While I was in Washington, I had a chance to visit with Dr. Abdul Said. Dr. Said had been my professor and mentor at American University's School of International Service, and we had developed a strong personal relationship that continued after I left the university. After spending an hour or so catching up, he looked me over for a moment and then casually mentioned that he thought I needed to update my wardrobe. He told me his wife was working as a clothing designer and placed clothing orders for Woodward & Lothrop, DC's flagship department store—the same place where Mom had bought the off-white dinner jacket I wore to the White House. Dr. Said insisted we drive there to meet up with his wife. They selected and purchased a beautiful pair of tan, bell-bottomed pants as a gift for me, and assured me that bell-bottoms were the latest in men's fashion.

When I returned to Moscow, I proudly wore them to an embassy event. With more access to western news media, the Americans knew I was dressed in the latest style from the States. The Soviet guards did not, and the astonished looks on their faces soon gave way to outright laughter. They thought I looked like a clown, proving once more that not every hot trend in the West made it behind the Iron Curtain.

I had initially wanted to spend another summer working with Kolya and our volunteer construction detachment before returning to the States. The plan was to work on Sakhalin Island, which is located off the far eastern coast of Russia, just north of Japan's Hokkaido Island, but it was not to be. Kolya had included me in the list of those who would be in the detachment, even though Sakhalin was closed to foreigners. Once the authorities found out, they not only excluded me, but removed Kolya as commander as well. The Physics-2 detachment was so loyal to their leader that once Kolya was replaced, they all refused to go.

Travels Home Through Asia

While in Washington for memorial services for Walter and May, Dad and I worked up an itinerary for my return trip to the States. Rather than flying west from Moscow to DC, I would head east. The two-month trip would take me to thirteen different Asian countries, then to Hawaii, and finally to San Francisco before finishing up in Washington. Dad was paying for it, and being his typically frugal self, he didn't book me into any exclusive hotels or resorts. His plan was actually better, in that it was far more interesting and educational. He arranged for me to be hosted by his many international trade union friends and acquaintances as I hopscotched across Asia.

I started in Karachi, then the capital of Pakistan, and went from there to Bombay (now Mumbai) and then Ahmedabad and New Delhi. I left India for Rangoon, Burma—now Yangon, Myanmar—hoping to reconnect with the Burmese grad student who had lived on my floor at the rooming house during my last year at Cornell. I understood he'd become a professor at the University of Rangoon, but university officials told me they had no record of his having taught there. At the time, Burma was ruled by a one-party military dictatorship, and I speculated that he disappeared because he'd done something to alienate himself from the government.

My next stop was Bangkok, Thailand, where I was the guest of Sukum Navapan, president of the Thai Military Bank. While I was growing up in Washington, Sukum and his brother Clive had each spent at least a semester living with us while studying at American University. After that I went on to Kuala Lumpur, Malaysia, and then to Singapore, Jakarta, the Philippines, Hong Kong, Taiwan, and Okinawa.

(With Sukum Navapan and his wife in Thailand)

After one final stop in Tokyo, I flew to Honolulu on the just-introduced, enormous Boeing 747, where I encountered one of the flight attendants I had met at the embassy in Moscow. She bumped me up to first class, which I had entirely to myself. I was thrilled to be able to do some skindiving again while in Hawaii, and even more thrilled to be back on US soil—and in US water.

From Hawaii, I flew to San Francisco, where I stayed with Eric. Eric was working as administrative director of the San Francisco Art Commission's Neighborhood Arts Program and had embraced what can only be described as a hippie lifestyle. He was renting a house in the Berkeley Hills with friends—he and his girlfriend, a nurse, lived in the basement. The upstairs tenants were therapists and UC Berkeley students. The therapists had installed a huge hot tub in the garage, but when they weren't using it with their patients, it was available to anyone who lived there. In keeping with the mood of the times, the tub was not clothing optional. To use it, it had to be just you and the water—birthday suit, not bathing suit.

Eric's house is where I had my first experience with marijuana. Years later, when the two of us were reminiscing about my visit, he told me that a friend of his girlfriend had also been staying in the house while I was there. According to Eric, she was a strikingly beautiful and quite uninhibited fashion model who got me stoned and naked in the hot tub. Apparently, I'd been very shy about all of it, which only made her like me more. But because even the fact that she was there at all came as news to me, I don't know for sure what happened after that...but I think I can guess.

CHAPTER 9

1970-1972

The Campaign Trail—Ted Kennedy and Birch Bayh

After returning to Washington, I met with Senator Bayh about the position he had offered me during his visit to Moscow. He still wanted me to work for him, but the job description he had in mind had changed. Bayh was planning to run for president in 1972 and now intended to hire me as a member of his campaign staff. When I told him that Ted Kennedy had asked me to work on his senatorial reelection campaign for the next few months, I could almost see the wheels turning in his head. By "loaning" me to Kennedy, he'd be doing Teddy a favor that he could call in down the road—a favor that would look a lot like his endorsement for Bayh's run for the White House.

I joined the Kennedy campaign with Senator Bayh's blessing, and in early fall I was off to Boston. I worked under Bill Foley, head of Kennedy's advance team, and we became close friends. An advance person—or advance man, which was the customary terminology at the time—goes to the designated location before the candidate arrives and makes all preparatory arrangements for the candidate's appearance. He then attends the event with the candidate to make sure all goes as planned—and fixes it when it doesn't.

Being an advance man required nimble problem-solving skills and the ability to think on your feet, and sometimes even when you did the right thing, it didn't turn out the way you planned. Kennedy was speaking before a large campaign luncheon at a Boston hotel. To facilitate an easy departure, I'd arranged with the doorman to hold a place for the senator's car just a few steps from the entrance. Leaving the hotel, I introduced Senator Kennedy to the doorman and mentioned his kindness. Kennedy reached toward him for a handshake, but the doorman held out his hand palm up—he expected a tip. Awkward. And yes, I should have anticipated that and taken care of it before the senator left the luncheon.

I was advancing a parade in western Massachusetts and saw a group of nuns who had lined up along the route. Senator Kennedy with a bunch of nuns—it was a photo op waiting to happen. As he walked in the parade and got closer to the sisters, I offered to take a group photo, but I took too long setting up the shot. Meanwhile the parade kept moving, leaving Kennedy further and further behind. He became increasingly impatient. "Take the photo, John!" he said in exasperation. "Take the photo!" The senator then had to double-time it to catch up to his spot in the line of march.

As I was advancing with Joseph P. Kennedy II, a future congressman and son of RFK, Joe was on the phone receiving information about the event and asked if I had some paper to write on. I gave him my little black book, which had all the phone numbers and addresses from my last two years in Russia and from my trip home through Asia. In the flurry of activity that is always part of a campaign, I forgot to get the book back from Joe, and never saw it again.

By the time Ted Kennedy won reelection that November, Senator Bayh had already named me National Youth Coordinator for his presidential campaign. My job entailed rallying student support for Senator Bayh at major universities around the country. Having encouraged the senator to accept a speaking engagement at Temple University in Philadelphia, I belatedly discovered that his appearance coincided with a crucial home game for the Temple Owls, the university's much beloved basketball team. Worse yet, the student organization sponsoring Senator Bayh's event had booked him into an enormous auditorium. With only the first few rows filled in the otherwise empty hall, the senator adroitly began his presentation by suggesting we change to a seminar format. Lesson learned: be sure to check what other events are scheduled at the time your candidate is due to speak.

As an advance man, I was still making mistakes, but my learning curve was going up. During the summer, there are always a lot of student interns working in DC, whether it's in Senate or House offices or at summer posts in federal agencies. In August 1971, we decided to promote Senator Bayh's presidential campaign among these interns by throwing a floating party. We chartered a vintage paddlewheel riverboat to cruise down the Potomac to a Virginia amusement park. The boat would drop off the kids for a couple of hours, then bring them back later that night. To make the trip even more fun, I convinced some Bayh supporters to spring for a few kegs of beer on deck, as well as a live band. It was an innovative idea with a lot of upside potential—sometime around Labor Day, the interns would return to their home states and universities across the country, carrying with them positive PR about Senator Bayh's candidacy.

A week or so before the cruise, I attended a reception at the Soviet Embassy, where I ran into Larisa Kuznitsova, a Russian woman who had worked in the foreign student office at Moscow State University while I was there. I'd seen her often enough at MGU—that's where I had to go to pick up visitor passes for guests. She recognized me right away, and introduced me to her husband, Vadim Kuznitsov, who was one of the young diplomats newly assigned to the Soviet Embassy. I invited Vadim and Larisa to join us for the riverboat party. At Vadim's suggestion, I also invited another young Russian couple from the embassy, Igor Filin and his wife Mayya.

After we'd cruised for some time that evening, Vadim suddenly asked me how many miles the Virginia amusement park was from Washington. I had no idea. At that time, our State Department limited travel by Soviet diplomats to a twenty-mile radius from DC. Anything further required a special travel permit. My Russian friends were worried that they might be inadvertently violating that State Department regulation. Thankfully, nothing ever came of this incident, or if it did, I never heard about it.

Sometime later, Vadim and Larisa invited me to their apartment for dinner. At one point Vadim took me into the kitchen and quietly advised me that it would not be a good idea for me to spend time with Igor Filin. I didn't know what to make of his warning. Was Vadim trying to caution me to avoid contact with someone who might have been something other than a diplomat? That wasn't out of the question. Embassies—ours and theirs—had envoys and attachés whose official titles were fig leaves that thinly masked the fact that they actually worked for their country's espionage organizations. Or was Vadim competing with Igor for a favorable relationship with me because of my position with Birch Bayh? If Senator Bayh were to be elected president, a "side door" into the Oval Office could be immensely valuable. That was plausible too, but there was no way for me to know whether it was one of these possibilities, or something else entirely.

A close associate of mine during the Bayh campaign was Clarence Martin, who was the regional coordinator for most of the South. While advancing a trip to Georgia, Clarence and I attended the first inaugural of Jimmy Carter as governor. We got to know Carter aides Hamilton Jordan and Jody Powell, who would later play key roles in Carter's White House: Jordan as chief of staff, and Powell as press secretary.

Another memorable time with Clarence was at a friendly staff party in suburban Washington. There was a pool in the backyard of this private home, and some of the guests who had brought bathing suits jumped in. Clarence and I wanted to join them, and although we had not brought swim trunks to the party, we had consumed a considerable amount of alcohol—enough so that stripping down to skinny dip seemed perfectly reasonable.

There was certainly quite a bit of astonishment for a while, but then, all of us had been drinking quite a bit, and most of the guests who had been swimming went back inside to continue partying, as did Clarence and I after getting dressed. I do remember the next day being somewhat embarrassed, but I also remember that a lovely young lady with whom I'd been swimming drove me home from the party that night to the basement apartment in my parents' home. It had its own entrance and she and I did a little more partying together there. Had the skinny dip been ill-advised? Jury's still out.

While working almost nonstop for the Bayh campaign, I somehow found an occasional weekend to make the two-and-a-half-hour drive to

Everett, Pennsylvania, about a hundred miles east of Pittsburgh. Everett is a small town in the Allegheny Mountains surrounded by beautiful open country, and it was far enough from DC that real estate was affordable. Wanting to spend more time there, I stopped at a local store to ask whether any property was for sale and was referred to a farmer named John James. Farmer James had ninety-two acres he wanted to sell, and as it turned out, his parcel was just what I was looking for. We drew up the bill of sale on the hood of my car, and with an $18,000 loan from Dad and a purchase agreement that allowed me to stretch out payments over many years, I became a first-time landowner.

The land was in its natural state when I bought it, but I soon built a log cabin on the property. I'd loved carpentry and woodworking since I was a boy—our DC house had a large basement, and Dad had installed a workshop down there. With his guidance, I learned to use both hand tools and power tools. As a teenager, I'd already put those skills to use on Martha's Vineyard to build a log cabin fort for the children of Phil and Leni Stern—and I'd gotten into a lot of hot water with Phil for having felled some of his trees to use for lumber. Now the trees I cut down would be my own.

The rustic cabin that I built with my own hands became my refuge and my safety valve, the place where I could regroup and recharge and immerse myself in the beauty and stillness of nature. Every time I went there, I returned to DC replenished. Once the cabin was finished, I hired a contractor with a bulldozer to create a small, stream-fed lake in a valley not far from the house. It fulfilled its mission as refuge for many years thereafter. I believe I didn't sell it until sometime in 2005.

In April 1971, the Vietnam War was still going on. Despite Nixon's claims of a successful "Vietnamization" of the conflict, Americans were still fighting and dying there. An enormous antiwar demonstration was planned in Washington for April 24, and young people were coming into the city from all over the country. The Bayh campaign office was located on an upper floor of a downtown DC office building, and we invited demonstrators from Indiana to bring their sleeping bags and camp out on our floor.

At the same time, history professor Vladimir Drobizhev, my master's research adviser at Moscow State University, was visiting with a Soviet delegation. After meeting him at my father's UAW office, I brought him to Bayh campaign headquarters. My goal was to show him how in the United States we work to change the government without violence, without a revolution, and how authorities in a democracy handle dissent. Soon after we arrived at the campaign office, the police knocked on the door. Someone had apparently noticed a lot of demonstrators entering and leaving the building at all hours and had complained about it. I explained the situation to the officers, introduced them to Professor Drobizhev, and told them that the comings and goings of the protestors were legit.

The next day, over half a million people gathered to demonstrate against the Vietnam War. As I was driving Professor Drobizhev toward the Capitol, he expressed his amazement at how well the police were dealing with vehicle and pedestrian traffic during the ongoing demonstration. "In Moscow," he said, "it would take the entire government to be involved in organizing such a demonstration, and that could only be a pro-government demonstration. Here, it is an anti-government demonstration so well organized by the police!"

I soon received a promotion from Senator Bayh and was named regional coordinator for the Mid-Atlantic area—DC, Maryland, and Virginia. My appointment was short-lived for the saddest of reasons. Bayh's wife Marvella had been diagnosed with breast cancer. When she made the announcement, it was a gutsy thing to do—at the time, no one talked openly about this disease. Marvella Bayh was one of the first public figures to disclose her diagnosis. The plan was to deal with her cancer aggressively, with a mastectomy, radiation, and chemotherapy, and Birch Bayh withdrew from the presidential race to care for his wife and support her during her treatment. Her therapies were successful for a time, but the cancer came roaring back six years later. Marvella Bayh died in 1979 at the age of forty-six.

The Campaign Trail—George McGovern

When Senator Bayh ended his candidacy, I was approached by Frank Mankiewicz. Frank had been Bobby Kennedy's press secretary at the time of his death in 1968, and our paths had crossed on the campaign trail several times since then. Frank was now George McGovern's national campaign director, and he offered me a job as Massachusetts state coordinator.

Arriving in Boston in the fall of 1971, I immediately saw several familiar faces from my time working on Ted Kennedy's senate campaign. I lived in a house with close colleagues of my Kennedy advance team boss, Bill Foley. In our office, I developed close relationships with our state press secretary, Ed Jesser, as well as with Robert "Skinner" Donahue, and Nick Mitropoulos, two of our top state organizers.

One of our most active and effective participants in the campaign was Barney Frank, who was then a candidate himself for the Massachusetts State House of Representatives. Frank would go on to serve in the Massachusetts State Senate before being elected to Congress in 1980, where he served with distinction until his retirement in 2013. In Congress, Frank was probably best known as the cosponsor (with Connecticut Senator Chris Dodd) of the Dodd–Frank Wall Street Reform and Consumer Protection Act (better known as just Dodd–Frank). Passed in 2010, it overhauled US financial regulations following the Great Recession of 2008.

Aside from the campaign itself, I have fond memories of frequent late-night trips to a popular local bar called the Bull & Finch Pub, a regular hangout for political campaign workers—it really was "the place where everybody knows your name." About a decade later, it would become the inspiration for the hit TV series *Cheers*, but while I was working in Boston, I got to know Sally, a beautiful blonde waitress who worked there.

In the fall of 1971, my parents were out of the country and asked me to represent them at a Soviet Embassy reception to celebrate the November 7 anniversary of the 1917 Russian Revolution. I invited Sally to drive with me to DC and accompany me to the reception. When we arrived at the Soviet Embassy, we went through a receiving line where we were greeted by the top embassy officials, including Anatoly Dobrynin. Dobrynin was the dean of the Washington diplomatic corps—his tenure as Soviet ambassador had begun during the presidency of JFK, and would extend into Reagan's second term, ending in 1986. I explained—in Russian—to Ambassador Dobrynin that I was there in place of my father, whom he knew, and that I had spent two years in Moscow studying Russian and doing graduate thesis research at MGU. Dobrynin was very interested in hearing more about my stay in Moscow, and we spoke long enough to seriously back up the receiving line. Ever the diplomat, he said nothing about my small gold lapel pin that spelled out the letters "McGovern."

Sometime thereafter, Henry Kissinger, Nixon's National Security Advisor and eventual Secretary of State, arrived at the reception. Kissinger had developed something of a reputation as a ladies' man, having dated a series of attractive women including Candice Bergen, Liv Ullmann, Diane Sawyer, and Jill St. John. As Sally and I introduced ourselves to him, Ambassador Dobrynin joined us. Dobrynin noticed Kissinger eyeing Sally appreciatively and couldn't resist a comment. "John has good taste, doesn't he?" he remarked.

Kissinger looked at Sally approvingly, nodded to Ambassador Dobrynin, then scowled at my McGovern pin. "In women, yes," he replied in his *Dr. Strangelove* German accent, "but not in politics."

The Rad/Lib Caucus

By December 1971, the race to become the Democratic presidential nominee to face off against Richard Nixon was heating up, and a number of progressives had already declared their candidacy. In addition to my candidate, George McGovern of South Dakota, Ed Muskie of Maine was running as well. Eugene McCarthy of Minnesota, whose strong showing in the New Hampshire primary in 1968 had convinced LBJ not to seek reelection, was also seeking the nomination.

Ted Kennedy, of course, was the X factor in Massachusetts Democratic politics, but in the lingering aftermath of the 1969 Chappaquiddick incident, he continued to deny that he intended to become a candidate. Muskie from nearby Maine was considered a frontrunner, but he wasn't active in Massachusetts, seemingly to leave a lane open for Ted in case he had a change of heart. That left McGovern and McCarthy as the two leading contenders for the state's progressive delegates.

Our campaign had purchased McGovern stationery and envelopes from a company owned by Jerry Grossman. Grossman reportedly had donated heavily to Eugene McCarthy's presidential campaign in 1968 and was openly supporting McCarthy again for the 1972 nomination. Many McCarthy backers, including Grossman, advocated for holding a liberal caucus well in advance of the primary. Candidates would be invited to make their pitch about why they should be the nominee, and then the assembled delegates would vote on who they preferred.

The idea was not just to pick a winner but to unify behind him. Everyone wanted to avoid the chaos and bitter infighting that had marred the 1968 Democratic convention. For the purposes of this caucus, if a candidate got 60 percent or more of the vote, the campaigns of the losing candidates pledged to support him, at least in Massachusetts.

Given Grossman's endorsement of what was being called the Rad/Lib caucus, many McGovern backers suspected that it was intended as a setup for McCarthy. Many, but not all, since a number of our campaign operatives were convinced that we were underestimating how much support there was for McGovern. Their confidence persuaded us to participate in the January 15 caucus. Now it was up to us to prove them right. (One of our most enthusiastic campaigners was a young Ed Markey, who would go on to be elected to the House of Representatives in 1976 and to the Senate in 2013.)

At the caucus, Senator McCarthy spoke on his own behalf. Senator McGovern was not available but was represented by eighty-four-year-old former Alaska Senator Ernest Gruening. Although Ted Kennedy himself stayed diplomatically neutral, I still had ties to members of his staff from my work on the senator's 1970 reelection campaign, and those connections paid off—the Kennedy staff loaned us walkie-talkies so we could coordinate and communicate with one another during the proceedings.

Once the voting began, it became readily apparent our optimism had been justified. McGovern scored an overwhelming victory, winning 62 percent of the vote on the third ballot. True to their word, Jerry Grossman and other McCarthy supporters promptly endorsed him. Hunter S. Thompson wrote about it in his book *Fear and Loathing on the Campaign Trail '72*:

> *Grossman ignored the obvious fact that he and other pro-McCarthy heavies had been beaten stupid, on the grass-roots organizing level, by an unheralded 'McGovern machine' put together in Massachusetts by John Reuther—a nephew of Walter, late president of the UAW. I spent most of that afternoon wandering around the gym, listening to people talk and watching the action, and it was absolutely clear—once the voting started—that Reuther had everything wired.*

R. W. Apple Jr. wrote in *The New York Times* that "Mr. McGovern's Massachusetts effort was put together by John Reuther, a nephew of Walter P. Reuther, the late president of the United Automobile Workers. The McCarthy backers complained that he had simply out-organized them."

I surely couldn't take all the credit. It was our campaign team, including Eddie Jesser, Skinner Donahue, Jerry Vento, Nick Mitropoulos, and many others who "had everything wired" and "had simply out-organized them." Our win at the Rad/Lib caucus gave our campaign a huge boost, leading to McGovern's win in the Massachusetts primary.

I was in Boston for victory night, but it was only temporary—the McGovern campaign had already moved me on to my next assignment. I was on the road nationally as part of the effort to bring organized labor into the McGovern camp, and it was sometimes a tough sell. Former VP Hubert Humphrey, whose robust ties with organized labor went back decades, had been reelected to the Senate, and was gearing up for another run at the presidency.

Not surprisingly, the national campaign office sent me to my birth state of Michigan, where the Reuther name was quite well known. Working with local and state campaigns, I would often station myself at factory gates and shake hands with workers on their way to or from work, introducing myself and letting them know that a Reuther was supporting McGovern.

I kept a busy campaign schedule, and my presence soon got the attention of local news media. I was written up by the Battle Creek *Enquirer* on May 11, 1972, under the headline "John Reuther campaigning for McGovern here today." The story said:

> *Reuther will begin his campaign here with a 2:30 p.m. visit today to the Battle Creek McGovern Campaign Headquarters... At 3 p.m., he will visit the Eaton Corp. on 20th Street for a handshaking session with workers. After a radio interview, he will meet for dinner with the Calhoun County Democratic Executive Committee... At 6:15 p.m. Reuther will address United Auto Workers stewards, Local 220 in the VFW Hall, Marshall... At 7:35 p.m., Reuther will tape a television interview and then head for more campaigning in Bay City.*

Later in May, Detroit *Free Press* Pulitzer Prize-winning journalist Saul Friedman spent the day with me, then wrote a lengthy article called "A New Breed of Reuther Walks McGovern's Road." Friedman's perceptive piece touched a nerve, because it identified a key contradiction between my union heritage and the impression I made in person.

"John Reuther has a pretty good working-class name," he began, "but among workers he has trouble figuring out just who he is." Friedman noted that, "Although he is from the working class, he is not of it, and the workers know it... In a way, his is the problem of the American working class and its sons. For it is the American dream that the son must rise above his class—but not too far. And John Reuther, Cornell graduate and world traveler, can't go home again."

Friedman understood how the American dream—home ownership, a better education for your children—worked at cross-purposes to the organized labor movement. Successful organizing and bargaining led to better lives for workers, but that hard-won upward mobility brought with it an inescapable conundrum for unions and their political power. Often enough, the college-educated children of men and women who worked the assembly line and walked the picket line now had more in common with the children of company executives—the young people they graduated with—than they did with union members fighting for workplace safety, health benefits, and a decent hourly wage.

And I personified the dilemma. Friedman wrote that I looked "like a prep school product of the Eastern establishment, tall, strapping… But behind a face that any mother could love, the Reuther dedication and commitment is there. And John Reuther has taken it up where his father and his uncles left it, going beyond the era and glory of old unionism, the picket line, and the New Deal, to the New Politics, which clashes with family friends."

After the Democratic Party convention in Miami in July of 1972, I became McGovern's national campaign coordinator for Hubert Humphrey's home state of Minnesota. Humphrey had run as Minnesota's favorite son, but his candidacy flamed out. Because he'd been LBJ's vice president, he could never jettison the Vietnam War albatross around his neck. The McGovern supporters in the state now faced the task of uniting the state party behind the Democratic ticket, and it was thought that a Reuther, whose family and the UAW had a long and close relationship with Hubert Humphrey, might help make this happen.

That year, Humphrey's fellow Minnesota senator, Walter Mondale, was running for reelection, and our paths crossed regularly. I greatly appreciated the guidance I received from his staff, and from Hubert Humphrey's staff as well. The offices of both senators were instrumental in helping me convince AFL-CIO leadership in Minnesota to endorse McGovern. The union had always been a strong supporter of Humphrey and had been slow to move on after he was no longer in the running.

I had initially been quite optimistic about our chances for a McGovern victory in Minnesota after we had done so well in Massachusetts, but I never really believed he would win the general election nationwide. We were running against an incumbent president, and I was also seeing the national polls. Nevertheless, I was enthusiastic about participating, as I felt I was making a contribution. I was as enthusiastic for McGovern as I had been for RFK, mainly due to McGovern's opposition to the war in Vietnam. At the time, I don't remember having thoughts about becoming a candidate myself, but I did feel that my work was important—that it mattered.

CHAPTER 10

1973-1974

Back to Michigan

In November of 1972, Richard Nixon won reelection in a landslide with almost 61 percent of the popular vote. George McGovern carried Massachusetts, but no other state. Having run his campaign in Minnesota, the only small measure of personal pride I took in the otherwise overwhelming defeat was that we lost our state by the smallest margin of any of the remaining 49 (Nixon's 51 percent to McGovern's 46 percent).

Prior to running the Minnesota campaign, I'd spent considerable time working with University of Michigan students in Ann Arbor. With their encouragement, I decided to re-establish my Michigan residency and run for Congress from the second congressional district. Michigan's congressional districts have morphed substantially over the years, but at the time, the second covered what was essentially the lower righthand corner of the state, stretching north from the Ohio border to include Monroe, Livonia, Ann Arbor, and the outskirts of these areas. I chose the second because of the base I had there with supporters at the University of Michigan. I also believed I would be able to appeal to a broad assortment of Democrats in this most diverse district.

The incumbent was three-term Republican Marvin Esch, first elected in 1966. Democrats were looking for someone who could unite this truly diverse district of college, suburban, and rural communities to defeat Esch in the 1974 midterm elections. The Democrats were heavily favored to make substantial gains in both the House and Senate, as the Watergate scandal had tainted the entire Republican Party. When I told the UAW Director of Political Affairs of my plans, he said, "With the name Reuther in Michigan, half of the people are going to love you, but the other half are going to hate you, so you're going to have to find a way to gain the respect and trust of the other side."

By "the other side," he meant people who identified with management, not labor, and we decided that the best way to earn their respect would be to get a management job in the auto industry. First, however, I had to solidify my bona fides with labor union members and their families. A local UAW member I had worked with in the McGovern campaign pointed out a problem that was obvious to him, but not to me. Although my name was Reuther, he said, I personally had never worked on the assembly line, nor was I a UAW member.

It wasn't that I felt superior to factory workers—I surely did not. That said, I understood that I could be perceived that way, and I'd had enough experience campaigning to know that in politics, perception is everything. Although I'd worked with my hands all my life and had been a busboy and waiter and member of Culinary Workers Union Local 226 in Las Vegas, that wouldn't help my "outsider" Ivy League image with assembly line workers in the second district.

The upward economic mobility created by the successful labor union movement brought with it an unwanted political side effect—my advanced degree could easily become a barrier between me and the blue-collar voters who otherwise would be my natural constituency. To combat it, this UAW member got me a job in the cut and trim department installing seating and upholstery at GM's Fisher Body Plant in Livonia. I became a member of UAW Local 174, the same local where Dad and Uncle Walter had begun.

When I first clocked in, both management and local union leadership were apprehensive, but for two very different reasons. My Fisher Body supervisor was worried that this college-educated Reuther might be gathering on-the-job evidence to write some kind of an insider exposé on working conditions at the plant. I got along very well with my coworkers, one of whom was the daughter of my supervisor. She and I dated for a while, which I'm sure contributed to his apprehension about my presence in his shop. At the same time, I was told that the head of Local 174 was hearing footsteps—he feared I was after his job as an opening gambit in a Reuther return to power.

Strangely enough, my brother Eric had had something of the same problem when he worked briefly at a UAW assembly line in California before going to Venezuela with the Peace Corps. Eric was still in California when I decided to run for office. He had become director of TELACU, The East Los Angeles Community Union, a nonprofit organization that was originally set up by Esteban Torres, one of my father's former UAW colleagues in the union's DC office. Ed, as we knew him, had been UAW's assistant for Latin American affairs. In 1982, he was elected to Congress. Eric served as his top aide until Torres retired in 1999.

While I was working the line at Fisher Body, I was angling toward a management job, preferably at Ford. Why Ford? Perhaps in part because of my acquaintance ten years earlier with Henry Ford II's daughter, Charlotte. Two influential letters of recommendation were sent to Ford on my behalf. The first was from former Detroit Mayor Jerome Cavanagh, who sent a "Dear Ted" letter with my résumé to Theodore Macke Jr., Ford's VP of Public Affairs. Cavanagh's letter was apparently a follow-up to an earlier phone conversation between them. Cavanagh's letter closed with: "My sense of the theatrical compels me to project how appropriate it would be to have a Reuther working for the Ford Motor Company. I am sure you can see these possibilities as well."

The second letter was sent directly to Henry Ford II by former Vice President Hubert Humphrey, who was now back in the Senate. In his response, Ford confirmed to Senator Humphrey that he had "asked our Vice President of Personnel and Organization, Mr. E. D. O'Leary, to follow through on this to be sure that John is given every consideration for any reasonable opportunity there might be here for him." The note was hand-signed, "Best Regards, Henry."

Perhaps not surprisingly, a Ford representative soon called to invite me to a morning interview. I was looking forward to sitting down with him, but the appointment time he suggested was going to be a problem. At that hour, I'd be installing bucket seats in Buicks, but I thought it best not to reveal that. After telling the hiring rep that I had a scheduling conflict because I had "an appointment with GM at that time"—not exactly a lie, but not exactly the truth, either—we agreed to set the appointment for later in the day. I took a business suit with me to the plant, changed after my shift, and went to the interview at Ford.

I was hired in March 1973 to work in the governmental affairs department at the massive Ford World Headquarters building in Dearborn, a.k.a. The Glass House. My primary responsibility was to set up and attend speaking engagements for top Ford executives and engineers around the country. In other words, I was an advance man—again—and my experience on the campaign trail with candidates like Ted Kennedy and George McGovern soon proved to be invaluable.

Building a Political Campaign

As I settled into my job that spring, I rented an apartment near Ypsilanti and began mapping out my campaign. I started by reaching out to local Democrats. I found them to be bruised and hurting from the trouncing in 1972, yet at the same time still bitterly at odds with one another. It was a microcosm of what was happening across the country. In the wake of the somewhat ignominious American withdrawal from Vietnam, the OPEC oil embargo, ongoing civil rights clashes, and the *Roe v. Wade* Supreme Court decision, Democrats were badly fragmented. In the second district, uniting them to support me would be a challenge. There was a very liberal constituency around the University of Michigan at Ann Arbor; there were more traditional establishment Democrats in the Wayne County/Detroit suburbs like Livonia (many of whom were anti-busing); and we also had rural Democrats along the Ohio state line in Monroe County.

The Monroe party was more like a farmer/labor party, and I felt especially welcome there, probably because of their admiration for the Reuther brothers. Since many people from Monroe crossed the state line to work at auto plants in Ohio—the Jeep factory in Toledo, for example—I campaigned in the Buckeye State as well as in Michigan. It also made sense to gravitate toward the Monroe Dems in terms of the current campaign. One of my Democratic primary opponents, Dr. Ed

Pierce, was very strong in and around Ann Arbor but not at all popular in Monroe, so I saw an opportunity to build a base there.

I attended every possible meeting, gathering, and picnic I could, and developed a close relationship with the county chairman and his family. My affection for these folks was so strong that one day after work, I drove forty-five minutes to Monroe to ride on a chartered bus with local Democrats back up to a Detroit Tigers baseball game, then back with them to Monroe, where I got in my car and drove back to Ypsilanti.

(On the campaign trail)

One of my greatest regrets was my failure to have an early meeting with Dr. Ed Pierce. Ed was an Ann Arbor physician, former city council member, Democratic mayoral candidate, and anti-Vietnam war activist who later became my strongest primary opponent. He gave up a lucrative medical practice to open a free medical clinic for low income, uninsured people in his community. If I hadn't run myself, I would have supported Ed for Congress.

At Ford, I tried to keep my intention to run for Congress below the radar, but after a November 18, 1973, article in the *Detroit Free Press*, that was no longer possible. Under the headline, "A Reuther in Your Future," it read, "John Reuther, nephew of the late UAW president Walter Reuther, plans to run for Congress against incumbent Marvin L. Esch in Michigan's Second District... Committees are already being formed for the campaign..." Because the article mentioned that I was a government affairs representative at Ford, I had to resign. Once I did so, however, I had no income, except for the few dollars I made from selling some of my Russian book collections. When voters asked what I did for a living, I referred to my work in politics with Ted Kennedy, Birch Bayh and McGovern. I was, however, living on a shoestring. To save money, I moved out of my apartment and rented a small, one-bedroom guesthouse in the backyard of an elderly retired couple.

I formally announced my candidacy on March 13, 1974. I had three opponents for the Democratic nomination: Marjorie Lansing, a political science professor at Eastern Michigan University, Ron Egnor, an assistant city attorney who had the backing of some of the building trade unions; and Ed Pierce.

We opened our main campaign office in a suburban Ypsilanti home leased from the local Democratic state representative. The headquarters was staffed primarily by student volunteers from the University of Michigan, but my good friends from the McGovern campaign in Massachusetts soon showed up to pitch in. First to arrive were Ed Jesser, who became my campaign press secretary, and demographic whiz kid Skinner Donahue, who studied and prioritized all the district precincts where I had the best chance to gain support. Nick Mitropoulos eventually joined the campaign as well.

All three were destined for prominent careers in the political and governmental arena. Skinner Donahue became a key strategist in Jimmy Carter's successful run for the White House; Ed would serve as press secretary for Carter's reelection campaign. Nick became a high-ranking administrator at the Kennedy School at Harvard, serving as the executive director of the Taubman Center for State and Local Government, director of the Forum, and deputy director of the Institute of Politics.

My candidacy soon attracted media attention. A story in *Newsweek* was picked up by the Associated Press and appeared in papers all over the country. One of the reasons I gave for running was that I wanted to be "among the Democrats privileged to upset President Nixon's vetoes."

Not all the press I received was entirely positive. There was also a story in *Congressional Quarterly* headlined "Carpetbagging Losing Negative Force," in which I was identified as "the carpetbagger most likely to succeed in 1974."

I had expected to be slammed with this kind of accusation, and Skinner, Ed, and Nick were ready for it. One of the things campaign staff does is anticipate the opposition research—the "oppo"—that will be used against you. Yes, I had moved to Ypsilanti to run in the second district, they acknowledged, but I had been born in Michigan, and my name had a certain ring to it.

Money is the mother's milk of politics, and Maria "Keach" le Grand chaired our Friends of John Reuther Committee. We soon organized a fundraising drive, collecting every address list we could in order to identify possible donors, including UAW retirees, Democratic Party supporters, friends from high school and college, and former colleagues from the Kennedy and McGovern campaigns.

Among those we solicited was Phil Stern, for whom I'd worked on Martha's Vineyard in '61 and '62. Phil, a well-known liberal activist and author, had always been vocally and unequivocally opposed to the corrupting influence of money in politics. He eventually wrote a book entitled *The Best Congress Money Can Buy*. As a result, I was both pleased and surprised when he wrote to Maria le Grand, saying, "In general I'm out of the business of political giving. But I admire John so much I can't say no, so here's a modest contribution." He enclosed a check for $200.

Another surprise donor was Martin "Marty" H. Peretz, an assistant professor at Harvard and a Gene McCarthy supporter. Marty had married an heiress to the Singer sewing machine fortune. During my 1974 campaign, he purchased *The New Republic* magazine and took over as editor-in-chief. Marty donated $1,000—by far the largest individual contribution. Many donations were in the $1 to $10 range, often from UAW members and other retirees who gave what they could afford.

My family was completely supportive of my decision to run for Congress. Both of my parents spent a good bit of time in Michigan campaigning for me, with Dad making a speech at the opening of my primary campaign headquarters in Livonia. In Washington, family friends assembled a list of potential supporters for a DC fundraising event. Unfortunately, someone went ahead and printed and mailed the invitations—which included a list of sponsors—before final approval from those sponsors had been secured. Among them was Ethel Kennedy, who did not want to take sides in a Democratic primary. Knowing the invitations had already gone out, the best I could do was call Mrs. Kennedy and apologize, and she was gracious enough to forgive us. Ultimately, the gathering was a success, and I was most honored that among those who attended were Senator Eugene McCarthy and Eleanor McGovern, wife of Senator George McGovern.

(With Dad, Eugene McCarthy and Eleanor McGovern)

Andy Manatos, my longtime friend from junior high through college, also hosted a fundraiser for me in Washington, gathering many of our close friends and former teammates from those early days. Politics runs in his family; his father, Mike Manatos, had been White House Senate liaison for both Kennedy and Johnson. Later in the 1970s, Andy would serve in the Carter administration as assistant secretary of commerce and would eventually join his father as a partner in the influential public policy/lobbying firm, Manatos & Manatos. The firm is still known as Manatos & Manatos today, except now Andy runs it with his son.

Andy's fundraiser was one of the most enjoyable evenings of the campaign. During the party, he showed a slapstick 8-millimeter home movie that he and some of our friends had made to show how they were raising money for my campaign. One scene showed a friend jumping out of the bushes and stealing the purse of one of our young lady friends.

Back in Ypsilanti, I got a call early one morning from a woman volunteering to work with my campaign. She explained that because of funding cutbacks and low seniority, she'd been laid off from her teaching job in a local public school. Because I was somewhat uncomfortable that she'd been able to get my home phone number so easily, I suggested that she call my campaign office.

Later that afternoon, Ed Jesser and I entered headquarters to see a striking young woman addressing campaign envelopes. While most of my volunteers wore jeans, this very lovely blonde wore a fitted hunter green dress, which showed off her beautiful legs. As Eddie and I stared at her from the kitchen, I said, "This must be the new volunteer who called me this morning. I should go over and introduce myself."

Ed scowled; he could see all too well where this might be headed. "Don't get involved with the volunteers, John!" he warned sternly. "If you do, Skinner and I are going back to Boston!"

"Don't worry," I told him. "I just want to thank her for joining our campaign."

I walked over to introduce myself and learned that her name was Jill Fitzgerald. She had been a high school political science teacher but had been laid off due to her lack of seniority. Her mother had seen an article about me as a candidate and had suggested that she volunteer with the campaign. While we chatted, I sat down on the couch next to her and soon heard Eddie's unmistakable Beantown accent booming from the stairwell. "Skinnah, pack ya bags! We're goin' back to Bahston!"

Jill became a regular in the campaign office, and I eventually learned that she was a divorcée with a young son. We discovered that we shared many important beliefs and values, including opposition to the war in Vietnam, support for civil rights and a woman's right to choose, and a strong commitment to the Democratic Party. She soon took over scheduling responsibilities and setting up meet-and-greet opportunities with voters. Some of my favorite events were the wine and cheese parties she organized at supporters' homes around the Detroit suburb of Livonia. Our hosts and hostesses invited their friends and neighbors, and Jill would often accompany me. After mingling with the guests over wine and cheese, I would make brief remarks.

After one of these parties, Jill and I sat talking in her car parked in front of the host's home for a long time. Finally, knowing nothing further was scheduled for that evening, Jill and I returned to the house and asked our friends if we could take a couple of glasses of wine and some cheese out to the car to continue our private party.

(With Jill at a campaign event)

In Monroe County, one of the most active and friendly Democrats was a progressive Catholic nun. She was from Sisters, Servants of the Immaculate Heart of Mary (I.H.M.), a local order based in Monroe that is dedicated to intellectual curiosity, ecological consciousness, inclusivity, and action for justice. In keeping with the doctrines of her order, she was an outspoken opponent of the Vietnam War and a strong supporter of civil rights.

The sister arranged for me to address the entire convent. The program called for me to give remarks, then take questions from the nuns. Eddie Jesser came with me, and as we entered the convent, both of us hoped we'd be able to tiptoe around the third rail of politics for Catholic voters: the subject of abortion.

My speech was very much in line with both my personal beliefs and the issues that the sister had been promoting. After I finished my presentation, I invited questions from the nuns. Most of them dealt with topics I had already raised, and for a time, Eddie and I dared hope we were home free about a woman's right to choose. Out of the corner of my eye, I could see him tapping his watch crystal to get me to wrap it up, but the last question turned out to be the one we'd been trying to avoid: What was my position on abortion? Eddie's head dropped to his chest.

The idea of lying to a convent full of nuns was a nonstarter, and in any event, I was already on the record on this issue with other voters. Under the circumstances, the best I could do was to address the issue forthrightly, acknowledge the validity of their point of view, state my position, and make sure the sisters knew why I felt that way. I told them that I understood that the Church's position on abortion was unambiguous and unwavering. Then I took a deep breath and told the nuns the truth as I saw it—that I did not believe it was my role as a man, nor should it be my role as a member of the House of Representatives, to decide this question for a woman, any woman. I believed strongly that this was a decision to be made by a woman and her doctor, not by me or the government. As I spoke, many of the sisters bowed their heads while fingering their rosaries and mouthing silent prayers.

My experience with the nuns was not that unusual. In my spring and summer campaign appearances, the constant challenge was to walk the tightrope—to be fully honest and committed to my values without losing votes in a badly divided but evenly split district. The battle lines had been drawn years earlier between traditional, establishment Democrats and progressive, antiwar, new politics Democrats, so trying to stake out a middle ground often meant drawing fire from both sides.

Like the question of abortion, amnesty for draft dodgers was another hot topic. In 1967, I'd been prepared to refuse induction over my opposition to the Vietnam War, but after deep reflection I realized that I was unwilling to go to Canada to avoid the consequences of my decision. That was my personal choice, but I had no quarrel with anyone who had faced the same situation and come to a different conclusion. I was openly in favor of amnesty for those who had left the country to avoid the draft. I thought it was time to allow these men to come home, but my position was seen as too liberal for some residents of Livonia and Monroe County, and not liberal enough for Ann Arbor. The same rifts and divisions were apparent on other issues as well.

News coverage of the primary was peculiar. In some parts of the district, it was almost as if I'd disappeared. The areas around the University of Michigan were an Ed Pierce stronghold, and it appeared that the *Ann Arbor News* was making an overt effort to downplay my candidacy. Just over a week before the August 4 primary, it published its election editorial on the congressional candidates. It went into detailed analysis of Ronald Egnor, Marjorie Lansing, and Ed Pierce, but all it said about me was that I was "formerly of Ford Motor Company."

This kind of favoritism wasn't happening just in Ann Arbor. On August 4, the *Detroit Free Press* published its candidate profiles. The only mention of my stand on the issues was this statement: "He has criticized the Nixon administration for failing to control inflation and has campaigned for tax reform to shift the burden toward corporations and wealthy individuals. He has called for a national health care system." Without further positive or even negative information about me, the article concluded by saying, "These three are, in our opinion, well qualified. Either could give incumbent Esch a run for his money… But when it comes to hard choices, we'd vote for Ed Pierce. We welcome his candidacy this year, as we have respected his views in other campaigns. He spoke out early against the Vietnam war, a good indication of a man who is willing to help form public opinion instead of merely being part of it."

On election night, August 6, the results were too close to call between Ed Pierce and me. In the wee small hours of the morning, I went to bed thinking I'd lost to him by 84 votes, but Eddie and Skinner woke me up a few hours later to tell me that I had gone ahead by a handful. The *Lansing State Journal* had me winning by five votes, 12,964 to 12,959. The article said I had "held a 3 to 1 lead over Pierce in Monroe County, and a better than 2 to 1 lead in Wayne County." As we looked at the precinct-by-precinct results, it became clear that despite my stance on abortion, the Sisters, Servants of the Immaculate Heart of Mary had cast their ballots for me in a solid bloc. The sisters had put me over the top.

The next day, Pierce's campaign manager called to say they were going to request a recount, but back then, recounts could take as long as a month. In the short campaign season between August and November, neither of us wanted to give Esch, the Republican incumbent, the advantage of having the two of us fighting, so Ed Pierce and I made the unprecedented decision to campaign together until the results were final. We also pledged to support whoever won the recount.

The UAW put my campaign in touch with a top national recount consultant, who advised me that it was not necessary to go back over the results in every precinct, only in the ones that had showed great strength for Pierce in areas where I was otherwise the stronger candidate. In a relatively short time, our recount produced favorable results, and my margin of victory began to grow. Ed Pierce conceded, then endorsed me, and I began gearing up for the November 5 election against Marvin Esch.

The left-leaning *Ann Arbor Sun* had supported Pierce but was slow to endorse me even after I'd won the primary. In an October 25 article, the newspaper said, "The 30-year-old Reuther is nephew to the UAW's Walter Reuther, and has the look of a man born with a golden spoon in his mouth. He came to live in the Second so he could run here; UAW coffers financed his handsome primary campaign, but in spite of the razzle dazzle he beat Ann Arbor's homespun Ed Pierce by only a few votes."

The statement was only partially correct. I had come to the second district to run for Congress, and I was never secretive about that, but they were wrong in saying that UAW had financed my campaign. Setting the record straight about that mattered to me—again, perception is everything in politics—and I didn't want to be known as the carpetbagger whose nomination had been bought and paid for by the UAW.

In the runup to the Democratic primary, I made public the names of all my donors. There were larger donations from the McGoverns, Phil Stern, and Marty Peretz, among others, but the average contribution to my campaign was $16.65. Contributions from individuals with a UAW connection amounted to a few hundred dollars tops.

My full disclosure proved conclusively that my campaign was not financed by the auto workers, but that didn't stop Republicans from saying that it was. Accusations that the UAW was underwriting my campaign were repeated by Robert Griffin, a Michigan Republican senator whose major claim to fame was that he was the cosponsor of the notoriously anti-labor Landrum-Griffin Act. Griffin sent out 10,000 fundraising letters on Esch's behalf, accusing the union of trying to buy me a seat in Congress.

I reacted sharply and publicly to Griffin's charges. As I told the *Traverse City Record Eagle*, "For a man who took four-figure contributions from the dairy and agricultural interests some weeks after the 1972 election, to accuse me of being bought is like Richard Nixon calling Archibald Cox a quitter." (Nixon, of course, had personally ordered the firing of Watergate Special Prosecutor Archibald Cox.) I demanded that "Mr. Esch repudiate Senator Griffin's allegations, and that Senator Griffin issue a public apology retracting his slurs and innuendos." Neither of them did.

The *Ann Arbor News* eventually endorsed me against Marvin Esch and included my citation of findings by Common Cause that "Only eight representatives out of 435 in the Congress received more money from wealthy business and agricultural groups than Marvin Esch."

During the fall campaign, I was humbled and honored to have some major national Democratic figures campaign with me and for me. George McGovern appeared at the University of Michigan, where his antiwar views were both well-known and popular. President Kennedy's brother-in-law, Sargent Shriver, campaigned for me as well. Shriver had been the founding director of the Peace Corps and was also the architect of President Johnson's War on Poverty. In that role, he headed up the Office of Economic Opportunity, which made him technically my boss when I had worked at OEO, even though he had been many rungs up the food chain from me. Sargent Shriver had also been George McGovern's vice-presidential running mate—eventually. McGovern's first VP choice, Senator Thomas Eagleton of Missouri, was forced to drop out just weeks into the campaign after damaging and ultimately disqualifying mental health issues came to light; he'd been hospitalized repeatedly for crippling bouts of depression and had undergone electroshock therapy.

(With George McGovern at the University of Michigan campaign event)

Senator Walter Mondale of Minnesota also campaigned with me, and of course he brought with him the shaggy dog story of Natasha, my German shepherd. I'd purchased her in DC in 1972, but soon thereafter I was working full time with the McGovern campaign and living in Minneapolis. While there, I took Natasha to a local veterinarian to get her shots, and as was common practice at that time, the vet affixed a tag to her collar with his name and address.

In the aftermath of the Nixon landslide, Natasha and I returned to DC. We were staying at my parents' home in northwest Washington, and one day she didn't return from her morning run. With the benefit of hindsight, letting her run off-leash in the city was a mistake. I guess both of us had become accustomed to her running free on the farm where I had lived in Minnesota. That said, this behavior was unusual for her—she had always gone out and then come right back home. I looked around the neighborhood for several days and finally took out a lost dog ad in the *Washington Post*. I described Natasha, the area where she was last seen, and listed our home phone number. Within a day, a neighbor called to say she had found Natasha and soon brought her to the house. The woman also mentioned that when she first saw the tag on Natasha's collar, she had assumed that some visiting Minnesota tourists had lost their dog. In an effort to reunite the dog with her owners, she had called the DC office of Senator Walter Mondale and given them all the details.

That phone call set off an unusual series of events. As a result of working in Minnesota for the McGovern campaign, I was quite friendly with many members of Senator Mondale's staff. After Natasha was returned, I went to his Capitol Hill office to let them know that Natasha had been safely returned, and to thank them for their effort. As I was describing the incident, Mondale's administrative assistant looked at me quizzically—as far as he knew, no one in the office had been contacted about a dog from Minnesota. I asked if he ever discovered who on the senator's staff had been involved in the search, to please thank them on my behalf. As I walked out of the office, I ran into Senator Mondale. "Well, John Reuther," he began, "so what are you up to these days—other than keeping me busy all weekend trying to find the owner of your dog?!"

"It was *you!*" I exclaimed. The senator himself had spent a good part of his weekend tracking Natasha's dog tags back to the local vet in Minnesota, who looked up his records and finally told him that Natasha belonged to me. What he'd done was the very definition of what has come to be known as "Minnesota Nice."

As I introduced Senator Mondale to the crowd in Ann Arbor, I told the story of Natasha, and when Mondale took the microphone, he confirmed it. "Yes, this is a true story," he began, "and now, John, whenever I see a dog, I think of you!"

Everyone got a kick out of Senator Mondale's folksy humor, and soon after his visit, I received a letter on Senate stationery.

> *Just a note to tell you how much I enjoyed campaigning with you last weekend. I was enormously impressed by the enthusiasm for your campaign, and I know you're going to be successful in November.*
>
> *Let me know if there is anything I can do to help.*
>
> *Warmest regards,*
>
> *Fritz*

In the end, the endorsements and the enthusiasm weren't enough. Although Democrats won a solid majority of 291 seats in the House, mine was not one of them. Esch was reelected with 52 percent of the vote. I received 45 percent. Following my defeat, I received many expressions of support and regret, including the following Mailgram from Sargent Shriver:

> *I am saddened by the fact that your maximum efforts, your courage, and your intelligences was not successful in this particular campaign. But I am sure you have got many future triumphs in store. Please be sure that I will always be one of your staunchest admirers and supporters ready to help in any way I can in the months and years ahead.*

Congratulations on an excellent campaign. Next time you will be victorious.

Best regards,
Sargent Shriver

I was in impressive company losing a seat in that election. Another Democratic congressional candidate who lost that year was Arkansas candidate and future President Bill Clinton.

CHAPTER 11

1975-1978

After the Campaign, What Next?

After my defeat, I don't think I was depressed, in part because I wasn't surprised. There had been polling that showed my defeat was likely. That said, I wanted to get as far away from politics as I could. I wanted to do something where I was dependent only on myself. I wanted to work with my hands, and I went back to what I'd loved to do since I was a kid—I became a carpenter. In March 1975, a Detroit friend whose father was a carpenters' union leader helped me to join Carpenters Local Union 95. Most of my jobs involved setting up and dismantling exhibit stands for major trade shows. Since that work was sporadic, I also accepted a part-time teaching job as a social science instructor at Wayne State University's College of Lifelong Learning.

Mostly I wanted to use my carpentry skills on something for myself, so I borrowed $4,000 from my parents as a down payment on a vacant, foreclosed property in Ypsilanti that was coming up for auction. The property included two buildings: a small, two-story, wood frame house at the front of the lot, and a one-story, flat-roofed, cinder block building behind it.

Before the property was auctioned off that winter, I went to look it over. Seeing a lot of footprints in the snow between the front and rear buildings, I concluded that there would be many bidders for the property. The minimum bid was listed as $12,000, so I submitted a written offer of $12,890. As it turned out, I was the only bidder. So much for my Sherlock Holmes deduction about what those footprints meant.

At some point, the cinder block building had been converted from a veterinary clinic into a one-bedroom living unit with a large living room, kitchen, and bath, but the place was in terrible shape. It had been vacant for a while—after the utilities were turned off, the water pipes had frozen and burst. I wanted to do the repair work myself, so I got a plumbing certificate from the City of Ypsilanti. Within a short time, the apartment in the rear building was ready for occupancy, and to have some money to live on, I rented it to a campaign acquaintance.

The end of the election did not mark the end of my relationship with Jill, but we did start seeing one another less often. Although Jill and I continued to date, I also occasionally saw other women. A few weeks after the election, I was still living in the small house in the backyard of the retired couple, having cocktails with a young woman, when the phone rang. It was Buffalo Springfield/CSNY musician Stephen Stills, who had supported my campaign and had performed on Halloween on my behalf in Ann Arbor. He was calling to tell me how sorry he was that I had lost. This was somewhat similar to what had happened in 1964, when President Johnson invited my date to dance with him at the White House. My date was hugely impressed, but in a way that had nothing to do with me.

After working with my campaign, Jill—five years younger than I—became a very successful model and actress. Despite my dating around, she and I remained close, and I got to know her parents, siblings, grandmothers, and her five-year-old son Chris from her previous marriage. Our relationship was deepening, and I could imagine a life together.

One evening, during a long, late night phone call, Jill and I decided to get married. We set the date for October 12, 1975. Jill's father, who worked for AAA travel, suggested we go on a weeklong honeymoon to the Adriatic resort of Dubrovnik in southern Croatia. There was an AAA package for the trip, and Jill's grandmothers offered to cover the cost as their wedding gift to us. I assumed that they would make all the plans for our honeymoon directly through Jill's father, so I left it all up to them.

We sent out wedding invitations to our families, friends, and campaign associates, knowing that not everyone would be able to make it to Michigan. One of the RSVPs was a telegram from Eddie Jesser and Nick Mitropoulos in Boston:

Jack and Jill went up the hill
to join in matrimony.
Nick and Ed would like to come,
but they don't have the money.
Best wishes,
Nick and Ed

Another was from Senator Walter Mondale, who had met Jill when he came to the second district to campaign for me. Mondale sent his "heartiest congratulations," but noted "Unfortunately, I'm committed to be in Minnesota. I'll be with you in spirit nonetheless, and Joan joins me in sending our very best wishes to you both. I hope we'll have a chance to get together again soon." He signed the letter "Fritz," then added in his own handwriting, "I *knew* why you were running!" clearly remembering how attractive Jill was.

As our wedding date approached, I found out that Jill's father had assumed I had made all the arrangements for our trip to Dubrovnik, just as I had assumed he was doing the same. Weeks before we were to exchange vows, there were no plans for a honeymoon, but by that time, the AAA tour package to Dubrovnik was sold out. I booked our honeymoon for Moscow and St. Petersburg, thinking it would be nice to show Jill where I had spent a couple of years of my life.

After we returned, Jill, Chris and I settled into the small wooden house, or tried to. The two-story house had a bedroom and bath on the second floor, another bedroom, bath, living room and kitchen on the main floor, and a small basement for the furnace and utilities. I replaced the gas heating system and much of the plumbing and upgraded the electrical system. Using the carpentry skills my father had taught me, I made new doors for the kitchen cabinets. I did my best to make the house more livable, but that meant a great deal of dust, noise, and construction upheaval on a daily basis.

Once there were no longer saws and drill presses in the kitchen and living room, we decided to sell it. The small profit we realized from the sale was enough for a down payment on another fixer-upper closer to

Ann Arbor—a ranch house overlooking a small pond. The new house was not nearly as spartan, but once again, my family was living in a home where my renovation work was disrupting our lives constantly.

It was also time to put my home improvement skills aside and get a job that would support my family. I once again took advantage of the long-standing Reuther connection with Jack Conway. Years earlier, Jack had arranged for me to work as a congressional liaison with the Job Corps after I graduated from Cornell, and he was now executive director of the American Federation of State, County, and Municipal Employees international union (AFSCME) in DC. In March of 1976, Jack appointed me assistant area director of AFSCME's Michigan office in Lansing.

I held that position for nine months. During most of that time, the area director position directly above me was vacant, so I assumed that job responsibility as well. During those same nine months, we got pregnant. On August 10, 1976, Jill gave birth to our son Alexander, whom we have always called by the Russian nickname "Sasha."

By the time Sasha was born, Senator Mondale had become Jimmy Carter's running mate—one popular campaign slogan touted them as "Grits and Fritz." Mondale must have forgiven me for his lost weekend tracking down Natasha the German shepherd because he agreed to become Sasha's godfather. A year later, on Sasha's first birthday, he sent formal birthday greetings addressed to "Master Alexander Fitzgerald Reuther" on his official stationery that read *The Vice President—Washington.*

(With Jill and Walter Mondale, who's holding one-month old Sasha)

Being Sasha's father came naturally to me, as I assume it does to most dads, but I think I could have been a better father figure to Chris. When Jill and I were first married, she and her former husband Eric weren't getting along and often argued by phone about Eric's plans to spend time with Chris. Not wanting to add fuel to that fire, I took a more hands-off approach to parenting Chris.

(With Sasha)

(Sasha and Chris)

I finished the renovations on the second fixer-upper home just in time to sell it—we were moving to Washington. AFSCME had offered me a position as southern states regional coordinator in their DC Field Activities Center. I was to start in December of 1976, and I was thrilled to link up again with my old friend Carl Wagner, who at that time was AFSCME's director of political action.

I'd first met Carl in 1970 in my father's office, shortly after returning from my studies in the Soviet Union. Carl was a bit younger than I was and worked for the Alliance for Labor Action (ALA). The ALA was an association of unions that had been formed in 1968 by the UAW and the International Brotherhood of Teamsters. Uncle Walter and AFL-CIO president George Meany had been unable to find common ground on issues of social policy and terms of governance for the combined unions, so Walter had pulled the UAW out of the AFL-CIO and linked up with the truckers' union.

I also became close to Carl's then-girlfriend, Swe Thant, who had immigrated to the US from Burma (now Myanmar). Carl and Swe married and had a daughter about a year after Sasha was born. Alex Wagner is as beautiful and accomplished as her mother, having worked as a journalist and television host for CBS News and MSNBC.

Carl held top-level positions in the presidential campaigns of many Democratic candidates and would go on to serve as co-chair of Bill Clinton's campaign in 1992. I first got to meet Clinton on a trip to the AFSCME regional convention, which was held in Arkansas. Bill Clinton, then Arkansas attorney general, was our keynote speaker. When I introduced myself to him, I was surprised that he not only remembered my name, but also that I'd been an unsuccessful congressional candidate in 1974.

All this time, I still had my wooded property in southern Pennsylvania, where I'd built the log cabin and five-acre lake. As Sasha was growing up, I often took him and some of his school friends to the cabin for overnight camping trips. Since Chris was six years older than Sasha, he spent more time independently with his friends and didn't come with us as often.

Sasha has said he remembers these trips as father/son bonding time. For us it was something akin to a Tom Sawyer adventure—hiking, fishing, cooking over a campfire, catching crayfish in the creek, and swimming in the lake. I recall those days fondly. I got to revisit all the fun activities I'd done with Phil and Leni Stern's kids on Martha's Vineyard, except now I got to do them with my own son!

CHAPTER 12

1978-1981

1978 Satra and Moscow

Moving back to Washington meant coming home to me, but it uprooted Jill. Nevertheless, she continued her modeling and acting work, both in DC and in New York. In the spring of 1978, while Jill was auditioning at a DC hotel for a New York agency, I went to the hotel bar and ran into Bob Keefe, Birch Bayh's former chief of staff. Bob had gone on to serve as executive director of the Democratic National Committee from 1972 to 1976 and now headed up his own lobbying and consulting firm. One of his clients was Satra, a New York-based international trading company whose name was derived from the first letters of the words Soviet American Trade.

Satra's owner and chairman, Ara Oztemel, was a highly entrepreneurial, highly successful American businessman of Turkish Armenian descent. After graduating from Northeastern University, he'd made a fortune exporting raw materials—primarily iron, nickel, and chromium ores—from the Soviet Union to the West.

Satra's trade in chromium ore, or "chromite," was especially lucrative. It was the height of the Cold War when Oztemel first approached the Soviet government about granting him an export license to sell chromite to US companies. His American colleagues and rivals all thought he was crazy. The Soviets would never allow it, they said, because chromium is an essential component of stainless steel, and has many strategic military and aerospace uses. The Soviets also thought he was nuts, but for an entirely different reason: they were certain that no Western buyer would be willing to pay for the ore in hard currency. Undaunted by the critics and pessimists, Oztemel brokered the deal and reaped the benefits—by 1975, he was worth $25 million.

Bob Keefe told me that Satra might be an excellent job opportunity for me, in part because Satra's Moscow office also represented other international companies looking to establish trade relations with the USSR. Oztemel, an active Democratic Party supporter, was looking for someone to replace his current chief representative in Moscow. He needed someone who was familiar with Russia and the Russian language, and who was willing to remain in the USSR for a minimum of three years. The time commitment was essential; turnover was bad for business, and Oztemel had already hired one representative who lasted only a year before quitting the company and returning to the States.

Oztemel invited Jill and me to come to New York to meet with him and discuss the position. Before agreeing to take the meeting, Jill and I talked it over. She was very forthright about not wanting to relocate to Moscow. The move would shut down her promising modeling and acting career, and she was anything but enthusiastic about the prospect of raising Chris, then seven, and Sasha, eighteen months, in a country where she didn't speak the language—and one that was notorious for its shortages of consumer goods to boot.

I told her not to worry, I was sure that the odds of Ara Oztemel hiring me as his chief Moscow representative were slim-to-none. Yes, I'd done graduate work in the Soviet Union, but my Russian language skills had atrophied in the years since, and I had absolutely no business experience whatsoever. I encouraged Jill to think of our trip to New York as an all-expenses-paid mini-vacation, courtesy of Satra. It was a chance for a little luxury—a chance we didn't get very often. We'd stay in a four-star hotel, have dinner in a great restaurant, take in a hit Broadway show, and go home.

That's not how it worked out. Somehow, I was exactly what Oztemel had been looking for. He was not concerned about my lack of experience—the company, he said, would teach me everything I needed to know. He offered me the job, and I accepted.

To get me up to speed, Satra sent Jill and me on a familiarization trip to Europe. We went to Russia, but we also visited our company facilities in Germany and England. Satra held the export rights to these two countries for Soviet-produced Lada automobiles—economy cars that were modeled on the Fiat 124 and manufactured in Tolyatti, a city I'd visited with Kolya, the leader of our volunteer student construction detachment. When we returned, Jill, the boys and I rented a house in the Westchester suburb of Rye, not far from Long Island Sound, and I settled in for a couple of months of training at Satra's New York office. The goal was to familiarize me with all aspects of Satra's business and with the materials that Satra was exporting from the Soviet Union at the time.

We left in August of 1978 to begin our three-year stint in Moscow. For the first three months, our home was the Hotel National—the same ornate, fin de siècle palace where my student friends and I had met with Senator Eugene McCarthy and where a government agent had mistakenly apprehended me, thinking I was a Soviet citizen illicitly using hard currency to purchase camera equipment.

We stayed in Suite 107, which was nicknamed the Lenin Suite because Vladimir Lenin and his wife Nadezhda spent a week there in 1918. Our windows looked out on Red Square, the Kremlin, and Lenin's Tomb. In later years, Suite 107 developed a certain international cachet, and considering who has stayed there, it's a pretty sure bet that it had been bugged for decades…and still is. Previous guests included Jack Nicholson, Donald Trump, and Barack Obama, which made the presence of the Reuther family—in particular our two rambunctious little boys—something of an anomaly. Hotel guests were astonished on a regular basis as Sasha and Chris raced up and down the corridors on their Hot Wheels Go Karts.

We were still in the Lenin Suite in early November when the building began to shake a little. Tons of military hardware—including tanks, armored trucks, artillery, rocket launchers, and other heavy weaponry—were rumbling across Red Square in a dress rehearsal for the annual November 7 parade. I immediately knew exactly what was going on, but some of our fellow guests did not. In the elevator on the way down to breakfast the next morning, I overheard one elderly British tourist ask her equally elderly companion if she had witnessed the military coup d'état that had rolled past the hotel the day before.

Before leaving Moscow, the departing chief representative taught me the finer points of his job, and I soon learned that Satra's business was a lot bigger than exporting raw materials. We had an active consulting division that offered our foreign clients everything they would need to establish and maintain an office presence in Moscow. We also facilitated connections with government contacts who were key for their particular business. In Moscow, as in most places, knowing who to talk to in the bureaucracy is essential. When I took over as chief representative, we moved from the Hotel National into a high-rise, three-bedroom flat and enrolled Chris in the Anglo-American school at the American Embassy. Two-year-old Sasha stayed home with Jill.

(With Sasha, Chris, Jill and her parents in Moscow)

Although there were shortages of some goods and other products were hard to find, we soon learned that there was a speedy and efficient work-around. Other foreign families showed us how to order American essentials like peanut butter and Cheerios from a company in Finland. In many ways, it was like a very early precursor to Amazon Prime—the Finns shipped the orders by overnight train from Helsinki, and we had our products by the next day.

One day our receptionist told me that a young American was in the lobby, looking for work. This was not unusual—American exchange students hoping to extend their stay after their coursework ended would go jobhunting at the Moscow offices of foreign companies. Thinking I would shake his hand and politely send him on his way, I went to our office reception area to speak with him. An hour later, Tom Laurita and I were still talking. I didn't have the authority from Oztemel to offer him a position at Satra, so I hired him to babysit for Chris and Sasha, at least for the time being.

Oztemel visited Moscow regularly, and on his next visit, I introduced him to Tom. Ara invited him to join us for dinner at a restaurant with live music. Before long, Ara, an accomplished jazz saxophonist, and Tom, who played a mean blues harmonica, were up on stage with the band. As the last set was winding down, Ara hired Tom as my deputy, and when my Moscow tour of duty ended in the fall of 1981, Tom Laurita took over as chief.

Life in Moscow, Part I

In 1979, President Carter appointed former IBM Chairman and CEO Thomas Watson Jr. as our ambassador. My friend, IBM's chief rep in Moscow, invited Jill and me to dinner at his apartment several times, often with Ambassador Watson and his wife, Olive. One of these dinners was Thanksgiving, 1980, when two other couples joined us: Illinois Senator Charles Percy and his wife, Loraine, and Motorola Corporation CEO Bob Galvin and his wife, Mary.

A week after this dinner, Senator Percy sent me a gracious letter and a *Congressional Record* printout of his kind and thoughtful remarks honoring Robert Johnson, who had recently passed away. Bob had been Region 4 director of the Iowa/Illinois UAW for twenty-four years and was a close family friend.

There was no problem, no issue that I could discuss with Bob without being impressed by his intuition, wisdom and common sense. His advice and counsel were practical, honest and direct. I shall miss him very much…

We are so pleased that you are going to be in Washington and trust that you will keep in touch with us and will let us know when you plan on arriving. Thank you for all that you have done to make life much more interesting and exciting for Olive and Tom Watson. Bob and Mary Galvin join me in sending our very best wishes to you.

The Anglo-American School was located on the grounds of the American Embassy, and while Chris was a student, Jill was an actively involved parent. She also was a member of the embassy's amateur theatre ensemble, which put on plays and musicals for the embassy community. Jill had the leading role in a show that was performed at Spaso House, the ambassador's residence, and Ambassador Watson brought a very special guest of honor to the program: Bob Hope.

Satra had a films division that distributed Soviet films in the United States. Our Moscow staff representative, Ludmila Davydenko, enabled us to build close friendships with our Soviet colleagues and business partners in the film industry, one of whom was the very talented and world-famous Russian filmmaker, director, and actor Nikita Mikhalkov. Mikhalkov would go on to direct *Burnt by the Sun,* which won the 1995 Academy Award for Best Foreign Language Film. Jill and I were thrilled that Nikita and his wife Tatyana came to a staff party at our apartment and later invited us to their *dacha*—country home—for a day of fun and partying.

At one point, Jill met an American woman who was setting up a Moscow marketing program for Estée Lauder cosmetics, and Jill was hired as a consultant. We soon had lots of Estée Lauder gift set samples, which came in handy at the most unexpected times.

My attention must have been wandering as I drove to the office on a Sunday morning—there was very little traffic, but I was driving in the central lane normally reserved for official vehicles. Not surprisingly, I got pulled over.

In these situations, once the Moscow traffic police realized you were a foreign businessman, they really didn't want to issue you a ticket. One of the first questions they asked was what products you sold, which was an indirect but not very subtle way of inquiring whether you had any samples you could part with.

I told this officer that our company exported chrome ore, which of course was not particularly helpful, but then added that my wife marketed Estée Lauder cosmetics. As soon as I offered him a perfume gift set, I was free to go.

One other traffic violation of mine was forgiven, even without the donation of samples. In the Winter Olympics of 1980, the US ice hockey team defeated the heavily favored Soviets to win the gold medal. We in the States still call it the Miracle on Ice, but at the time, all of Moscow was in shock.

Several days after the American victory, I was keeping pace with other vehicles on the highway, but we all were exceeding the speed limit, and I got pulled over. Unlike in the United States, in Moscow you were expected to exit your vehicle with your documents and walk to the police car. As soon as I gave the cops my auto registration, drivers permit, and passport, the four officers in the car started talking about the Miracle on Ice. After a few minutes, they very kindly concluded that in honor of the US hockey team's gold medal victory, they would let me go with a warning. I considered myself lucky—at the time I was fresh out of Estée Lauder samples.

The Boys and Me, Part I

I was still in training at Satra's New York office when Ara pulled me aside for a confidential conversation. "John, I want you to know that I talk to 'the boys' on both sides," he said. Despite his somewhat cryptic language, I knew exactly what—or who—he meant. "The boys" were our respective espionage agencies: the KGB and the CIA. "Our governments are not talking to each other," he continued, "so someone else has to keep those channels of communication open." To Ara, dealing with "the boys" was a basic fact of doing business between the US and the USSR, and as far as Satra was concerned, I would be that "someone else," when I got to Moscow.

I soon learned exactly what he meant. During my first months in Moscow, I was contacted by Igor Filin, one of the Soviet diplomats who'd joined us for the Birch Bayh campaign paddlewheel cruise down the Potomac. Igor was on home leave and invited me to join him for lunch with his friend, who had a last name, but I'll just refer to him as "Boris." Boris was in his mid-forties, spoke excellent English, and seemed well-educated. Ostensibly, he was a pal from Igor's university years and worked for the Soviet Main Administration for the Export of Raw Materials. This was an agency Satra dealt with regularly, and I assumed this would be a valuable connection to make for the company. After sympathizing with me about the challenges that foreign company reps and their families experienced in Moscow, Boris offered to help me not only in my work, but also with any arrangements that would make life more comfortable for my family.

I asked him whether he could find someone to stay with our children and help with cooking and cleaning so Jill could get out on her own. Boris quickly arranged for Nona, a kind, personable woman who was a terrific nanny/playmate for the kids, a great cook, and a wonderful housekeeper.

In those days, all Russian staff working for diplomats and foreign companies had to be hired through the Soviet Foreign Ministry's Main Administration for Service to the Diplomatic Corps. Although Nona told us she spoke no English, we learned that she previously had worked for the political attaché at the US Embassy.

Hmmmn. No English… really? To me, that was telltale indicator that Nona was more than a housekeeper and probably had additional job responsibilities of a more clandestine nature. Nevertheless, we loved her, and her supposed lack of English language skills were a great incentive for Jill and the kids to learn some Russian. Boris also arranged for Rya, a young Russian language teacher, to start tutoring Jill. They became very close and traveled together to many cities in the Soviet Union while I was occupied with my work.

I wasn't really bothered by the fact that our nanny/housekeeper might have been a spy. I pretty much understood that it came with the territory. Any Russian employee assigned to work with foreigners back then probably had additional responsibilities to keep certain Russian government agencies informed of anything unusual that the foreign individuals might be doing or saying. It was just the nature of the relationship between our countries at that time. Although I expected this of Nona, I never thought of her as a spy, and Jill, the kids and I liked her very much.

Early in my work with Satra, Senator Edward Kennedy came on an official visit to Moscow, and the embassy invited a large group of guests to meet the senator at a courtyard reception. I attended, and when the senator reached out to shake my hand in the receiving line, he remembered me and pulled me aside for an extended conversation. It was some time before he returned to the receiving line.

Apparently, the "boys" were watching, possibly from the windows or balconies of the adjoining apartment buildings. Perhaps some of them were also in attendance. Not long thereafter, Oztemel came to Moscow, and when we spoke privately after he himself had met with the boys, he said that the authorities were quite impressed with my relationship with Ted Kennedy and the lengthy amount of time he had spent with me at the embassy reception.

Lunches with Boris

Boris and I began to meet regularly for lunch, and it was always an event. He booked us at Moscow's top restaurants and arranged for us to have a private dining room to ourselves. Our lunches always included a medium-sized bottle of vodka with the meal, and a similarly sized bottle of cognac over dessert and coffee, which meant that lunch often lasted almost till dinner. We discussed any questions or needs I had at work, sometimes talking about other foreign firms and their representatives, and sometimes about how I perceived the current state of US-Soviet relations.

Boris seemed genuinely interested to learn about the attitudes of the American business community and usually had lots of questions. At first, he insisted on paying each time, but I was increasingly uncomfortable with that arrangement; I didn't want to feel like I "owed" him anything. I finally told him that I would only continue meeting for lunch if we alternated who picked up the check.

He never hesitated to reveal whatever details he had learned about either my business life or my personal life. At Satra, I got along well with our staff—at least I thought I did—in part because I didn't ask them to do anything I wasn't willing to do myself, including helping to paint the office. I often stayed with them after hours, partying and drinking vodka when we had special occasions to celebrate. Over one of our 80-proof lunches, Boris confirmed that the staff liked and respected me. Jill and I periodically invited Satra staffers and their spouses to dinner parties at our apartment.

Boris was both sincere and effective in his efforts to assist me, but he sometimes attached conditions whose rationale became clear only in hindsight. When I told him that my predecessor's request for a chemical engineer had gone unfulfilled for six months, he followed through immediately with the name of an applicant. Strangely, he told me to hire the man only as a temporary employee. Our new, permanent engineer, he assured me, would apply shortly thereafter.

As Boris had directed, I brought the applicant on board for a one-month probationary period. Hiring him on an interim basis was odd enough, but I was even more uncomfortable doing so since he currently worked at IBM. There was a great deal of camaraderie among foreign representatives in Moscow, and the IBM chief rep was a friend of mine. As a result, I felt a little uneasy poaching his employee. It got even weirder from there. The guy never reported for work, and after a week of his being AWOL, I called Boris. "Don't worry. All is well," he told me. "You'll have your permanent engineer in a few days."

And that's exactly what happened. The permanent engineer Boris sent me was extremely well qualified, and he stayed with Satra long after I left Moscow. We remain friends to this day. Sometime later, I met up with my friend, the IBM rep. As soon as he saw me, he thanked me profusely for helping him solve what had been an intractable personnel problem. IBM had been trying to figure out a way to terminate the engineer for a long time, he said, but because of Soviet employment laws, they'd been unable to do so. Only when the man informed them that he was quitting IBM to work for Satra were they able to get him off the payroll.

There was little doubt that Boris, most likely in concert with another of his KGB colleagues, had orchestrated this entire operation. It was enough to make me think that perhaps the boys had a Boris for each foreign company doing business in Moscow, and that we were all being "handled" in one way or another.

The Boys and Me, Part II

Toward the end of 1978, Jill, the kids and I were due to return to the States for the winter holidays. Boris and I had lunch right before we left, and he warned me not to try to get in touch with Igor Filin while I was home. Igor, he said, was no longer with the Soviet Embassy. I found out later that there was a lot more to the story. Our government had accused Igor of being a KGB agent and had expelled him from the country.

While we were home, I met privately in New York with Ara Oztemel. By this time, I had no doubt that Boris was a KGB operative, and I thought he needed to know that. "I think I'm talking to the boys in Moscow," I told him.

"Well," he replied without hesitation, "then it's time to talk to the boys here." Ara set up a meeting in his private office and stayed just long enough to make the introductions. He then left me alone with the CIA officer.

I was surprised when he presented me with his business card, which clearly stated his title at the Central Intelligence Agency. I told him all about Boris, how I had met him through Igor Filin, and as much as I could remember about our regular conversations in Moscow. When I told him that Boris was likely to ask whether I'd met with the CIA while I was home, he suggested stonewalling it and denying that this meeting ever took place.

"That's not going to work," I said, shaking my head, "because I'm the world's worst liar. Whenever I lie, my face turns red. It's a dead giveaway."

The CIA guy remained impassive. "Well, this is our policy," he replied, "and this is our advice to you."

Soon after I returned to Moscow, Boris and I had our first lunch. We were past the vodka on to dessert and cognac before he finally asked the question. "So… did you meet with the CIA while you were in the United States?"

I nodded. "Yes, I did," I replied.

Evidently, that was not the answer Boris was expecting, because he couldn't maintain his poker face. "What did you tell them?" he asked as his eyebrows converged over the bridge of his nose.

"Everything," I said calmly. "I told them everything."

"You told them about *me*?" he said incredulously, his voice rising in both pitch and volume. "Did you tell them my name—my family name?"

"I did," I said.

Boris sank into his chair. "You may have ruined any chance I could ever have to go to the United States," he said sadly.

"In my defense," I responded, "I never believed for a minute that you told me your real name."

One might think that this would have ended our relationship, but it didn't. We continued to meet and discuss life and business for the rest of my time in Moscow. We also got together for longer periods of time outside the city, going on overnight fishing trips and camping out by a lake or river. I enjoyed going fishing with him and the open discussions we had regarding world events, at least until one unpleasant incident. As we were leaving a restaurant after lunch, he said something very offensive to a woman who had said or done something he didn't care for. In that moment, I lost a lot of respect and affection for him. It never came back.

When the new Moscow World Trade Center, also known as Sovincentr, was completed, Satra became one of its first tenants. This complex of three high-rise buildings was a vertical city unto itself and included contemporary offices, convention space, restaurants, a large international hotel, and apartments occupied primarily by members of the foreign business community. The complex had been designed and financed with the help of Armand Hammer. As a result, it was often referred to as Hammer Center...

But never by us. Ara Oztemel considered Armand Hammer a bitter rival, and not without cause. He believed Hammer had set him up for a sham press interview, a poorly veiled fishing expedition whose real purpose was to find out as much as possible about Satra's chromite business. Hammer had been planning to compete head-to-head with Satra to export chrome ore from the Soviet Union and apparently arranged the fake interview in an effort to gather as much information beforehand as he could.

My time with Satra in Moscow gave me a chance to renew my friendship with Kolya. One evening, he met me at the new office so we could go to dinner together. We left our coats behind and walked to one of the Sovincentr restaurants, listened to live music, and reminisced about old times. It was quite late when we headed back to my office, and for some reason, the office tower elevators had been shut down. Kolya, ever resourceful, did some exploring through the back halls and discovered a functioning freight elevator, which we took up to the nineteenth floor.

I used my key to enter the Satra office, and as we walked into the reception area, we quickly discovered we were not alone. There in total darkness were two men in suits and ties. They had flashlights and a ladder and were working on something above the ceiling tiles. My assumption from day one at Satra had always been that our offices and living quarters harbored listening devices. The only conclusion I could draw now was that the ones in the ceiling of our Satra reception area needed repair.

As soon as we walked in, they packed up their ladder and left. There was no need to question them about it—I knew what they were doing, and I also knew they would never admit it. When I mentioned it to Ara, he came to the same conclusion and just shrugged it off. The next day, Boris called to say he'd heard of our evening encounter, and that he knew that I'd been with Kolya. Boris gave no explanation of how he was aware of this, but I didn't need one.

During my work for Satra in Moscow, my relations with our embassy were warm, and I had an especially close personal relationship with Jeff Barrie, the Army Attaché. I assumed he had to be some form of intelligence officer, but he was also outspoken about the need to improve US-Soviet relations, and I liked that a lot. When Ara Oztemel first hired me, I understood that he knew Jeff, who had graduated from The Citadel and had a master's degree in Russian studies. My guess was that Jeff would have been Ara's first choice for Satra's chief rep in Moscow, but Jeff had already committed to his twenty-year hitch in the Army. Ara did hire Maureen, Jeff's wife, as my assistant, which led to a long and enjoyable social relationship between the Barries and the Reuthers in Moscow. Maureen and I both took Russian language lessons from the same instructor at Sovincentr, Natalia Uvarova, who also became a close friend, often entertaining Jeff and me at her apartment.

Life in Moscow, Part II

The 1980 Summer Olympics took place in Moscow. It was the mid-1970s when the Soviets put US broadcasting rights up for bids, but their requested minimum of roughly $100 million was so high that neither ABC, nor NBC, nor CBS made an offer. Oztemel, ever the entrepreneur, saw an opportunity—securing TV rights for the Olympics would give him a leg up on creating a fourth major network in the States.

In December of 1976, Satra signed a contract with the Soviet Olympic organizing committee for exclusive US broadcast rights. There is considerable evidence to suggest that the Satra agreement was a chess move by the Soviets to get more money out of American network television, especially since early in 1977, the Soviets—possibly under pressure from the International Olympic Committee—reneged and signed a new deal with NBC instead. Oztemel was understandably upset and sued NBC and the Olympic Committee for $275 million each. The suits were settled about ten months later, with Satra being granted theater and video cassette rights to the Moscow Games.

It all went south in December 1979 when the Soviet troops marched into Afghanistan. President Jimmy Carter delivered an ultimatum to Leonid Brezhnev, giving him until February 1980 to order his troops out of Afghanistan. When Brezhnev refused to comply, Carter withdrew the United States from the Moscow Games.

It was the opening salvo in a long proxy war between the superpowers: the USSR and its pro-Soviet client state, the Democratic Republic of Afghanistan, battled guerrilla efforts by the *mujahideen*—Islamist fighters who were armed and financed by the United States. President Carter also imposed numerous trade sanctions on the Soviet Union, including a grain embargo and a ban on high technology trade. Those sanctions crippled the ability of Satra's consulting division to represent and assist US tech firms looking to do business in Moscow.

While I was deeply engaged with Satra, Jill missed her career as a model and actress and began looking for things to fill her time. She and Rya, her Russian language tutor, toured other parts of the USSR, including a trip to Tbilisi, the ancient capital of Soviet Georgia, which was then a quasi-independent republic within the USSR. When she returned, Jill told me that a musical theater performance was the highlight of her trip, and that Rya had arranged for them to go backstage after the show. They socialized with the performers, including a very famous Georgian lead actor and singer. Jill didn't go into a lot of detail, but she did let me know how impressed she had been with the lead actor.

Non-Soviets living in Moscow had to register travel plans to another part of the Soviet Union with an official agency, and we routinely did so for Jill's trips. However, when Jill and Rya decided on short notice to go to Riga, the capital of Latvia, I belatedly realized just after their departure that we hadn't registered their trip. I urgently called Boris, who took care of it.

The Boys and Me, Part III

Natasha, one of our secretaries at Satra, had previously been a dancer with the Moiseyev Ballet, a troupe that combined folk dance with classical ballet technique. Jill and I had a wonderful relationship with her and with her husband; they were frequent guests at our apartment. At one luncheon with Boris in late 1980, he suddenly told me that I had to fire Natasha but gave no explanation.

I was not about to do that without first consulting Oztemel. He was expected back in Moscow shortly, and I put off any action until we spoke. After telling Ara what Boris wanted me to do, he met with the boys, then confirmed that yes, I had to let her go. As with Boris, however, he gave me no rationale for the firing, which meant that when I spoke with Natasha, I'd have to make one up.

I brought Natasha into my office and told her that because the Soviet occupation of Afghanistan had resulted in US trade embargos against the USSR, Satra's business was down. As a result, we had to make staff cuts, and unfortunately, that included her position. She was shocked but then asked if I would go home with her that evening and tell her husband that she was being laid off.

I drove Natasha home and told her husband the same thing I had told her earlier in the day. Without hesitation, he looked me directly in the eye and said, "They made you do this, didn't they?"

"Yes, they did," I admitted.

The next time I had lunch with Boris, we went through the usual business discussions over the main course, but as soon as we got to dessert, cognac and coffee, he brought up Natasha. "You told her husband that I made you fire her, didn't you!" he said angrily.

"Yes," I responded.

Even before he said anything, I was already convinced that Natasha's firing was retribution. Most likely, her husband had done something—or not done something—that upset the boys. Removing Natasha from a very desirable job with a foreign firm was the KGB's way of punishing him.

Boris, like the rest of the boys, was into consequences, and now it was my turn. He needed a way to get back at me for exposing what they'd done to Natasha and her husband, and he found it—not in my role at the office, but in my personal life. "That Georgian is having sex with your wife," he said much more crudely.

"Yes, I know," I responded, which was sort of a lie, but not really. Until Boris spoke up, I hadn't known, but the possibility was on my mind. The Georgian acting troupe was performing in Riga at the same time that Jill and Rya were there, and I struggled to make myself believe that was a mere coincidence.

That evening, I didn't say anything to Jill about what Boris had told me, mostly because I assumed our apartment was bugged. Whatever we said at home would be overheard by the boys. My first opportunity to talk with her about it was several days later, when we went to the Bolshoi. During intermission, I told her what Boris had told me. I said that if there were secrets between us, the boys could exploit them and use them to manipulate us. I also confessed that I had been unfaithful to her on a business trip to Texas during the time I was working as a regional coordinator for AFSCME. While Jill has since denied having had a relationship with the Georgian actor, my memory is that she confirmed it to me at the time. Nonetheless, standing there in the bar room of the Bolshoi theatre that evening, we agreed that we would have to be open with one another from there on out.

Boris and I continued to go on overnight fishing and camping trips. On one of them, I was fishing downstream from him when an elderly fisherman appeared and asked me something in Russian that I didn't understand. I repeated it to Boris, who translated the expression as, "What are you using for bait?"

In the late summer of 1981, my Moscow tour of duty was about to end. Jill, Chris, Sasha and I were headed back to DC. Ara had promoted me to vice president and had assigned me to run Satra's Washington office. Before leaving for good, Jill and I made a short trip back home to buy a house. We started looking in our previous Silver Spring neighborhood but were disappointed to discover that although the same house we had hoped to purchase in 1978 was back on the market, the price was now 30 percent higher. We passed and bought a more affordable fixer-upper instead.

Before leaving Moscow for the last time, I had one final luncheon with Boris. I lamented how much more expensive houses were now than they had been three years earlier. I told him that financially, I would have been better off to have purchased that home in 1978, then rented it out while we were overseas.

Boris nodded sympathetically before speaking. "John," he began, "why don't you let us pay for half of the cost of that house?"

It was the perfect opening to use that fishing expression he had translated for me. "What are you using for bait, Boris?" I responded in Russian.

That was the first, last, and only time I was ever offered compensation by the boys.

CHAPTER 13

1981-1986

Satra's Washington Office

Jill, Chris, Sasha, and I returned from Moscow and moved into the fixer-upper house in Silver Spring, Maryland. I became a businessman/government intermediary by day and a carpenter/handyman by night. My spare time was consumed with major renovations to our home. I enlarged our first-floor master bedroom, opened an archway between the living room and dining room, spruced up the boys' bedrooms on the second floor, and finished the basement with a recreation room for Chris and Sasha and a carpenter's workshop for me.

(With the kids, Jill and my mom in Maryland)

As vice president of Satra and head of the Washington office, I now managed the company's interactions with Congress and the federal government, as well as with the Soviet Embassy and trade office. Our office was just me and Barbara Salkin, my secretary. Barbara had been a Democratic Party activist when I was Senator Bayh's presidential campaign regional coordinator in 1971 and supported me in my congressional campaign in 1974.

Dealing with Congress on one particular issue was a little awkward for me—more than a little, actually. Our Soviet trading partner, AvtoExport, had granted Satra the rights to import Soviet-built Lada automobiles into the United States, and my job was to facilitate that. What made it uncomfortable was that my last name was synonymous with protecting the rights of US auto workers. Wouldn't the influx of these inexpensive imports decrease sales of American cars and thus jeopardize the job security of UAW members? It didn't take long for the press to take notice of the irony. An article in the *Indianapolis Star* described my predicament:

> *The Soviet-American Trade Association is now quietly lobbying to disarm congressional opposition. It is doing so—believe it or not—in the person of John Reuther, son of Victor Reuther and nephew of Walter Reuther, the brothers who organized American auto workers in the mid-1930s. The younger Reuther, who spent the last three years in Russia working for the trade association, argues that his lobbying is not inconsistent with the family tradition of supporting international trade. "We as a nation sell far more to the Soviet Union than we buy," he said.*

The rationale I put forth was that because the US-USSR balance of trade was heavily in our favor, more American jobs were generated across the board than might be lost in Detroit. Nevertheless, it still felt like I was on the spot.

Like all vehicles sold in the United States, imported cars had to meet both Environmental Protection Agency admissions standards and safety requirements established by the National Highway Traffic Safety

Administration. Satra set up a lab to test the Ladas for compliance, but AvtoExport made a costly blunder. At the time, new car standards in the UK were quite different from those in the States, and some items on the safety checklist were contradictory. British standards mandated that when a vehicle was crash-tested, as much windshield periphery glass as possible flew out of the window frame. In the United States, the more glass remaining in the frame, the better. Unfortunately, AvtoExport somehow got this crossed up, and cars manufactured to be sold in the UK were shipped to the States. Of course, they failed to meet EPA and NHTSA standards.

All too soon, Lada's crash-test failures became irrelevant. Late in 1981, President Reagan imposed numerous tough trade sanctions on the Soviet Union for having backed/urged the declaration of martial law in Poland. Poland's Communist leaders, in a ham-fisted effort to crush increasingly strident political dissent, had put tanks in the streets and imposed a nighttime curfew in major cities. The primary target of this effort was Solidarity, a union that had originated at the Lenin Shipyard in Gdansk and was led by Lech Walesa. As part of the Russian-approved crackdown, Solidarity was outlawed, and Walesa and other union leaders were jailed.

Reagan responded to Poland's martial law with sweeping trade sanctions on the USSR that included suspension of all licenses for export of electronics and a refusal to renew US-Soviet exchange agreements on energy, science, and technology. These measures were a direct hit on Satra's wheelhouse—in effect, we were considerably restricted in our business volume, and I quickly accepted Oztemel's offer to leave Satra with a reduced retainer for twelve months.

Real Estate and ICDP

Meanwhile, I had to support my family. With an urgent need to reinvent a career, I took the necessary real estate coursework at the University of Maryland and became a licensed realtor. I was hired as an agent at Robinson Real Estate, a company opened by Terri Haddad Robinson, an old friend from the Office of Economic Opportunity. Terri was of Lebanese background and had contacts in the Arab community.

I started my real estate career in dramatic fashion. My first client was the Washington office of the Palestine Liberation Organization (PLO). They were looking for office space, but landlords were quite resistant to having them as a tenant. I finally had to pre-screen buildings and owners so I could show the PLO only offices where the landlord had confirmed in advance that they would be willing to lease to them. I soon found an acceptable space, and we closed the deal. In celebration, the PLO reps took me out to dinner, and I was quite pleased that we were joined by a State Department representative who was dealing with the PLO office, and by a Palestinian poet who was famous in the Arab world.

During my nearly three years with Robinson Real Estate, I kept up with US-Soviet relations and periodically attended functions at the Soviet Embassy and social events with other Americans interested in improved relations between our two countries. At one of these gatherings I met Lindsay Mattison, director of the nonprofit International Center for Development Policy (ICDP). The ICDP was active in efforts to reduce the use of military force to deal with international conflicts and brought together various experts to discuss and promote possible alternatives.

The President of the ICDP was Robert White, who had been ambassador to Paraguay and El Salvador until he was fired by President Reagan. The circumstances of his firing were concerning. "In 1981, as the ambassador to El Salvador, I refused a demand by the Secretary of State, Alexander M. Haig Jr., that I use official channels to cover up the Salvadoran military's responsibility for the murders of four American churchwomen," he wrote. "I was fired and forced out of the Foreign Service."

Lindsay offered me a job at ICDP as director of a newly formed commission on US-Soviet relations. Our objective was to bring together US and Soviet specialists on Third World conflicts to analyze causes and find solutions that did not involve military support from either Cold War superpower, but we were also ready to travel to the countries where such conflicts were ongoing. Our goal was to end the proxy wars that were ongoing in various areas of the world, including Afghanistan and several parts of Latin America.

We flew to Moscow in late April of 1986, where we were to discuss rising tensions in Latin America with our Soviet counterparts. While we were there, the No. 4 reactor at the Chernobyl nuclear power plant in Ukraine blew up. As the rest of the world was learning about the dire consequences of the explosion, we remained completely in the dark—there was a total news blackout in Moscow.

The Soviet government first denied that anything had happened, then acknowledged that a "minor" accident had taken place, even as they were evacuating 100,000 people from the surrounding area. Only in August, more than three months later, did they reveal the full extent of the disaster to the International Atomic Energy Agency. Meanwhile, airborne radiation levels soared to unsafe levels across Europe, including along the route our delegation took to fly back to DC. I learned what had happened only after we landed, and in hindsight, my first reaction was almost comical: I took everything in my suitcase to the dry cleaners.

CHAPTER 14

1987-1988

Moscow Peace Forum

In February 1987, ICDP was invited to bring a delegation to Moscow to attend a peace forum organized by Soviet President Mikhail Gorbachev. Actor/singer-songwriter Kris Kristofferson was a financial supporter of ICDP; he was also starring in *Amerika*, a new TV miniseries about life in the United States ten years after a hypothetical Soviet takeover…

And that was a looming problem. The drama, which was heavily anti-Soviet, had been filmed before the recent thaw in relations between East and West. Kristofferson was concerned that the miniseries would set back the progress we were starting to make building bridges through the Iron Curtain.

I invited Kris to come to Moscow with our delegation. He and his wife Lisa joined us in New York for a press conference announcing his participation, and their presence brought us a lot more publicity than we would have generated otherwise, including coverage in the *New York Times*:

> *While disputes swirl around the television series Amerika, in which he stars, the actor Kris Kristofferson will weather the storm in an unlikely place—the Soviet Union. The seven-part, 14½ hour series, which portrays Mr. Kristofferson as a freedom fighter of the future in a United States that has been taken over by the Russians, begins Sunday on ABC affiliates…*
>
> *Plans to air the series have drawn protests, including demands that it be withdrawn, from organizations including the United Nations, which has suggested it might take legal action if the series is aired.*
>
> *In the drama, which is set in the year 1991, the Soviet takeover of the United States grows out of the posting of Soviet soldiers here as part of*

a United Nations peacekeeping force. ABC announced Tuesday that it would introduce each segment with a declaration that the series is fiction and organizations depicted "are not intended to bear any resemblance to today's counterparts."

When asked about the non-fit between his role in the *Amerika* mini-series and his participation in the conference, Kristofferson, a Rhodes scholar, offered a thoughtful, well-considered reply. "It's better," he said, "to have someone (in the series' starring role) who is then willing to go over to Russia with an open mind to improve communications… We have to go on beyond the old stereotypes of the Russians as the enemy in order to save the planet."

(With Kris Kristofferson, his wife Lisa and my former Satra colleague Natasha Mikulinskaya, who was working as a translator)

The Moscow Peace Forum, whose theme was "A Non-Nuclear World for the Survival of Mankind," attracted scientists, educators, and entertainment figures from around the globe. Among those attending were former Canadian Prime Minister Pierre Elliott Trudeau, former Austrian Chancellor Bruno Kreisky, Norman Mailer, Gore Vidal, Gregory Peck, and Marcello Mastroianni. Also attending was prominent Russian dissident Andrei Sakharov. Originally a nuclear physicist, Sakharov had become a passionate advocate for disarmament and nonproliferation. Awarded the Nobel Peace Prize in 1975, the Soviet government had barred him from traveling to Sweden to collect it. Yelena Bonner, his wife and fellow activist, went to Stockholm and accepted on his behalf.

Despite heavy government pressure to remain silent, Sakharov continued to speak out. In 1980, after openly criticizing the deployment of Soviet troops to Afghanistan, he was exiled to Gorky (now Nizhny Novgorod). In the early 1980s, Gorky was a closed city because of the many military research and production facilities located there. By confining Sakharov to a place where foreigners were banned, Soviet leadership hoped to curtail the reach of his ongoing critiques.

In December 1986, just months before the Peace Forum, Gorbachev lifted the banishment and allowed Sakharov to return to Moscow. Once the Forum began, he and Yelena agreed to meet separately with our delegation and invited us to spend an evening with them at their Moscow apartment.

At the time, the most popular music group in the Soviet Union was Mashina Vremeni, a rock band whose name translates as Time Machine. In Russia, they were comparable to the Beatles. They attended sessions of the Peace Forum, and Andrey Makarevich, their lead singer, invited Kristofferson to join them at their next concert. All 13,700 seats in the Luzhniki Palace of Sports were filled, and those of us in the ICDP delegation were fortunate enough to attend. Among the songs Kris sang with the group was an up-tempo version of the civil rights anthem "We Shall Overcome," and it brought the entire arena to its feet.

Cuomo Delegation to the Soviet Union

As Democratic New York Governor Mario Cuomo was eyeing a run for the presidency, his advisors identified a potential campaign vulnerability: the governor had very little foreign policy experience. His aides asked ICDP to organize a meeting schedule for the governor that would begin to fill the void. We planned a series of conversations for him with an array of Soviet leaders during a trip that would take place in the fall of 1987. By then, however, Cuomo had decided against throwing his hat in the ring. Nevertheless, he still made the trip.

Returning to my role as advance man, I arrived in Moscow several days before the governor. I was accompanied by Fredrica "Fritzy" Goodman, a key member of Cuomo's staff whose title was director of the Office of Special Projects and Protocol for the State of New York. Perhaps not surprisingly, my KGB friend Boris from my Satra days soon contacted me at my hotel. As in the past, he invited me to dinner and drinks. In the process of catching up on what had transpired since our last get-together, we consumed even more than our usual quota of vodka and cognac. I was quite tipsy when I returned to the hotel, and when I told Fritzy about my relationship with Boris, perhaps I didn't choose my words as carefully as I should have. What I know for sure is that after I mentioned the concept of talking with the boys on both sides, she passed that on to Governor Cuomo.

Cuomo met with a number of high-level Soviet officials, including Anatoly Dobrynin, former Soviet Ambassador to the United States, Vitaly Vorotnikov, chairman of the Russian Soviet Federative Socialist Republic Council of Ministers, and Georgy Arbatov, founding director of the Soviet think tank that studied Canada and the United States. He also met with Yevgeny Primakov, director of the Institute of World Economy and International Relations of the USSR Academy of Sciences (IMEMO). Primakov was a rising star in the Soviet Union. In the years that followed, he would go on to become first deputy chairman of the KGB, foreign minister, and finally prime minister, but only briefly—he would soon be replaced as prime minister by another rising star, Vladimir Putin.

(With Mario and Mrs. Cuomo at a Moscow press conference)

(Ceremonial wreath laying in Moscow)

The final destination for Cuomo was Leningrad, where the governor continued his discussions with national and local leaders. In the hotel elevator on our last day, Governor Cuomo recalled what Fritzy Goodman had told him about my talking with the boys on both sides, but it was clear that it had lost—or gained—something in her retelling of it. "John," Cuomo said loudly, "I know you work for either the CIA or the KGB and I don't know for which, but I want to thank you for all your help on this trip."

In Governor Cuomo's follow-up written report to the ICDP, he summarized his assessment by saying, "It seems clear to me that there is an opportunity now—perhaps the best in forty years—to break out of the grip of the Cold War and move gradually and surely toward a greater mutual security and cooperation… I wish to thank Mr. John Reuther, the Executive Director of the Commission on US-Soviet Relations, for his invaluable assistance to me and my state delegation throughout our stay in Moscow and Leningrad. Without his help, we would not have had as successful a trip as we did."

Joint Soviet-American Delegation to Afghanistan

While in Moscow with Cuomo, I had taken advantage of his meeting with Yevgeny Primakov to sound out our IMEMO colleagues about forming a delegation to travel to Afghanistan. I proposed meeting jointly with representatives of various Afghan factions to discuss the ongoing conflict. IMEMO responded positively to the idea, and we began planning for a US-Soviet trip the following year.

Soviet troops had rolled into Afghanistan in December of 1979; in the spring of 1988, they were still there. While they were propping up the government of Mohammed Najibullah, CIA operatives were funneling large quantities of both arms and money to the Islamist guerrilla forces of the mujahideen.

We left for Afghanistan on April 18, 1988. The fifteen-member Soviet delegation was headed by IMEMO director Yevgeny Primakov. The eleven-person US group was led by two veteran diplomats: ICDP President Robert White, who had served as US Ambassador to Paraguay and to El Salvador, and

William Sullivan, who had been our last ambassador to Iran before relations were severed and had also served as ambassador to Laos and the Philippines as well. Joining us were a number of top academicians and regional specialists, as well as six journalists, including a team from ABC News.

As we prepared to leave on this trip, Gorbachev had already announced a planned Soviet troop withdrawal, but it had not yet begun, and fighting was ongoing. A preliminary peace accord had also been signed in Geneva by the governments of Afghanistan and Pakistan, but that, too, had yet to translate into a cessation of hostilities. Pakistan was a signatory because at the time, it was our proxy supporter of the mujahideen. Primarily through a program that the CIA dubbed "Operation Cyclone," the US government used Pakistan as a training base for insurgent forces, and also as a first stop for weapons delivery. Arms were flown into Pakistan and then carried over the border into Afghanistan.

Before leaving for Moscow, our ICDP staff attended a series of meetings in DC, including a briefing with the second secretary of the Afghan Embassy to the United States, and a separate meeting with the deputy chief of mission of the Embassy of Pakistan. We also held two meetings at the State Department, one with the Afghan desk chief and the other with our former deputy chief of mission in Kabul.

Because of ongoing US support for the mujahideen, we consulted with three mujahideen leaders in DC. They were aware that ours would be a joint mission with the Soviets and strongly disapproved. When the three mentioned that they knew we would be staying at the Kabul Intercontinental Hotel, we took it as a lightly veiled threat.

On the way to Moscow from DC, I had some downtime in the airport in Frankfurt. While waiting to change planes, I noticed an American couple sitting nearby in the restaurant. It took me a while, but I finally figured out why the man looked familiar. He was San Francisco 49ers quarterback Joe Montana. I approached him to get an autograph for Sasha, and he graciously complied.

Once we arrived in Moscow, members of the Soviet delegation ran down the itinerary for our week in Afghanistan, and the next morning, the Afghan foreign minister joined us for the Soviet commercial flight to Kabul. ICDP member John Nicolopoulos, our Moscow liaison, was supposed to join us, but canceled at the last minute. Galena, his Russian wife, had hidden his passport. She wasn't going to let him make her a widow, she explained, by going to Afghanistan.

Kabul International Airport is more than a mile above sea level and sits in a bowl ringed by the Hindu Kush mountains. Because there is no straight approach to the runway, we circled to lose altitude in preparation for landing. As we did so, the sky lit up. Soviet ground forces and helicopters were sending up flares to divert heat-seeking missiles launched by the mujahideen. Those flares gave us little or no sense of security. The US had equipped the mujahideen with the best and latest Stinger missiles, and they had already brought down a number of Soviet aircraft.

On the afternoon of our arrival, we checked into the Intercontinental and were taken to view the Museum of Seized Arms. The exhibit of weapons captured from the mujahideen brought home the shocking human cost of the war in the starkest possible terms. The room showcased barbaric weaponry that included booby-trapped children's toys, but perhaps worse, people who had been wounded and maimed by these weapons were also on display.

(At the Museum of Seized Arms)

That evening, the Afghan Academy of Sciences held a reception to welcome us. Many guests approached our American group without hesitation, expressing their desire to improve relations and to resume meeting with US academicians and university colleagues. The following morning, the US delegation members were given a breakfast briefing by John Glassman, the chargé d'affaires at the American Embassy. He passed out American flag lapel pins and advised us—warned us, actually—to wear them at all times. If mujahideen fighters saw us on the streets and suspected that we might be Soviets, the pins would help identify us as Americans. Our Soviet colleagues found this humorous, but in photos taken of me during the trip, I was always wearing my pin.

Over the next several days, we met with the Peace, Solidarity and Friendship Organization, the Ministry of Foreign Affairs, the Afghanistan Chamber of Commerce, and Afghan refugees who had returned to Kabul. We also visited a Soviet military installation, where the Soviet base commander, together with Ambassadors White and Sullivan, held an outdoor press conference. The outdoor meeting site was shaded by camo netting, but I suspected that its ancillary purpose was to shield us from American reconnaissance aircraft.

(With Afghan troops and Russian armored carriers)

(Ambassadors White and Sullivan with a top Soviet general)

The following day we flew to Mazār-i-Sharīf, capital of the northern province of Balkh, a more peaceful and Soviet-friendly area along the border with Soviet Uzbekistan. We met with local political leaders, toured a fertilizer plant, an Afghan military base, and a beautiful, historic mosque. After the tour, we were brought to the ranch-like home—complete with backyard swimming pool—of Mohd Rasul Barat. Barat was the very wealthy, thirty-year old head of his own trading company, and was engaged in several joint ventures with the Soviets. They were working to develop a number of industrial enterprises, including the processing, drying, and marketing of raisins, sausage production, and the manufacture of plastic bags. Barat told us that he owned "half of the city" of Mazār-i-Sharīf and also mentioned that both his father and his brother had been killed by the mujahideen.

While we were waiting by his pool for the barbeque to be served, I noticed a number of our Soviet colleagues going into the house and coming out with cold beers. I decided to join them, and when Barat heard me speaking Russian as I entered the kitchen, he assumed I was part of the Soviet delegation. I was invited with the rest of the Russians into an adjoining room and after we were seated on floor cushions and offered shots of vodka, he proposed a toast to welcome us to Mazār-i-Sharīf. Still unaware that I was an American, he concluded with a bold declaration: "We will show these son-of-a-bitch Americans that we know how to entertain!" At that point, I approached Barat and told him I was an American. He was quite impressed, not just with my knowledge of Russian, but with the rapport I had with my Soviet colleagues.

Despite that awkward beginning, I developed a rapport with Barat, in part because I realized that he possessed an immensely valuable skill. To assure the flow of goods, Afghan trading companies, including his own, had shown a remarkable ability to navigate between the official government and the resistance. I asked Barat to tell me how he did it—I thought it would be useful to political leaders on both sides.

We flew back to Kabul that evening, and once again it was readily apparent that a ceasefire was a long way off. Our hotel offered a great vantage point from which to observe the many flares launched to protect aircraft arriving and departing from nearby Kabul International Airport. We could also watch the steady stream of fully armed Soviet military helicopters as they took off and headed for battle.

The ABC News team accompanying us wanted to see where they were going—they wanted eyewitness battle footage. We chartered a small plane to fly to Jalalabad, which was about a hundred miles east and roughly halfway to the Pakistani border. It was also a hot zone for skirmishes between Russian-backed Afghan forces and the mujahideen.

Not everyone thought this was a good idea, and some members of our delegation preemptively opted out of the trip. Sitting on the tarmac waiting to take off, I started having misgivings myself, and for the second time that day, I worried about my own mortality.

It had already been a long day. The sun was not yet up when I'd started getting dressed for the trip to Mazār-i-Sharīf, and I remembered that I'd left Sasha's Joe Montana autograph back in Moscow, along with some other things I wasn't going to need in Afghanistan. Not knowing what the day would bring, it occurred to me at the time that if anything happened and I didn't return, Sasha might never get his souvenir.

In the predawn darkness on the morning of April 22, I sat down at my hotel room desk and wrote my son a short note, letting him know there was a sports celebrity autograph waiting for him in Moscow, and telling him how much I loved him, his brother Chris, and his mother. I left the note with my clothes and other belongings in the hotel room, assuming, perhaps naïvely, that it and the rest of my "effects" would be sent on to my family in case I didn't make it home.

The first part of the day at Mazār-i-Sharīf had gone well, and while we were there, I'd never really felt like I was in imminent danger. Now, buckled into my seat for the flight to Jalalabad, I was grateful that, if anything happened, there would be some written record of my love for my family. Meanwhile, however, we remained on the ground. The crew said we were in a weather hold, but we all suspected it was far more likely that local fighting in and around Jalalabad had compromised our ability to land safely. I started to wonder whether the mujahideen fighters in Jalalabad had the same Stinger missiles that they had here in Kabul.

I fell asleep in my seat and awoke an hour later. We were still on the tarmac, but all of our Soviet colleagues had deplaned in favor of the airport lounge. We Americans stuck it out until Ambassador White decided that he, too, had had enough. Our ABC News crew was undoubtedly disappointed when the ambassador stood to leave, but the rest of us were immensely relieved, and after retrieving our Soviet colleagues from the bar, we returned to the Intercontinental.

The morning of our departure for Moscow, our joint delegation was invited to a private meeting with Afghan President Najibullah. Najibullah had formerly been the director of KhAD, the Afghan state intelligence agency, which also had a grisly track record of torture and assassination. He spent two hours with us and urged the Americans in the group to pressure or otherwise encourage the Reagan administration to cut off military support for both the mujahideen and for Pakistan. After saying he wanted democracy for his people that was free from outside influence, he indicated his willingness to negotiate with rebel leaders under his policy of national reconciliation.

Ambassador White was openly skeptical, telling Najibullah that he could see no proof that his policy of national reconciliation was working, and added that in any event, it could not be dictated from above. Nevertheless, the ambassador did feel that our trip had been productive, since we'd added to the reservoir of knowledge on both sides and equipped a large group of influential Afghan citizens to speak intelligently on ending the conflict.

(Ambassador White with Afghanistan President Najibullah in the front row center, along with Ambassador Sullivan directly behind them)

We returned to Moscow for follow-up meetings with our Soviet colleagues, including a wrap-up session with Yevgeny Primakov and his associates at IMEMO. Primakov, ICDP director Lindsay Mattison, and I also were interviewed by the Soviet newspaper *Izvestia*. I was quoted in the article as having made what I thought were a number of salient points:

> *We met with Afghans from different sides of the firing line, and we sensed that they all are tired of war... [This was] a remarkable precedent for multilateral dialogue on questions of solving regional conflicts. Its participants unambiguously advocated a political settlement as opposed to military methods for solving such disputes... The solution of the Afghan problem could become a model for the settlement of other international conflicts.*

After this quote, the article concluded with Primakov's comments: "I think that we can end our conversation today on this note of optimism."

On our final day in Moscow, we met with Georgy Shakhnazarov, personal adviser to Mikhail Gorbachev and president of the Soviet Political Sciences Association, who was considered to be the author of Gorbachev's policy of "New Political Thinking." After a formal, farewell luncheon with Soviet members of the delegation, a tour of the Kremlin, and an evening at the Bolshoi Ballet, we flew home to Washington.

Financial Issues

Harsh financial choices were waiting for me when I got home. The limited real estate work that I had been able to do from 1983 to 1986, followed by a modest income from ICDP, had not been enough to provide my family with the lifestyle we'd enjoyed when I worked for Satra. Jill's modeling and commercial advertising career was blossoming, but the fees she earned were not enough to make up for my reduced salary.

Our downward economic mobility had adversely affected my relationship with Jill. She was not thrilled with our modest lifestyle in Silver Spring, especially since many of her model and actress friends had husbands who were doctors or lawyers and lived in impressive homes in the tonier Washington suburbs. In general, our marriage had become frayed and was at an impasse.

Early in 1988, Jill told me she was planning to move out. This was difficult to hear, but I understood and accepted her decision. I began looking for an apartment for Sasha and me in our neighborhood so he could continue at the same middle school. Chris was about to graduate from high school and go off to college at Boston University in the fall of 1988.

When we told my parents about our plans to split up, they believed that our problems were related to our finances. They strongly encouraged us to stay together and provided a modest loan to help us make things work. It helped for a while, but I knew there was more money trouble on the horizon. In 1988, the ICDP suffered some major losses;

by the time I returned from Afghanistan, it was under financial stress. Lindsay Mattison, the director, informed me that staff cutbacks were likely that summer.

It was time to look for another job. I reached out to Wade Greene, a member of our Afghanistan delegation who was a philanthropic adviser to the Rockefeller Family Trust Foundation, about setting up an Afghan relief study program, but it proved to be a dead end. Lindsay Mattison tried to find me a position in the private sector, without success. I also pursued commercial consulting work, including with Mohd Rasul Barat, the Afghan businessman I'd met at his northern Afghan home.

Barat, whose company exported 500,000 tons of raisins annually to the Soviet Union, had reached out to me by telex to see if I could help him find American manufacturers of raisin-cleaning equipment and polyethylene bags. I found a California company that could provide the equipment Barat was looking for and negotiated a commission for me on the sale, but the company had reservations about going through with the deal. They feared the possibility of US restrictions on the export of American technology to Afghanistan, and were also concerned about how, when, and whether they would be paid. After that deal fell through, the other shoe dropped on June 22, 1988, when I received a formal letter from ICDP Director Mattison, confirming that the time had come to give me official notice.

CHAPTER 15

1988-1990

Perestroika Joint Venture

I was in my last days with ICDP when I met Paul Von Ward at a US-Soviet relations get-together. Paul headed Delphi International Group, a consulting company that made travel, hotel, and entertainment arrangements for visiting foreign delegations meeting with government agencies in DC. He had a connection with Andrei Stroyev, the young, personable general manager of Mosinzhstroi, a huge Moscow city government construction company. It was a valuable connection to have: Stroyev's company had 35,000 employees and a monopoly on the construction of roads, utilities, and other infrastructure in Moscow.

Paul and Andrei had already done the preliminary work to establish what would be Moscow's first US-Soviet joint commercial real estate and construction venture. In June of 1988, they formalized their collaboration and called their newly registered enterprise Perestroika Joint Venture, or PJV. *Perestroika* in Russian means reconstruction. Mikhail Gorbachev had used the term to describe his policy of restructuring the Soviet Union's economic system and saw perestroika as a way to begin stepping away from Marxist hardline central planning. By doing that, he hoped to nudge open the door to more economic interaction with the West.

Perestroika also means reconstruction in the physical sense. Moscow had been a focal point of Russian life and culture for centuries. Like most urban centers with a long history, its streetscape was dotted with older buildings whose architecture echoed the glory of the past. Unlike New York or Paris or London, however, Moscow's historic buildings had not been upgraded to meet the needs of changing times. Basic heating, plumbing, and electrical systems were archaic—or worse.

Telecommunications systems that businesses increasingly relied on were absent or inadequate, as were the amenities that foreign office workers had come to expect. Some structures were unsafe; others were eyesores that had been completely abandoned.

And that was an opportunity disguised as a problem. Many of these buildings were located in key areas of downtown Moscow, where quality modern office space was scarce. Paul and Andrei established PJV to renovate—to *reconstruct*—these architectural treasures to create modern business spaces that would rent out at top of the market prices. Their target lessees would be foreign corporations willing to pay a hefty premium for a pleasant and functional work environment as they began doing business in the Soviet Union. For PJV and for Andrei Stroyev in particular, "perestroika" truly was a double entendre.

My real estate background and Russian business experience made me an ideal candidate to represent Delphi in PJV, and Paul Von Ward and I met to discuss my role. Shortly thereafter, he flew to Moscow to meet with Stroyev, and I sent him a list of contacts I thought would be helpful. The names I gave him included Georgi Shakhnarof, Gorbachev's personal advisor and first deputy chief of the Communist Party Central Committee, and three members of the Soviet delegation to Afghanistan, including Yevgeny Primakov.

When Paul returned, he made me a formal but conditional job offer. He proposed that I travel with him and two other Delphi associates to make preliminary presentations to Moscow authorities to secure a site. Getting an official site designation from the city was an essential first step because all existing buildings set for renovation were government-owned structures and sat on city-owned land.

That trip was scheduled for July. If all went well, Delphi would retain me on a short-term contract. I would remain in Moscow from September to December to aid in negotiations and get the project off the ground. Once they confirmed that I was a good fit for the job, they would bring me on board for three years as PJV director of foreign affairs, with an annual salary of $75,000, plus 800 rubles per month (then about $960) to cover personal expenses. My contract would also include a family residence in Moscow and other perks normally associated with an expat executive position in the Soviet Union.

After I got laid off at ICDP in June, Jill and I had discussed the cold economic reality that the best and perhaps only way for me to bring in a comfortable salary was to take a position in Moscow, where a premium was paid to people with my background and experience. That income was going to be more essential than ever because we now had college tuition to pay—Chris was headed to Boston University in the fall. For Jill, however, returning to Moscow was going to put a severe damper on her modeling, advertising and film bookings—again. She'd already sidelined her career to do that once and was unwilling to do it a second time. I was not surprised. We had already discussed separating, and I was prepared to take this on alone.

PJV Math

PJV had a designated capital fund of $12.5 million. Since Delphi, Paul's company, had 20 percent of the equity, he was responsible for providing $2.5 million of the total. The remaining $10 million was to come from four Russian legal entities participating in the joint venture:

- 60 percent from the Moscow City Main Administration for the Construction of Engineering Structures (Mosinzhstroi)—the company headed by Andrei Stroyev;
- 8 percent from the High-Rise and Hotel Administration of the Moscow City Council;
- 7 percent from JV Dialogue, a Soviet-American joint venture; and
- 5 percent from the Moscow City Main Administration for Architecture and City Design and Construction.

In addition to their share of the capital fund, each of the three Moscow city entities contributed their expertise and invaluable insider government contacts, but JV Dialogue had a unique role. Established in 1987, it had been one of the first joint ventures in the Soviet Union, and

Dialogue staff members were very helpful in showing us how to navigate the rules and regulations involved in creating and registering a joint venture. Its founder was Joe Ritchie, a multimillionaire Chicago options and commodities trader. For several years, he was the exclusive distributor for Microsoft products in Russia. As a result, much of Dialogue's participation in PJV was not payment in cash, but in-kind contributions in the form of computers, software, and accessories.

Much to my surprise and delight, I soon learned that the Dialogue staffer who had signed the founding documents of PJV was Greek journalist John Nicolopoulos. I'd met John in Moscow on my way to Afghanistan with the ICDP—he'd been our media liaison, and it was a pleasure to link up once again with him and his wife Galena.

During our July meetings, PJV secured its first site: Bolshoi Gnezdnikovsky Lane No. 7, a gutted six-story apartment building constructed in 1906. What we saw was just the shell of a six-story structure, with only iron beams holding the exterior brick walls together. Ideally located, it stood in the very center of Moscow, directly across Pushkin Square from what would become the most popular McDonald's restaurant in the world.

Once Perestroika JV was awarded the site, things started to move quickly. Andrei Stroyev put together a team of Russian, Italian, and American architects to draw up plans to convert this shell of a structure into a contemporary office building that included luxury suites on a seventh, mansard rooftop level. He then secured Codest International, an Italian construction company, as the contractor. Why use a foreign contractor? Soviet construction companies at that time had no experience developing and building modern office buildings that would be suitable for contemporary international corporations, and Stroyev knew this all too well. Space built by Russian construction companies may have been historically beautiful, but not especially functional as modern office premises.

Glitches began to appear shortly thereafter. The problem, as was often the case in the Soviet Union at that time, was hard currency, or the lack thereof. Hard currency was the only payment that foreign construction companies like Codest would accept, but rubles contributed by Soviet partners were not convertible, and JV Dialogue was making most of its contribution in electronic equipment. Although Delphi was expected to provide its share in Western currency, it had not been obligated to contribute until the first site had been approved. Now that Bolshoi Gnezdnikovsky Lane No. 7 had been secured, however, Paul Von Ward was having trouble coming up with Delphi's $2.5 million share.

Nevertheless, he quickly contracted with me to become PJV deputy director. Most of my time was spent working directly with Andrei Stroyev, who was not only general director of Mosinzhstroi but also general director of PJV. Working together for long hours as we developed plans and a budget, Andrei often welcomed me to his apartment for dinner with his wife, Yelena. I also joined them at their summer cottage on the island of Serebryany Bor, a resort area formed by a branch of the Moscow River not far from the city.

Andrei spoke excellent English and loved the Beatles. We quickly established great rapport and a relationship of mutual respect and trust. He was anxious for change in the Soviet Union and embraced the concept of perestroika in all its meanings. His staff did as well. As I came to know them, I began to understand how much it meant to them to be part of an international joint venture at this pivotal time in their history.

(With Andrei Stroyev)

Their resources, skill and enthusiasm meant that the weakest link in PJV was Delphi Group, specifically Paul Von Ward himself. I soon realized that, although Paul had been in the right place at the right time to create PJV with Stroyev, going forward he was not a strong construction and development partner. Andrei had wanted to set up PJV so that Mosinzhstroi could earn hard currency—which would enable them to purchase foreign-made roadbuilding equipment, spare parts, and infrastructure construction technology—but his motivation was much deeper than that. I wrote a note to Paul because I wanted him to understand how much this JV meant personally to Andrei and the other Russian staff members.

> *To the individual Soviet PJV staff members, including Andrei Stroyev, the JV represents more than an organization for the "transformation of ruble-based economic units to convertible currency assets." They see working for a joint venture as a means of breaking away from the constrictions of the stagnant, centralized Soviet economic system. Jobs with a JV are highly prized and represent a major career move leading to travel and hard currency earnings and salaries more on the world market scale. The Soviets are looking far down the road, with the immediate priority of launching the JV and reinvesting profits to see that it survives and grows.*

When Paul arrived in Moscow, it became clear that he and Andrei were still at an impasse. Andrei was doing everything he could to forge ahead as quickly as possible, but because Paul was having trouble raising Delphi's share of the funds, he kept his foot firmly on the brake. Paul's company was causing other problems as well. Andrei was struggling to get city approvals because officials were unimpressed with Delphi's bona fides. In addition to being short of cash, Delphi had no background in construction or commercial real estate development.

Ultimately, Paul and Andrei agreed to a parting of the ways. Although I'd been retained by Delphi, I was now determined to stay with PJV. The hunt was on for an American partner who could buy out

Delphi— one with funds to invest, one that would value the working relationship I had developed with Andrei and other PJV staff. In short, one that would hire me.

Worsham

During these months in Moscow, I had kept in touch with Steve Lundy, president of Trout Unlimited (TU), the American flyfishing organization. Quite by coincidence, he came to Moscow soon after Andrei and Paul had made their decision to split up. I was living in the Budapest Hotel and invited Steve to join me for lunch. When I shared our need to find a new American partner, he mentioned one of their TU leaders, Earl Worsham. His company, Worsham Group, was a successful commercial property developer based in Atlanta. Lundy said that Worsham had led delegations to the Soviet Union and was interested in pursuing real estate development in Moscow.

I faxed Worsham with information about PJV and our interest in finding a new American partner to replace Delphi. I also told him that Andrei Stroyev and I were flying to the States in late December to meet with possible investors, and that we would like to meet with him, if he was interested. Not only was he interested, he took over planning much of our trip.

When we landed at JFK, Earl Worsham and Alan LeBlanc, his partner and son-in-law, were waiting with a stretch limo. We rode together to the hotel on Central Park that they had booked for us and had a series of meetings with them over the next day and a half. Worsham arrived well prepared with documentation and brochures about his many commercial real estate projects, including Hyatt hotels, high-rise office buildings, and senior living facilities. One of his key projects was CenTrust Tower, a landmark forty-seven story office building in downtown Miami. Designed by I. M. Pei, it was known for its three glass tiers, which were colorfully illuminated at night. During our meetings, Worsham was quite the salesman, which surprised both Andrei and me. We had expected that we would be the ones selling him on the benefits of joining PJV, but what happened was quite the reverse—he was selling us on the Worsham Group instead.

We left New York for Chicago and met with JV Dialogue founder Joe Ritchie, but he was not prepared to buy out Delphi's interest in PJV. We then sat down with Bernd Chorengel, president of Hyatt International Corporation. PJV was already in discussion with Hyatt about a hotel in Moscow. Chorengel told us that although Hyatt would not be the investor to replace Delphi, it was most interested in managing a hotel under contract with PJV.

When Andrei told him that in all likelihood we had found a new partner in commercial developer Earl Worsham, Chorengel looked shocked. "Earl Worsham, of the Worsham Brothers?" he asked.

"No," Andrei replied. "His company is called Worsham Group."

Both of us were taken aback when Chorengel declared that he wouldn't have anything to do with any project in which Worsham was involved. Worsham had built the Hyatt Regency Hotel and Convention Center in Miami, which was completed in 1984. "I'm not going to set myself up for a lawsuit by telling you details," he added, "but talk with anyone who has done business with Earl Worsham, and you'll learn why I won't do business with him."

This was potentially serious—Andrei and I were about to fly from Chicago to Atlanta to solidify a deal with Worsham Group to buy into PJV. If Earl Worsham was somehow untrustworthy, we needed to know. When we asked Chorengel to put us in touch with some of Worsham's former business partners, he gave us the name of a man who'd been involved with the CenTrust Tower. We tried to contact him by phone but were told that he was out of the country and would not return soon.

That evening, Andrei and I called Earl. When we told him about our discussion with Hyatt International, he immediately said there must be some mistake—his company was Worsham *Group*, not Worsham *Brothers*, and led us to believe that Chorengel must have been thinking of someone else. Although I believed Chorengel and doubted there had been any misunderstanding, Andrei was already pretty much sold on Earl. He was ready to do a deal with him to get him to buy out Delphi.

Andrei and I flew to Atlanta, where Earl rolled out the red carpet once again. As if to counter Hyatt, he set up a meeting with the president of Ritz-Carlton International, who was clearly interested in opening a hotel in Moscow. He also covered all our expenses. That evening, Earl asked whether I was an investor in Delphi and PJV. I told him that I was an employee, not a stakeholder, and that I was being paid by Delphi.

"John," he said, "if I become the American partner in PJV, I want you to have equity in my company. I believe that my company executives should feel that this company is also *their* company." I was quite impressed with Earl's offer and took him at his word. I looked forward to his company buying out Delphi.

Andrei and I flew from Atlanta to Washington for talks with Delphi. They did not go well. Paul was clearly upset that our schedule had been oriented around Worsham, and he was still having trouble agreeing with Andrei on the details of the buyout. I felt bad leaving Andrei alone in his hotel after our acrimonious meeting with Paul, so I convinced him to stay in my parents' home until he returned to Moscow. Mom and Dad had years of interaction with people from other countries, and they were charmed by Andrei and his friendly, personable manner.

I also invited Andrei to spend some time with me at my home. Jill, Chris, and Sasha were in Michigan visiting her mom for the holidays. He was quite impressed with my renovations, most of all with the workshop and its power tools. In those days, even top Soviet officials lived modestly. Andrei's home was a no-frills two bedroom/one bath apartment, and I could tell by his face that he was comparing it unfavorably with my middle-class suburban house in Silver Spring.

Baker & McKenzie

Before Andrei and I left for New York, Delphi associate Larry Kaufer had contacted a number of Moscow-based foreign company representatives, including Paul Melling, a British attorney with Baker & McKenzie, a prominent international law firm. Melling was working out of the Moscow offices of the British/Soviet Chamber of Commerce but was interested in leasing offices through PJV. Kaufer set up a meeting to discuss this, after which Melling sent a summary message to Baker & McKenzie offices in key locations around the world, including their DC office.

Unbeknownst to me, one of their top Washington attorneys was my old friend Gene Theroux, the former associate director of Young Citizens for Johnson (YCJ) who had arranged for me to host Barbra Streisand at the 1964 Democratic Party convention. Gene reached out to me after he got Melling's memo, and we agreed to meet when Andrei and I arrived in Washington.

Gene told me how anxious Baker & McKenzie was to open its own office in Moscow and emphasized how difficult it had been to find office space there. Andrei and I agreed to offer Baker & McKenzie interim space in our own PJV office, and to do so under a barter agreement. Two Baker & McKenzie attorneys would provide PJV with a specified number of hours per month in legal services. In return, PJV would provide them with office space, sponsor their Soviet visas and their authorization to have cars in Moscow, and give them access to our international phone lines, fax, and telex.

True Colors

Earl and Paul finally came to an agreement. Worsham Group bought out Delphi's equity in PJV and was on board by early 1989, but that didn't solve our hard currency problem. It soon became apparent that Earl was in no hurry to make any major cash contributions to the PJV capital fund that were anything close to what we needed to finance construction of our first project. He did offer to cover some administrative expenses and the purchase of imported Japanese cars for top PJV executives. That, however, was substantially offset by his filing for reimbursement from PJV for all the expenses he had covered for Andrei and me while we were in New York and Atlanta. In essence, he billed the cost of our trip back to us.

With that as a preamble, I guess I shouldn't have been surprised that I had difficulty getting Earl to come to terms on my own employment contract. Delphi International had covered my salary through December of 1988. I now had to negotiate a new arrangement with PJV, but Earl was in no hurry to do that, either. Meanwhile, I continued working without pay. I finally faxed him a proposal that included the salary agreement (the same one I'd had with Delphi) as well as ancillary benefits that were common at that time for expats in Moscow:

- Multiple-entry visas for all members of my family;
- An apartment comparable in size and location to those afforded accredited American firm representatives in Moscow, with a minimum of two bedrooms and two baths, washer and dryer, fully paid rent, and all utilities;
- Annual tuition (then $6,000) for Sasha to attend the Anglo/American school in Moscow;
- Payment of the fee for family use of American embassy facilities;
- Moving costs;
- Annual home leave to the US for our family, twice-yearly family trips to Western Europe, and a yearly round-trip travel allowance for Chris to fly between Boston and Moscow;
- A car and gasoline; and
- A base annual salary of $75,000 USD and 800 rubles monthly, plus a family medical/dental plan that would cover us in the US and well as the USSR.

After long negotiations and much pressure from me, Earl ultimately agreed to these terms. I then reminded him of the commitment he had made to me in Atlanta, that I was to have an equity position when he became a PJV participant. When I asked him how he was going to structure this, he replied as if that conversation had never happened. "John, in business there are employers and employees. I'm an employer, and you're an employee. You may not like it, but that's the way it is."

It was upsetting, to say the least, but I wasn't the only one Earl stiffed. When Michael Morgenstern, PJV's American financial manager, was hired, he too was promised an equity position, but Earl reneged on that commitment as well, just as he had with me. Michael and I became very close friends—we remain so to this day.

On his next visit to Moscow, Earl wanted to show Moscow officials that his company had the right experience and qualifications to take on these PJV rehab projects. As proof, he brought with him a great deal of promo literature about his previous commercial real estate developments in the States. When I browsed through these brochures, I noticed that some of his buildings had been developed under the name Worsham Brothers, just as Hyatt president Bernt Chorengel had told us—and as Earl had denied to Andrei and me.

Cyprus and OPM

Our Baker & McKenzie attorneys advised us that it would be better if PJV's American partner was not registered in the United States but in a foreign country that had a double taxation treaty agreement with the Soviet Union. Without that protection, any American partner in PJV would be obligated to pay both Soviet and American taxes on income and capital gains, without the ability to reduce the amount paid in US taxes by the amount paid in Soviet taxes.

The small Mediterranean island nation of Cyprus catered to many corporations with this need for tax shelter, and Worsham distributed almost all of his PJV equity among several separate, wholly owned Cyprus companies. Over time, we learned that this web of interlocking companies was a key component of Worsham's business model. If there were claims against one company, his other holdings, as separate legal entities, remained insulated from those claims. Worsham Group itself retained a scant 1 percent of PJV, but it was this percentage that allowed PJV to claim to be a Soviet-American joint venture.

Early in 1989, Moscow city authorities told Andrei Stroyev that it would be a conflict of interest for him to continue as both general director of Mosinzhstroi and general director of PJV. Since Mosinzhstroi was his base of power in the Moscow government, he resigned his position with PJV. He and Earl agreed that I would step up into his post—at a considerable increase in pay. Andrei wasn't leaving PJV entirely, however. He and Earl would serve as co-chairs.

There is a time-honored principle in real estate: in any individual development project, invest as little of your own money as possible. This principle is known as OPM, which stands for Other People's Money, and in the Soviet Union in the 1980s, it was a hard rule to follow. As we geared up to begin construction on Bolshoi Gnezdnikovsky Lane No. 7, we needed OPM, but where would it come from?

The answer emerged from a conversation I had with Slobodan Kostic, Dow Chemical's Moscow rep. As soon as I showed him the reconstruction plans for the building, he was sold. "We'll take it!" he said.

I quickly had to backpedal and confess that we were still trying to organize the financing. "We'll pay you rent in advance," he offered. When I told him that a year's rent would not be enough to finance the reconstruction, he came back with a proposal that became the solution to my OPM problem. "We'll pay you five years up front," he declared.

Five years' rent paid in advance would cover the cost of construction, which meant we could make this project work. I then met with the top Moscow representatives of other major international corporations, including BASF Chemicals of Germany, DuPont Chemicals, and Monsanto. I told them that Dow was prepared to pay us five years rent in advance during construction to finance the building, and all of them forwarded this information to their top management.

As it turned out, Slobodan Kostic was unable to get Dow's top management to approve the arrangement he'd offered me, but Dow was the only one. The boards of the other companies all ratified payment of at least five years rent in advance, and one ultimately offered six and a half years up front.

We negotiated first with BASF, a German chemical company, and drew up a preliminary agreement. In early June of 1989, however, it looked like the deal would fall through after BASF attorneys inserted several unacceptable revisions into the contract. After laying out our specific objections, I wrote to the BASF board:

In 45 minutes, I have the third round of negotiations with the company DuPont, which is, as are most foreign firms in Moscow, in desperate need of contemporary office space. They are requesting exactly 1,500 square meters of space and are clearly in the position to finance such space. Yesterday I held similar negotiations with an Austrian company in conjunction with an Austrian Bank. The conditions for prepayment of rent are exactly the same, however the rental rate is now at $700/m2, ($65/ square foot) per year.

My memo brought BASF back to the table. Within a few days, they agreed to rent 1,550 square meters (16,684 square feet) of Bolshoi Gnezdnikovsky Lane No. 7 for ten years. Five years of that rent would be paid during construction. At an annual cost of $700 per square meter, that was enough to finance full reconstruction of the building.

Earl was ecstatic, and sent me a short, handwritten fax:

John, that letter of yours of June 7th to Schraudolph is the very best letter I have ever read. A real motivator, yet friendly and businesslike. It should be sent to Harvard Business School as an example—no kidding— the Best. Thanks, Earl

Codest finished the reconstruction of Bolshoi Gnezdnikovsky Lane No. 7 in nine months at a cost of $3.4 million. Due to its proximity to Pushkin Square, it became known as Pushkin Plaza. BASF became the prime tenant, and we leased the balance of the square footage to other companies, including Mitsubishi and Baker & McKenzie.

(The Pushkin Plaza building, with the large arched window on the top floor, can be seen in the upper right corner of this image. The line of people around the park are waiting to get into the newly opened McDonalds restaurant.)

(The BASF representative in his office in the Pushkin Plaza building)

PJV Takes Off

Going forward, the Pushkin Plaza agreement with BASF became the template for financing other PJV projects. As we undertook renovation of additional buildings, I negotiated similar contracts with Länderbank of Austria, Monsanto, DuPont, and Hoechst Chemical, among others. Since these construction/lease agreements all included premium rental payments for up to six and a half years in advance, more money began pouring in than we needed to cover the cost of construction.

PJV's success made Andrei Stroyev an international media personality. His photo appeared on the July 16, 1990, cover of *Newsweek*'s international edition. In an October 10,1990, CBS Evening News interview with correspondent Anthony Mason, he talked about the changes that were happening in the Soviet Union. Some Russians feared that change would lead to instability, but to Andrei, that was a positive, not a negative. The country had been stable for seventy years, he said, then added, "I'm happy that it's not stable now, because it will lead to something new, something much better."

Mason also interviewed me and asked whether I believed Stroyev would be successful. "I'm betting on him," I replied.

Despite—or perhaps because of—our success, I started seeing signs that Worsham was generating extra money from PJV, money that I didn't feel he had earned. By March 1989, Worsham Group had executed a separate development and management agreement with the joint venture. The agreement called for PJV to pay Worsham Group $500,000 for services that included negotiation of tenant leases and preparation of lease paperwork. I knew that Worsham was billing for tasks his company wasn't doing, and I knew this because I was doing them myself.

I had negotiated a construction/lease agreement with Monsanto, whose chief Moscow representative was my old friend and former Satra colleague, Tom Laurita. Tom invited Andrei and me for dinner with his wife at their apartment and explained that Monsanto needed a building with both office space and hotel rooms because they wanted the ability to house their executives when they came to Moscow for meetings.

Andrei was able to secure the rights to reconstruct a large mansion and we designed it to have not only offices but also an upper floor with six hotel rooms.

Jill and Sasha

Jill hadn't moved out of our house in Silver Spring, but we had been living separate lives on two different continents. By August of 1989, however, I convinced her to come with Sasha to join me in Moscow. PJV moved us into a two-bedroom suite in the Hotel Ukraina, then the tallest hotel in Europe. We were in good company—my friend Michael Morgenstern, PJV's American financial director, was just down the hall. The hotel itself was conveniently located just across the Moskva River from the American Embassy, where Sasha, now thirteen, was enrolled in the same Anglo-American School that Chris had attended.

(With Sasha in front of St. Basil's Cathedral on Red Square)

Sasha's feelings about leaving Maryland for Moscow were mixed. On the one hand, his parents were back together, and there were new family adventures to be had and new memories to be made. On the other hand, he was a thirteen-year-old boy who was really bummed to be pulled away from what was in many ways a classic American suburban teenage life: pals and sweetheart crushes, videogame arcades and Sunday football, bike rides and beach trips. I was fully aware that for kids of that age, those experiences are hugely important.

Frequent trips to the Moscow McDonald's were a bittersweet reminder of home. The fast-food establishment opened on January 31, 1990, and was an instant sensation. Customers lined up for blocks, but Sasha and his friends enjoyed an unusual privilege—they didn't have to stand in line. The father of one of them was an exec at McDonald's Canada, the arm of the parent company that had opened the Moscow venture, and he made sure the kids could walk right in.

Jill's modeling career was on hold, but she found ways to make use of her talent. Her good friend Pauline was an interior designer, and she and Jill set up a business to provide interior design services to PJV lessees. Monsanto was their first client, and they designed the Monsanto office space and hotel rooms, even making a trip to Yugoslavia to select finishing materials through Jastrebac, our general contractor. Although Codest had done an excellent job on Pushkin Plaza, we were able to significantly lower our costs by retaining Jastrebac, a highly qualified construction company based in Yugoslavia.

The design work helped Jill take her mind off the break in her modeling career, but life was still not all she wanted in Moscow. While she and Sasha enjoyed a very close bond, living in a hotel and making school lunches for him was less than fulfilling, and she longed to be back in DC and New York.

In all our lease agreements, clients paid not just for office space but for their prorated share of common areas. In the case of our project at Yuzhinskiy Lane, that included the underground area, including parking spaces, driveways, and a street access ramp. As we finalized a lease with DuPont, things became complicated when they asked that an elevator be installed, at their cost, from the garage up to their offices. The plan was to use one of their designated parking spots as the location for the elevator shaft. The question was how to charge them for it. In the end, because DuPont agreed to pay an upfront premium for a full six and a half years, we included two of their ten parking spaces at no additional charge.

With all this success, my only major disappointment was with Fiat. We were very close to signing an agreement for one of the six Yuzhinskiy Lane mansions, but Fiat pulled out at the eleventh hour. Several weeks later, the Fiat chief rep in Moscow invited me to his office and introduced me to his brother, who represented the IRI Group. The *Istituto per la Ricostruzione Industriale* (IRI) was an enormous conglomerate and the parent company for several major Italian firms, including Alitalia Airlines. I welcomed this introduction and began negotiations with IRI to lease not only the mansion that we had offered Fiat but also two additional mansions in this project.

After my introduction to the IRI representative, the Fiat chief rep walked me to my car. He wanted to know how long I had worked for Earl Worsham. I explained to him that Earl had replaced our original partner in PJV, that I had not worked for him or known him before that, and that I was working directly for PJV, not as a member of Earl's firm. When I asked the Fiat rep why he wanted to know, he told me that the Fiat general counsel had researched Earl Worsham and had reported back to the board with astonishing findings. The Fiat rep told me that, according to the Fiat counsel, Worsham's reputation was so unsavory that if he crossed the border of certain states—he specifically mentioned Indiana—he would be arrested. Not surprisingly, Fiat decided against signing the lease agreement with PJV.

I shared this disturbing news with Andrei, and we decided to ask Baker & McKenzie to investigate Earl and his US companies, and to do so confidentially. Their report was transmitted to me through a European colleague of theirs who was in route to Moscow. We didn't want it to land by fax or telex in our PJV offices, where incoming documents might easily have been forwarded by fax automatically to Earl by whoever was there at the time.

The lengthy report that Baker & McKenzie passed on to us found that Worsham Group and its affiliates had been involved in considerable litigation. Most claims were relatively small, except for a judgment of more than $102,000 owed to former partners in connection with an unsuccessful real estate transaction. "It should be noted," Baker & McKenzie continued, "that a suit was filed against Worsham Bros. Co., Inc. by Hardin Construction Group, Inc. for $5,000,000 in connection with renovation work performed by Hardin. Our data base was unable to determine the status of this suit, indicating that it may have been dropped or settled." At the time, Andrei Stroyev was as disturbed by the findings as I was, especially since we had lost Fiat as a client, apparently because of what Fiat felt was Earl's unsavory reputation.

Early on in my work with PJV, my old friend Boris called. Rather than meeting for a long lunch with vodka and cognac, he invited me to his apartment for dinner. He introduced me to his wife, but he now had an entirely different surname. He said he was now the general director of a joint venture importing medical equipment and supplies from England to the Soviet Union. Since Satra had also imported English medical supplies, I assumed it was likely that my old boss Ara Oztemel had helped set Boris up in this business.

CHAPTER 16

1990

Putnik Joint Venture

In March of 1990, Andrei Stroyev invited me to join him at a meeting with Andrei Popov, general director of Putnik Joint Venture. Putnik was planning to convert a gutted apartment building into a modern hotel, and Popov was hoping to contract with Stroyev's construction company, Mosinzhstroi, for building materials and foundation work.

Although Popov had envisioned only a narrow scope of work for Mosinzhstroi, Stroyev asked me to join him because he had something bigger in mind. He wanted to propose that Perestroika JV and Putnik JV develop this project together. Popov, however, was not interested. He felt that this project was his, and his alone.

After our meeting, I walked Popov to the elevator, and he confided that he was looking for a new foreign partner. He had teamed up with Rostik International, a Venezuelan company whose initial success in the Soviet Union had come with a string of photo shops selling and processing Kodak film. Rostik's later ventures would become even more well known and more lucrative: branches of Western restaurant chains, including Kentucky Fried Chicken, Planet Sushi, and TGI Fridays. In 1990, however, Rostik was either unable or unwilling to finance construction of a Moscow hotel and wanted to withdraw from Putnik JV. At the elevator, Popov asked me if I knew of a possible new investor.

From my perspective, the timing was opportune. I and two other senior Perestroika JV employees—finance director Michael Morgenstern and contract specialist Mikhail "Misha" Pankin—had become increasingly unhappy with Earl Worsham. We distrusted him, and for good reason.

We were doing the work, and he was reaping the benefits. Through our efforts, we had made PJV a success, but it appeared that Worsham was pulling out more and more of the revenue we generated and squirreling it away in offshore accounts. Because he'd also made it clear that the three of us would never have an equity position in the venture, we were ready to strike out on our own. Nothing in our Perestroika contracts prevented us from investing in the Putnik project, so we decided to create a company and propose it to Popov as the new 50 percent foreign partner for Putnik JV.

Michael, Misha and I invited Andrei Stroyev to join us as a fourth individual investor. He had the financial resources to do so, and his participation would help expedite crucial Moscow city approvals. In confidence, I told Stroyev that Michael and I were going to set up a company that we as individuals would own, and that this company would buy out Rostik's percentage of Putnik JV.

Stroyev wanted to be involved, but insisted that we invite Worsham and his son-in-law, who was also working with Worsham Group. Morgenstern and I agreed, but when Stroyev approached Worsham about the concept of participating in such a project with PJV employees—without mentioning Putnik—he apparently declined. Nevertheless, Michael, Misha, and I decided to secretly proceed. Stroyev confirmed that he still wanted in but was adamant that we not reveal anything to Worsham. Why was Stroyev so determined to keep his involvement a secret? From my standpoint, I assumed that once he understood that Worsham was opposed to PJV employees having equity in a development company like Putnik, Stroyev wanted to make sure that neither Worsham nor the city of Moscow learned of his personal participation.

To avoid the punitive 20 percent Soviet surtax then levied on profit distributions to an American company, we set up an LLC in Cyprus called Kanopa Holdings Company Limited. (This was before Cyprus offshore holding companies developed a bad reputation due to Russian money laundering activities.) At the time, Soviet citizens did not have the legal right to own foreign companies, either in whole or in part, so Michael and I set up Kanopa in our names. Since we believed that Stroyev's ability to access building materials and expedite permit approvals was critical to the success of the project, we agreed that ultimately he would be entitled to twice the percentage of equity in our project than Michael, Misha, and I would each have.

Popov's determination to reconstruct the building as a hotel was a sticking point. He knew the hotel business well—he'd been deputy director of the Moscow Metropol Hotel and director of the Cosmos Hotel, both part of the massive, government-owned Intourist chain. That said, his extensive hotel experience was not particularly relevant to the task at hand: getting the reconstruction funded, built, and leased out. I knew how to finance an office building through advance rental payments, and I knew that from a business standpoint, Popov's insistence on a hotel made it nearly impossible to proceed—nobody was going to pay five years in advance for a hotel room.

Popov was stubborn, but we eventually convinced him that an office building was by far the best option. We ultimately compromised: four floors of the Putnik building would be offices, with a large underground parking garage. The fifth, mansard level, would be either apartments or a boutique hotel. Once we learned that tenant companies were also looking for contemporary apartments, we convinced Popov that these would be more profitable than hotel suites, in part because we could negotiate prepaid lease agreements. Accordingly, Putnik was officially reregistered with Kanopa as the 50 percent foreign partner in July 1990.

The other 50 percent of Putnik was divided among three Soviet equity partners:

- 17.1 percent to Popov's hotel management cooperative (Putnik Cooperative);
- 17 percent to the Moskvoretsky Regional Council, a division of the Moscow City Council; and
- 15.9 percent for the Moscow division of Zhilsotsbank, a Soviet state bank, later reorganized as the independent Unikombank (Universal Commercial Bank).

Cyprus and Kanopa

Earl Worsham had divvied up most of his Perestroika JV equity among several Cyprus companies. His bank there, Wardley Cyprus, handled all his company accounts. Michael, Misha, and I already maintained US dollar accounts at Wardley Cyprus Bank, because each month, Perestroika paid a portion of our salary in US dollars into them. When we opened the Kanopa account at Wardley, Michael, Misha and I each transferred our equal shares of the equity contributions into it. Misha and Michael transferred their payments to Kanopa's account in their own names. I wanted to make sure that my participation did not become known to Worsham accidentally, so I opened a numbered account in Cyprus and made my payment as an otherwise unidentifiable contribution.

Stroyev transferred his share of the equity fund from a numbered account in Germany. I don't have any evidence of this, but I suspect that this account might have been opened for him by German construction equipment companies who were selling machinery to Mosinzhstroi and possibly had been providing Andrei with some form of hard-currency personal kickback or finder's fee. Since Popov had not wanted to bring Stroyev into the management of his JV, Michael, Misha, and I kept Stroyev's involvement in Kanopa a secret. Michael, Misha, and I were able to fund the balance of our percentage of Putnik JV over the next several years with the fees Kanopa earned from Putnik JV for negotiating advance rental payments from Putnik building tenants.

The Putnik building was located at Bolshoi Strochenovsky Pereulok No. 22/25. It stood in a prime location, but it was in terrible shape. The only original structural elements still standing were three stories of exterior walls, two of which were considered to be in good condition, since they had been built in the pre-Revolutionary period. We wanted to build an underground parking garage—up until then, underground garages were virtually unheard of in the Soviet Union—but to do so meant replacing the existing foundation section by section to create a much deeper basement. By law, only Soviet contractors could do underground excavation, so Putnik hired Andrei Stroyev's Mosinzhstroi company to do this work. For our main general contractor, we hired Jastrebac, the same Yugoslavian company that was working for PJV.

(The Putnik building's original three stories of exterior walls)

At Perestroika JV, we'd been asking tenants for five or six years rent in advance. For the Putnik building, however, we knew that this would be more than we needed to finance construction, so we decided to ask for three years instead. Since I was still general director of PJV and still doing all the PJV leasing, I was scrupulous about avoiding any conflict of interest. Although I could not and would not promote the Putnik project to clients who were considering leasing from Perestroika, once a possible tenant had declined premises in a PJV project, I felt that from an ethical perspective, I no longer had a conflict. At that point I would draw up an offer for them to lease space from Putnik and have it faxed to them in the name of Andrei Popov.

Michael Morgenstern had some close friends working for the international accounting firm Price Waterhouse, and in the autumn of 1990, we began negotiations with Price Waterhouse for both office premises and possible apartments in the Putnik building. Our Baker & McKenzie colleagues also anticipated a need for more space, so I told them of my participation in Putnik JV, and they indicated they might eventually lease space in the reconstructed Putnik building as well.

Not long after setting up Kanopa in 1990, Michael, Misha, and I decided that each of us also should have our own individual Cyprus companies. In this way, future anticipated business transactions among us would not represent personal transactions. In January of 1991, I opened my wholly owned Cyprus company, JSR Holdings Company Limited.

Meanwhile, Perestroika was having more and more success. With Russia's new openness to capitalism, this did not go unnoticed by the local and international press, and some of the credit came my way. In the August 1990 issue of a local English language publication, *Barometer—First Hand Information on Business in the USSR*, a piece by Igor Akhmerov entitled "Link of the Month—Perestroika Will Win" had this:

> *If Mikhail Gorbachev were to call John S. Reuther, Director-General of the Soviet-American joint venture Perestroika, and ask for advice on economic reform, Reuther would probably say: "Advance to a free market more quickly, but without copying the experience of the West. Capitalize on positive elements in the two systems." If I were Gorbachev, I would heed John Reuther's advice.*

At about that same time, we found another project in Moscow for Kanopa. Since returning to Moscow in 1988 to work for PJV, I had stayed in touch with Yevgeniy Molchanov, who had been our Satra company driver. Yevgeniy called to say that a division of the Moscow militia—similar to the police in the States—was looking to generate hard currency. To do so, they hoped to renovate their small, two-story building in central Moscow and lease it to a foreign firm. The building was located in a very prestigious, high-priced area just off Bolshaya Polyanka Street, a block from the bridge that crosses the river to the Kremlin. The militia had been given use of the building as a sports center, but it was too small for that.

After I discussed this project with Misha and Michael, Yevgeniy set up a meeting for Misha with the militia. They worked out an agreement to lease the building to Kanopa for ten years. In return, we would completely renovate the building to convert it into contemporary offices. Our anticipated reconstruction costs would be amortized over the first four years, during which we would pay the militia $80,000 per year in rent. After that, our rent would go up to $135,000/year through the end of the ten-year period, when we would no longer have any financial rights to the building.

CIR, an Italian industrial holding company, had been leasing a small office in the basement of PJV's Pushkin Plaza. They now needed larger premises, but PJV had nothing to offer them. I negotiated an agreement with them to pay rent to Kanopa in advance, and we used those funds to renovate the militia's sports center. During this time, however, Moscow city authorities passed legislation that forbade the militia from accepting hard-currency income. We evaded this restriction with a work-around that involved a payment-in-kind arrangement. After obtaining some police supply catalogues from the Pennsylvania State Police station near my property and cabin in Everett, Pennsylvania, I showed them to the leaders of the Moscow militia. They selected protective shields and other equipment from the catalogue, excluding any firearms, and Kanopa placed the order, which was then delivered to militia offices in Moscow.

Vera

Many things were changing in Moscow, both for me personally and for the city as a whole. When Sasha's school term ended in June of 1990, Jill took him back to DC for the summer. Since we had rented out our Silver Spring home, she leased a house in Bethesda. Before Labor Day, however, she told me they would not return to Russia.

Among the other changes in Moscow was the introduction of Western-style nightclubs and restaurants. Some shows featured scantily clad dancers. Earl Worsham came to Moscow that October and remembered one of these places fondly—the Olymp—and asked me to take him there again. As we were enjoying dinner and drinks, our attention was drawn to a nearby table, where a group of people was partying. Since the group included several attractive young women, Earl and I kept glancing in that direction. When I finally asked the maître d' what the occasion was, he told me that it was a birthday dinner for Alla Makarevicha, wife of Andrey Makarevich, lead singer of Time Machine, the iconic Russian rock band.

I had already met Andrey and Alla in 1987, when I was part of the ICDP delegation—that was the trip when Kris Kristofferson sang with Time Machine for a few numbers during their concert. After I reintroduced myself, Alla invited Earl and me to join their table, and one of the other women asked whether I spoke French. When I told her I did, she walked me over to a chair she had freed up next to Alla and her friend Vera. Vera began conversing with me in French, but I soon asked whether we could switch to Russian instead.

Vera was in the fashion business and made regular trips to Paris to purchase haute couture women's clothing for select Russian clients. She didn't have a company, as we in the States or Western Europe would commonly understand it. Her business was entirely off the record and off the books—Soviet authorities would have considered her a black marketeer. Vera was an astute businesswoman. She was also a great conversationalist, and the two of us were soon talking as if we had known each other for years. We danced together several times, and I think even then we both sensed that this was the start of a relationship.

After the show, everyone agreed that it was too early to call it a night. We drove to Alla's apartment to pick up her guitar, and then the party moved to my place, where we sat in the living room and sang Russian songs. Vera and I danced some more, and I could already feel that I was falling in love.

(With Vera at my apartment in Moscow)

If this was going to be a serious relationship, I had to be honest and tell her that I was still married. Vera replied that she also was married: Valery, her husband, was Time Machine's manager. That said, their relationship was complicated. Everyone had the sense that communism in Russia was in its last days, but there were, of course, no guarantees. If communism somehow prevailed, Vera and Valery had agreed to terminate their marriage so that Vera could marry a Parisian businessman, which would enable her and Anya, their seven-year-old daughter, to become French citizens and leave Moscow for Paris.

CHAPTER 17

October 1990

The Financial Consequences of the End of Communism

On November 9, 1989, after a period of civil unrest, the East German government announced that its citizens would be allowed to visit West Germany. Crowds of East Germans flooded into West Berlin with great rejoicing. It was the beginning of the end of communism.

After that, the dominos began to fall. Weeks later in Poland, former Solidarity union leader Lech Walesa was elected president. At about the same time, the Velvet Revolution established democracy in Czechoslovakia. For much of 1990, one common looming question across the former Iron Curtain countries was what would become of the assets that had belonged to the various Communist governments, and who would determine how they got liquidated or parceled out to new owners. Those assets included hard currency, properties, and businesses, and the people who controlled how it all got reallocated were in a position to make themselves and their friends extremely wealthy.

The German Money Transfer Scandal

The German Democratic Socialist Party (the new name of the Communist party after the Berlin Wall came down) had been the richest political party in Europe, having inherited the massive holdings of the East German government. In July of 1990, those businesses and properties had been valued at $300 million, but in late October, on the eve of the newly unified country's first free election, the party was forced to acknowledge that it had illegally transferred more than $70 million out of Germany.

The party chairman told reporters that leaders had sent the money to Soviet-held bank accounts in Norway and the Netherlands, and that they had done so to evade the agency responsible for liquidating East German government assets. The deputy chairman and finance chief were soon arrested by Berlin police.

The story was big news all over Europe, but what did that have to do with me?

A lot. Those "Soviet-held bank accounts" in Norway and the Netherlands—the accounts where those millions had been deposited—were secretly set up in the name of Putnik Joint Venture. In the summer of 1990, we had set up Putnik JV with a capital fund of 500,000 rubles, which was worth several hundred thousand dollars at most. Four months later, there were over 107 million deutschmarks ($71 million) in Putnik JV accounts in Oslo and Amsterdam.

Before the scandal broke, Michael Morgenstern and I were completely unaware that there were any Putnik accounts in Oslo and Amsterdam whatsoever. They had been opened secretly—by Popov, I assume—to receive funds from the East German Communist party. None of this money would ever have gone to the benefit of Putnik, but only to the benefit of certain individuals—which is why they had tried to withdraw the funds in cash.

I found out about it pretty much by accident. Not long after I met Vera, I took her to the Putnik site to show her our project and noticed some men in suits and ties talking to our staff. Hoping they might be potential tenants looking for rental information, I approached them, introduced myself as the Putnik JV leasing representative, and gave them my business card. They turned out to be German news reporters.

The illegal transfer had been discovered when a former East German Communist party official named Karl-Heinz Kaufman tried to withdraw a large sum of cash from the Oslo account. When he presented a power of attorney letter to the bank, ostensibly from Putnik JV, bank officers became suspicious, froze the funds, and notified German police.

Police raided the German Democratic Socialist party offices and seized a lot of correspondence between Putnik JV and the board of directors of the party—correspondence that had been transmitted from Moscow on our Putnik telex machine. The messages revealed a scheme to open accounts at banks in Western Europe in the name of Putnik JV, then illicitly transfer East German Communist Party funds into those accounts. Karl-Heinz Kaufman was apparently the go-between—many of the telex messages mentioned him by name.

As soon as I understood what had happened, I assumed that Andrey Popov must have had something to do with it. Popov had high-level connections within the Soviet Communist party and government system. Beyond Popov himself, one of his aides—a top Putnik JV staff member—had previously worked at the Soviet Embassy in East Germany, which meant he surely had ties to the leadership of the East German Communist party.

Were members of the Communist party of the Soviet Union also involved? I don't know. What I do know is that Popov gave me the impression that higher-ups in the Soviet Communist party had instructed him to do this. When I questioned him about his involvement, he replied, "When certain high authorities in this country ask you to do something, you do it and don't ask questions."

That was as close to a confession as anyone was going to get, but with the Communists still in power in Russia, it was, of course, something Popov would never dare to say publicly. At an emergency Putnik JV board meeting, we unanimously decided that, pending the results of a Soviet investigation, Popov would resign as board chairman and general director. Meanwhile, he would be replaced by Nina Galanicheva, the board member representing Zhilsotsbank.

We began to realize that we would have to watch everything that Popov was doing as closely as possible, but in the short term, the main focus had to be damage control. This involved twin strategies of communication and transparency, but since Michael and Misha were on a Perestroika JV business trip to India, that task fell exclusively to me. The timing was terrible. The scandal broke just as I was about to leave for the States to spend time with my family for the holidays. I scrambled to reassure potential tenants, and quickly contacted the Moscow representatives of Price Waterhouse, Rank Xerox Corporation, and Hewlett Packard. I informed them that the Putnik board had removed Popov, and that the first action of the new general director was to authorize me to continue negotiations for the lease of space in the Putnik building.

I also confirmed that renovation work on the building was ongoing, and that we fully expected to complete construction by August 1, 1991, as scheduled. I gave everyone my US contact information and encouraged them to call or fax me with any and all questions.

(At the Putnik building during construction)

(Putnik building construction from above)

En route from Moscow to Washington, my layover in Frankfurt gave me time to look over various international newspapers and magazines. What caught my eye was *Der Spiegel*—the German money scandal was the cover story. I noticed that the author referred to Putnik JV as a "Soviet-Venezuelan" joint venture, and realized that it was only a matter of time before investigators and reporters discovered that Kanopa had bought out Rostik as the foreign partner in Putnik JV. I knew I had to do whatever I could to prevent Kanopa from being dragged under by the scandal. To get out in front of the story, I contacted German security officials at the Frankfurt airport in the hope that I could aid the investigation and declare in the strongest terms that Kanopa had no role in moving deutschmarks into Putnik accounts in Oslo and Amsterdam.

Carrying a copy of *Der Spiegel,* I approached one of the heavily armed airport guards and asked to speak with security officials. He led me to the main security office, where I spoke with an administrator and explained that I represented Kanopa, the foreign partner in Putnik JV. I detailed what I knew of the scandal, and I left him my contact information for any follow-up questioning.

By the time I arrived in Washington, investigation of the scandal had already reached far and wide. Jastrebac, our Yugoslavian contractor, had been contacted by Interpol, and similar inquiries had been made to the Cyprus office of the local attorneys who were the designated Cypriot directors of Kanopa Holdings Limited.

Because protecting the integrity and reputation of Kanopa was my primary goal, I asked my father to set up a meeting in DC at the West German Embassy—their labor attaché was a personal friend. Once again, I shared all the details and left all my contact information and travel schedule with the embassy and reiterated my willingness to speak with Interpol or any other agency investigating the German money scandal.

Interpol never contacted me, but in March, 1991, our Cyprus-based Kanopa legal director copied us on an email to our banker at Wardley Cyprus Bank. Cyprus police had visited his office as part of their investigation "pursuant to a request by the Cyprus Embassy in relation to an October article in the Soviet official state daily newspaper, *Izvestia*, and an Interpol message." The police asked many questions about Kanopa, its legal status, the roles of Michael Morgenstern and me, and our relationship to Putnik JV.

A few days later, Michael and I met in Moscow with the Cyprus ambassador to the Soviet Union. We made a full report to him about our participation in Kanopa, the role of Kanopa in Putnik JV, and the efforts we had made to make it clear that our business in the Soviet Union had nothing to do with the German money scandal. I sent a report on this meeting to our Cyprus director and confirmed that Michael would be traveling to Cyprus within the week to meet with the Cyprus Department of Interior.

The Russians, of course, conducted their own investigation, and all of us testified at the formal hearing in Moscow. When it concluded, the ruling was that "someone" had falsified documents and stolen Putnik JV stationery to illegally open those accounts—someone outside Putnik.

That someone, however, was never identified by name, and no one from Putnik JV was ever officially implicated.

It all left me with the impression that higher-ups in the party in Moscow were involved, but with all the corruption going on in the Soviet Union at that time at all levels, there is no way of knowing whether this was done officially or as a corrupt scheme to move party money into individual pockets. In the aftermath, however, what was clear was that there had been a concerted effort at extremely high party/government levels to insulate and protect Andrey Popov, and to deep-six the story as soon as possible.

Even though he was officially off the hook, Popov did not regain either the chairmanship or his former position as general director at Putnik. He never officially conceded any involvement in the German scandal, but even after the initial crisis was over, Michael, Misha, and I were never confident that he wouldn't do something like this again.

CHAPTER 18

May 1991

German Money Scandal Fallout

Although the official investigations into the German money scandal and the worst of the bad publicity it generated were both behind us, we still had to convince major international corporations to proceed with leasing space from Putnik JV. Largely because of our willingness to be transparent and to make ourselves available for questions and conversation, we as individuals created a positive atmosphere of success and trust—and it paid off. In March of 1991, Price Waterhouse (PW) became the first company to lease both office space and apartments in the Putnik complex. In addition to expansive office premises on the fourth floor, PW also planned to lease three apartments on the mansard level. Two months later, the law firm Baker & McKenzie leased a large office on the first floor. Both firms agreed to pay three years rent up front, which we would use to pay for construction.

We were most grateful to Price Waterhouse and to Baker & McKenzie, not only for their vote of confidence in Putnik, but also for their wise counsel. They advised us to set up an offshore bank account into which the advance rent moneys would be paid, and from which we would pay our construction contractors. This was reassuring both to the lessees we already had, and to potential future tenants as well. If any claims against Putnik arose from the German money scandal, all of our tenants would know that their prepayments were not at risk.

Whenever I began negotiations with a potential client, I always described what had happened as fully as possible. I strongly believed that this was an essential step, and that it was crucial to clear the air. I wanted to make sure they knew we weren't keeping any secrets, and that

I had provided them with sufficient information to reassure not just themselves, but their corporate headquarters overseas as well.

For some companies, it was not enough. Hewlett Packard's property specialist had recommended to HP management that they lease a full floor in the Putnik building, but in the wake of the money scandal, HP bowed out. Baker & McKenzie, however, introduced British Gas to the project. We also began negotiations with Imperial Chemical Industries (ICI), which at the time was the largest manufacturing company in the UK.

To further reinforce tenant confidence, we facilitated the formation of a future tenants' committee and established the principle that no tenant would be required to make rental prepayments until 70 percent of the space was committed. At 70 percent, we were confident that we had enough financing to complete the renovation, but in the wake of the German money scandal, it was a struggle not just to get to 70 percent, but to stay there. Several times we surpassed the 70 percent threshold, only to have a potential lessee like Hewlett Packard drop out.

Fiat, a Price Waterhouse client, learned about the Putnik building through PW, and was most interested in taking space with us. Since Fiat had previously and specifically declined to lease from Perestroika because of Earl Worsham, they wanted to be sure he was not involved in Putnik, and they wanted that assurance in writing. They agreed that the letter would be acceptable if addressed to Price Waterhouse, but insisted that it be from both Stroyev and Worsham, or, if from only one of them, that the other be copied in.

Earl was then in the States, so I wrote a fax informing him that Andrei Stroyev had received a call from Price Waterhouse regarding PW's concern about the Putnik building under construction, due to the German money scandal. My fax included a copy of a fax to Price Waterhouse, as signed by Andrei as Chairman of PJV and General Manager of Mosinzhstroi, with Earl Worsham also copied as Chairman. It contained a strong confirmation to PW that Perestroika was not a participant in the building, as Earl thought that PW might still be interested in a possible Perestroika building. I provided both Fiat and Price

Waterhouse with extra signed original copies of the fax from Stroyev to PW. As a result, Fiat was prepared to continue negotiations with me for space in the Putnik building.

An Early Morning Surprise

As the Putnik project proceeded, I was still general director of Perestroika JV, but in May of 1991, my involvement in Perestroika came crashing down—and it happened on a fluke. It began with an early morning phone call from Worsham that woke me out of a sound sleep. He was in London with Stroyev for talks with Hyatt International about a hotel in Moscow, but that's not why he was calling.

Earl's Perestroika companies had their accounts at Wardley Cyprus Bank, the same bank where we had opened our Kanopa account, and the Putnik offshore account as well. Wardley Bank routinely faxed monthly statements for Earl's companies to the Worsham office in Atlanta, but someone at the bank apparently got crossed up and sent copies of our Kanopa account statements there as well. The statements showed all Kanopa financial transactions, including our initial equity deposits. Contributions from Michael Morgenstern and Misha Pankin were listed by name; anonymous transfers from Stroyev's German account and from my own numbered account at Wardley were shown as well.

Earl asked what I knew about Kanopa. I had a bad feeling as soon as he asked the question, but I had no idea how bad it would get. I told him that I believed it was a Cyprus company doing business in the Soviet Union, and I asked him why he needed to know. He then told me about receiving copies of Kanopa bank statements that showed transactions by Michael Morgenstern and Misha Pankin. I responded that most likely Michael was helping Misha with some investments. Earl said, "John, over a million dollars has come into this company's accounts, and most of it has been paid out to Jastrebac!"

When Earl asked whether I had anything to do with Kanopa, I confirmed that I did and told him that I was also an investor. I pointed out that I was well within my rights to do so, since nothing in my contract with PJV in any way prohibited my investing my income in other projects or companies of my choosing. I also reminded Earl that he had promised me equity in his company and then had reneged on his promise. I informed him that Kanopa was a partner in Putnik JV and mentioned that Putnik was constructing a multitenant office/apartment building using Jastrebac as the general contractor.

In a voice that was pretty much stone cold, Earl demanded that Michael, Misha, and I fly to London to meet with him and Stroyev that weekend. Flying to London was not a problem for Michael and me. As Americans, we could travel to the UK on short notice, but Misha was a Soviet citizen and would need a visa, which could take weeks. Before leaving, Michael and I talked about strategy, and I believe we spoke to Misha by phone. We had no idea what Earl would propose, but all three of us were prepared to fight.

Michael and I arrived in London and found a note from Andrei waiting for us when we checked in at the Hyatt. Joining us in my room, he informed us that Earl would not see us until we had agreed to his terms. We were to transfer 70 percent of the equity of Kanopa to PJV.

The terms were draconian, but not complying would have catastrophic consequences. In this particular showdown, Perestroika held all the high cards, and Worsham knew it. If we did not accede to Earl's ultimatum, Stroyev—as the contractor providing all local construction materials to the Putnik project—was prepared to stop work. Because Stroyev was also someone who wielded immense influence within the Moscow government, Michael and I felt we had no choice but to agree. We did, however, demand Worsham's guarantee that work on the Putnik building would proceed.

Stroyev conveyed our acquiescence to Earl, who said we could come to his room to confirm the deal. When we entered Earl's room, I told him that we were prepared to transfer 70 percent of the Kanopa equity to PJV, but only on the condition that nothing would be done to negatively affect Putnik in any way. Earl agreed, but when I reached out my hand to confirm the deal, Earl kept his hands at his sides. Our verbal agreement thus lacked even the grace of a handshake confirmation.

When Michael and I returned to Moscow, we told Misha what had happened. He was absolutely opposed to transferring 70 percent of Kanopa to PJV, but since Michael and I were the only two legal owners of Kanopa, we were in a position to proceed.

On May 20, Earl sent a fax from Worsham Group as Co-Chairman of PJV. It was addressed to both Stroyev as Chairman and to me as general director of PJV:

> *As we have become aware, some of the senior executives of Perestroika Joint Venture may be directly or indirectly involved in the development of a competitive project in Moscow, known as 'Putnik.'*
>
> *If this is true, these actions represent a direct and very serious conflict of interest, for Perestroika Joint Venture does not have any equity position in the above-mentioned project, or any contractual relations with the owners of the 'Putnik' project. Many details are not clear at the moment, but we must take all necessary measures to obtain full and complete information as soon as possible. Only after full disclosures will we be able to take the appropriate steps with regard to this project.*
>
> *Until this situation is fully remedied, and all necessary decisions are made, and legal documentation is in place, I request that you investigate the case further in Moscow. I further request that you immediately prevent any direct or indirect participation or involvement of PJV executives and staff members in any business connected with the 'Putnik' project or any other project that may be competitive with Perestroika Joint Venture. I would appreciate your prompt attention to and conclusion of this matter. Please inform me of the steps and measures you have taken to implement my request.*

Earl went on to address Andrei on the "moral aspect of the aforementioned conflicts of interest" related to Mosinzhstroi, Andrei's company, working on the Putnik project. Although Earl conceded that they were legally permitted to do such work, he added, "My personal recommendation would be to temporarily, until all is clear, withdraw your trusts from the project." Andrei told us that he had informed Earl of his participation in Kanopa, but I never believed he'd really done so. It was clear that Earl wanted PJV to have complete ownership and control of Kanopa, which is why he was behaving as if to confirm there had been no handshake deal made in London.

PJV had a young staff member who had also been working as a Putnik construction manager on behalf of Andrei's company. Not long after we received the fax from Earl, this young colleague told me that Andrei had announced to his staff that Mosinzhstroi was stopping work on Putnik. When I heard this, I went to Andrei's office and told him that if this was true, then we no longer had a deal. There would be no transfer of 70 percent of Kanopa to PJV, because he and Earl had violated a key term of the agreement—namely, that nothing would be done to negatively affect Putnik. Andrei confirmed he was pulling out, then added that Earl was now considering demanding 100 percent of Kanopa, not just 70 percent.

I told Andrei the deal was off and tendered my resignation from PJV on May 27, 1991. At the time, I was still in final negotiations with the Italian industrial IRI Group for the lease of three of the six mansions in PJV's Yuzhinskiy Lane project. Earl was aware that these negotiations were pending and asked me to remain with PJV to successfully conclude them, which I did. Earl had lied to me, threatened me, and repeatedly demonstrated his bad faith and lack of integrity, so why did I agree to stay? I had a family to support, and I was playing for time. I needed to keep drawing a salary while I figured out what to do next.

Another interesting development occurred when PJV decided to have an "annual meeting" in the Caribbean. Worsham and Stroyev tried to force us to sign agreements which in essence would have syphoned off over $50 million of PJV's pre-tax earnings to a string of offshore companies. Ownership of these companies was dubious, but most likely included many of PJV's board members who were also high officials in the Moscow city government. We refused to sign. Michael told Stroyev that on the way back to Moscow, he was stopping off in NYC for a job interview as finance director for an oil and gas joint venture elsewhere in the Soviet Union. Stroyev scoffed, thinking he was bluffing, but

Michael went through with his plan, and ultimately left PJV for a much higher paying job.

Soon after I had been successful in completing the lease agreements with the Italian IRI Group, Earl came to Moscow, and the PJV board met in Andrei's office. It turned out to be a convening of the executioners. First Misha was called in and fired, then Michael. Clearly, I was next.

While I was waiting, Victor Shtil, our PJV staff coordinator, demanded that I hand over the keys to my company car. He also told me that I would not be paid the outstanding rubles PJV owed me, nor would I be compensated for the additional week of leave I was owed, nor would I be paid my dollar salary or bonus commissions owed through the end of my employment contract that month.

I told Victor that by taking away my car and not paying me what I was owed, PJV was violating the terms of my employment contract. As a result, I felt no obligation to walk to the wall and voluntarily don the blindfold for the convenience of the firing squad that awaited me in Stroyev's office. I collected my personal belongings and left. I then approached Putnik JV management and asked them to hire me as director of leasing. I came on staff for a salary of $150,000 and 24,000 rubles per year.

After Michael was terminated, he accepted the offer made to him earlier for a much higher paying job as director of finance for the "White Nights" Joint Venture with Phillips Petroleum Company, operating both in Moscow and the large Siberian industrial city of Tyumen.

CHAPTER 19

June-August 1991

Worsham Declares War

The firings were just the beginning of Worsham's vendetta—and I found myself thinking back to the warning from Berndt Chorengel about not doing business with Worsham. As he had threatened, Stroyev withdrew Mosinzhstroi from the Putnik project, which left us without a provider of basic site work, including local building materials like bricks and cement, and officially approved hookups for utilities like heat, water, and electricity. However, Andrey Popov found a new local Soviet contractor, so work on the Putnik project continued.

Worsham attacked on the legal front as well. Putnik JV was soon contacted by the law firm of White & Case, LLP, informing us that Perestroika JV was filing damage claims of approximately $36 million, not just against Putnik, but against Michael, Misha, and me personally. The suit alleged that we had transferred valuable knowhow—insider secrets—to Putnik from Perestroika, and that Putnik had used that information to negotiate lease agreements with our tenants. It claimed that the text in the Putnik lease agreement was one I had developed as general director of PJV, which meant it was proprietary to Perestroika and that I had, in effect, stolen it.

The dispute between Perestroika and Putnik threatened to do a lot of collateral damage within the Moscow foreign business community. Many prominent law firms had clients negotiating leases with either PJV or Putnik, and they were caught in the crossfire. One such firm was Coudert Brothers, who represented Price Waterhouse. In an attempt to mediate the dispute between PJV and Putnik, Coudert's lead attorney reached out to me to say that Andrei Stroyev wanted to meet for a private conversation.

Through the Coudert Brothers intermediary, we agreed to rendez-vous on a designated street corner in the center of Moscow. I was waiting when Andrei's car pulled up. He got out, and we started to walk and talk together like the good friends we used to be. Finally, he got to the point. He said that he had something very important to tell me but first asked that I promise not to tell anyone, since it was information from a very high and confidential level.

The hugger-mugger struck me as overly dramatic, and I told him so. I said that he was acting as if this were an issue of national security when in fact it was a relatively simple business dispute.

Andrei was unfazed. "What I am about to tell you is very important," he began gravely, "both to your family and to your business, and you must promise not to share it with anyone."

I shook my head and took a deep breath before responding. "Andrei, if this is something that will affect my family, I will share it with my family," I replied. "And if this is something that will affect my business, I will share it with my business partners."

Apparently, that was not the answer Andrei was anticipating, and his face became somber. "Something is going to happen to either you or your family," he said ominously. "It may be a car accident or something entirely different. Earl and I are not in any way related to what will happen, but when it does happen, call me!" With that, he turned on his heel, walked back to his chauffeur-driven car, and rode away.

My assumption is that this was all Earl's idea, and I believe Andrei told me exactly what Earl had told him to say. I also assume that they told me in this fashion so I would know that if anything happened, they were the ones who'd made it happen.

The threat Andrei delivered had the desired effect. I was scared for my family, my partners, and for myself. As soon as I got back to the office, I gathered the leadership of Putnik JV and told them about my conversation with Stroyev. Nobody thought I was overreacting. We all understood it for exactly what it was—an overt threat of bodily harm made against me and my family, or all of us. We agreed on next steps: I would inform both the US Embassy and the KGB about this blatant attempt at intimidation, *and* I would do so in a way that would ensure that Earl and Andrei would be made aware of what I'd done. This would put both of them on notice that if anything happened to me, my Putnik partners, or anyone in my family, all suspicion would be focused on them.

I told Jill, Chris, and Sasha about the threat. I warned them to be especially observant and vigilant and to keep an eye out for anything out of place, strange people or incidents. It was a bit of a tightrope to walk; I wanted them to understand that I was concerned, but I did not want them to be overly frightened. I was frightened enough for us all.

That same day, I spoke with the commercial office attaché at the US Embassy, who was already aware of the dispute between PJV and Putnik. Meanwhile, Andrey Popov set up a meeting for me with the KGB. I briefed the officer on my conversation with Stroyev and provided him with background information on the dispute. He said his office would investigate.

A few weeks later, I met for lunch with this same KGB officer at the Budapest Hotel, where I was still friends with the maître d'. He arrived in the company of another officer—both were wearing business suits, not uniforms. A bit sheepishly, he said that he hoped I would understand that, as part of their investigation, it had been necessary for them to look into my background, and especially my history in Moscow. While going through my file, he said, they noticed that I already had a contact within their organization.

(At the restaurant in the Budapest Hotel)

I smiled because I immediately knew he was talking about my old friend Boris, and I found that ironic. In all the years we'd known each other, Boris had never acknowledged that he was KGB, nor had we ever discussed it. That said, I'd always assumed he was one of the boys, and I had no doubt that he knew that I knew. Simply put, it had been a tacit mutual understanding that was part of our relationship from the beginning.

The officer asked why I had not reached out to my old contact within their organization about the issue with Stroyev and Worsham. Somewhat surprised by the question, I responded that I'd last met with him about a year ago, and that he'd told me that he had become a businessman and now headed up a trading company importing medical equipment and supplies into the Soviet Union from the UK.

The officer's eyes briefly darted around the room, but otherwise his facial expression remained unchanged. There's an old Russian saying that there's no such thing as a former KGB officer, and I took his poker face as a sign that the old saying was right on the money.

The officers then asked whether I'd ever considered doing commercial real estate work outside of Moscow and mentioned a project that involved office space around a commercial airport in a city hundreds of miles away. As soon as they asked the question, I immediately understood the subtext. Listening between the lines, it was clear that the boys had no appetite to take on Andrei Stroyev, who as general director of Mosinzhstroi was a ranking city government official. His position gave him a great deal of cover in any dispute with an American businessman, and the KGB higher-ups had decided that the problem could best be resolved by relocating me away from Moscow. To put it in purely American terms, they were telling me to get out of Dodge.

The story about the PJV-Putnik conflict was covered with great drama in the Soviet press, with an article in both the Russian and English versions of the Soviet newspaper *Kommersant* (*The Businessman*). The article covered the fact that both Michael Morgenstern and I had secretly invested our money in Putnik, and that we both had been fired from PJV. The author continued by saying, "It is unclear what impact Reuther's departure will have on Perestroika… Reuther is considered an expert on the Soviet construction market and an excellent marketing specialist. Perestroika owes much of its foreign clients to Reuther, informed sources say."

At Putnik, we continued to market office and apartment premises, but it was an uphill battle all the way. As part of a plan to poison the Moscow market against us, Worsham and PJV launched a concerted effort to undermine our reputation. They were badmouthing us at every opportunity, and part of their campaign included efforts to tie the Putnik project to the German money scandal. I struggled to attract and retain clients in an atmosphere of rumor, innuendo, and outright slander.

My friends at Baker & McKenzie were sympathetic to our position, but as PJV's former attorneys and current PJV tenants, they had to stay out of it until the Putnik building was finished. Because they were sidelined, they referred me to Peter Barnes of Swidler & Berlin, a DC law firm. I retained Peter not only to defend us against the $36 million pending lawsuit that White & Case had threatened to file, but also to fight back against PJV's smear campaign.

In that climate, many clients got cold feet. Philip Morris had previously declared their intention to lease both office and apartment space. Because their commitment would once again put us over the 70 percent threshold, it was an important milestone for the project as a whole. Once they signed, it would trigger other lessees to make their initial 40 percent payments. As had become the pattern, however, I received indications from Philip Morris that their management was waffling and might back away from the deal.

Searching for another client for this key space, I connected with the Interest Section of the Republic of South Africa. They were seeking an office suitable to become the South African embassy once diplomatic relations were restored with the Soviet Union. On July 26, the South Africans confirmed that they had received the green light from Pretoria to proceed with their advance payment on space in the Putnik building. Beyond the office itself, the South Africans were also ready to work with Putnik to sublet interim office space and apartments across the street.

It soon became apparent, however, that PJV's defamation campaign was ongoing. When I met with the South Africans on July 29, they informed me that they had also met with Perestroika and had been warned to steer clear of the Putnik building. There were serious doubts, they'd been told, about whether we would be able to complete construction. PJV had also been extremely negative about me personally—they said that I would soon be facing criminal conspiracy charges resulting from my participation in the Putnik project while I was general director of PJV.

The South Africans told me that they had informed PJV that in all their dealings with me, I had never said anything negative about Perestroika. When they added that they were confident that the Putnik building would be completed because Baker & McKenzie and Price Waterhouse were already paying tenants, Perestroika informed them that conspiracy charges would likely be brought against those two firms as well.

The South Africans assured me that they wanted to work with me and still believed that the Putnik building was best suited for their purposes, but they wanted to avoid getting caught in the midst of any dispute between Perestroika and Putnik. At that point, I opened up to them and briefly summarized the history of Putnik and of my participation in Kanopa, and the participation of Pankin and Morgenstern, all of us Perestroika employees, in Putnik. I also included a summary of our personal history of disputes with Earl Worsham. Following this discussion, the South Africans informed me that they might be willing to proceed, but that we would need to find a way to minimize their financial risk during construction.

Mr. Morrison

My conversation with the South Africans on July 29 was actually the second time that day that I was told I would potentially face criminal conspiracy charges. I'd met earlier that morning with Baker & McKenzie attorney Paul Melling and someone calling himself Mr. Morrison, who purported to represent Perestroika Joint Venture. By claiming to "represent" PJV, the implication was that he, like Melling himself, was a member of the bar.

I doubted it. He was dressed in a coat and tie but didn't carry himself as if that was his normal daily attire. After indicating that he was originally from Florida, he said that he was now practicing in New York. I doubted that as well, in large measure because he offered no business card with a law firm name or address. During our meeting, Mr. Morrison informed us that PJV was gearing up to take legal action against several co-conspirators, including not just Michael Morgenstern, Misha Pankin, and me, but against Baker & McKenzie and Price Waterhouse as well.

Litigation, however, was not all he threatened. Morrison said that the suit would be accompanied by a massive negative publicity campaign in the States, a crusade that would use print and broadcast media to trumpet the complicity of both Baker & McKenzie and Price Waterhouse in our wrongdoing. In effect, he was declaring Worsham's intention to drag both firms through the mud, much as PJV was trying to ruin Putnik's reputation in Moscow. To avoid such action, Morrison demanded that Kanopa turn over 70 percent of its equity in Putnik to Perestroika Joint Venture by 5:00 p.m. Moscow time on July 31. If we failed to do so, the suit would be filed, and the poisonous publicity campaign would commence within two weeks.

After the meeting, Paul Melling conferred with his Baker & McKenzie colleagues in Brussels and London. They indicated that although they would prefer to sidestep what Morrison was threatening, it was their assessment that Perestroika was engaged in saber-rattling and borderline extortion. Their logic was sound: the case for conspiracy quickly fell apart because we could easily prove that Andrei Stroyev, a PJV co-chair, was not only aware of the involvement of Michael, Misha and me in Kanopa but was himself initially a willing participant with a stake in the action. Melling also confirmed that the lease agreement I'd been offering possible Putnik tenants was absolutely standard. There was no way Perestroika could allege theft of intellectual property for paperwork that was in common use by real estate brokers and developers all over Moscow.

On August 16, 1991, I signed the lease agreement with the Interest Section of the Republic of South Africa for the entire third floor of the Putnik building, a full 20 percent of the premises. Those offices would eventually become the Embassy of the Republic of South Africa. The next day I left for DC to begin a two-week family vacation with Jill, Chris, and Sasha. The four of us flew to California to see Disneyland and Universal Studios, but meanwhile, all hell broke loose in Moscow.

Soviet hardliners opposed to Gorbachev's policy of perestroika attempted to seize control of the government. The coup was short-lived, but the fact that it had occurred at all destabilized the country and hastened the dissolution of the USSR. During the event, three Russian civilians were killed. Because their deaths occurred just a few blocks from where I'd been living, we returned to Washington from our California vacation to find a pile of "Are you all right?" faxes from concerned friends and family.

Please Copy Locally

In real estate as in many endeavors, timing is everything, and I began to understand that the timing of all this ham-fisted PJV thuggish behavior was not coincidental. I'd recently concluded Putnik building deals with the British/Soviet Chamber of Commerce, Fiat, and the British chemical company ICI. It appeared that Rockwell International, Hoechst Chemical, and IBM were positively inclined. Even Philip Morris was coming back around. With these signed and probable tenants, we were nearing 100 percent commitment.

Like their defamation campaign, Perestroika's threat of legal action was intended to create so much fear and intimidation that prospective clients would shy away from the project—but that tactic only worked *before* they'd committed to taking space in the building. Once the Putnik building was leased and financed, those threats were toothless. What remained thereafter, however, was a lot of dangerous exposure—not for us, but for them.

We did not answer PJV or Mr. Morrison by his July 31 deadline, but in the meantime, I prepared a different sort of response to his ultimatum. My fax subject line was "Regarding Meeting with a Mr. Morrison," and I addressed it to Andrei Stroyev in his capacity as chairman of PJV.

My plan was to send it first to Stroyev alone, but I also wrote *Please copy locally*, indicating that eventually there would be other recipients as well. Those recipients were listed by name and included members of the Executive Board of PJV as well as the chairman and members of the PJV Advisory Committee. All of these individuals were high-ranking Moscow city officials who most likely had been on the receiving end of PJV monetary generosity—under the table, I assumed. I also included the name of the German bank where Stroyev had an account, his account in number only.

That *Please copy locally* did a lot of heavy lifting. It let Stroyev know that although I was not including these people immediately, I was more than prepared to include them if and when it became necessary. Before sending the note to Stroyev, I sent a draft to Peter Barnes, who read it and advised me not to change a single word.

The fax:

Dear Andrei:

*On Monday, July 29th, at the request of Paul Melling of Baker &
McKenzie's Moscow office, Paul and I met with a Mr. Dennis (or Douglas?)
Morrison, who asked for the meeting with me ostensibly on behalf of
Perestroika Joint Venture. I am not sure of Mr. Morrison's full name, and
I confess that I do not know the name of his firm, as he was unable or
unwilling to produce a business card or any other identifying information.*

*Mr. Morrison, allegedly acting on behalf of Perestroika Joint Venture,
said in his meeting with us and/or in a previous meeting with Paul
Melling earlier in the day, that if the owners of Kanopa Holdings Company
Incorporated did not by a certain time and date transfer to Perestroika Joint
Venture (he was unable to confirm with certainty if this was PJV USSR,
PJV Cyprus, or PJV USA) seventy (70) percent of the equity of Kanopa
Holdings Company Inc, that a negative publicity campaign—including
TV talk shows—and legal proceedings would be initiated, involving the
filing of criminal conspiracy charges against certain individuals and
several companies which are to be tenants in an office project under devel-
opment by Putnik Joint Venture in Moscow.*

*The demands conveyed by Mr. Morrison, accompanied by the threat
of such a negative publicity campaign and legal actions, are certainly
intimidations not to be taken lightly in any way, if indeed Mr. Morrison
was taking this position and threatening these actions on behalf of PJV.*

*I thought that it would be most appropriate, prior to giving instruc-
tions to our attorneys to begin preparing the necessary documents required
for defense against such threatened charges and actions, to ask you, as
Chairman of Perestroika Joint Venture, or your attorney, to confirm to me
in writing that Mr. Morrison either does or does not in actuality represent
Perestroika Joint Venture, or PJV Cyprus, PJV USA, or possibly some other
entity affiliated with PJV, and that the position taken by Mr. Morrison
and the threatened actions against certain individuals and firms does or
does not represent the position of Perestroika Joint Venture or other affiliated organizations of PJV.*

*I hope you will be so kind as to give me the courtesy of a response to
this request, before either party should undertake any actions which might*

otherwise be avoided. As you can imagine, the defense against such charges would likely necessitate the subpoena for testimony of certain individuals, such as the Board Members and Advisory Committee Members of PJV, possibly certain officials of Mossoviet who are knowledgeable of construction and development projects and site acquisition or transfer terms in Moscow, the Chief Prosecutor and officials of the Ministry of Finance who participated in a lengthy investigation into the activities of Putnik Joint Venture, the invitation as witnesses of certain business associates in Moscow and elsewhere, whose firms may be tenants of PJV buildings under operation or under construction, the subpoena of certain bank representatives of the Soviet Union, Cyprus, the USA, and Germany, together with transfer records and audits which may be necessary to confirm sources of funds and to prove or disprove alleged losses or damages by the parties to such actions, etc.

Unless I hear further from you or your attorney in writing, I will give instructions to our attorneys to begin the preparation of such a defense and possible counter claims.

With best wishes to you and to the employees of PJV, for whom I continue to have the greatest respect and appreciation for their friendship and cooperation throughout my three years with Perestroika Joint Venture. Belated greetings to all of you for the day honoring Soviet construction workers.

Sincerely yours,
John S. Reuther

Tick. Tick. Tick. Stroyev clearly understood the time bomb embedded in my fax. I was putting him on notice that the tables had turned. Proceeding with a lawsuit against us would bring the harsh light of unwanted public and official scrutiny to the finances of everyone involved in Perestroika Joint Venture, and I was convinced that there was plenty to hide. It was quite possible that Soviet citizens in PJV leadership had opened both company and personal accounts in Cyprus, in the United States, and in other offshore tax havens, and considerable sums of PJV money most likely had been transferred out of the country. Exposing this information would have particularly adverse consequences for Stroyev personally because we would publicly reveal the existence of his German bank account—the one from which he'd wired his initial contribution to Kanopa. As for the Russian officials I'd named, Stroyev would not be happy to see any of them called upon to testify, because, most likely, everybody listed had been on the take.

Although correspondence continued for several months between Peter Barnes at Swidler & Berlin and PJV's attorneys, Stroyev eventually convinced Worsham that any further pursuit of these charges against us would not only be futile, but dangerously counterproductive.

Months later, I ran into Stroyev at an international business conference in Moscow. "That was quite a fax that your attorney drafted," he said.

"My attorney didn't write that," I replied. "I did."

"Oh, sure," he said, then laughed derisively in disbelief.

Two years later, I had the last laugh. In 1993, Andrei Stroyev was forced to flee Russia because of allegations of corruption, failure to meet city obligations and tax payments, and other questionable financial dealings.

CHAPTER 20

1992-1994

Construction Management

A notice on the bulletin board at the embassy cafeteria advertised some stereo equipment for sale. The seller was Tom Weber, a young American who had been doing renovation and carpentry work on the embassy under contract to Bechtel Corporation. When I bought the equipment from him, Tom told me that he was looking for additional work. He had a BA in business administration and finance and a top-secret security clearance and was on a month-to-month contract with Bechtel. I thought he would be an ideal construction manager for Putnik.

Our construction manager would have to fulfill multiple roles, not only closely supervising our contractors and keeping them on schedule, but also monitoring communications and interactions among architects, contractors, tenants, and Putnik staff. That person would also be required to keep track of percentage completion documentation. This was a critical task, because meeting completion milestones and getting them signed off enabled us to invoice tenants for incremental payments.

Because construction had dragged on much longer than we had anticipated, these payments had become increasingly vital. Putnik's hard-currency administrative fund was exhausted. Since moneys in our Cyprus account could be used only for construction/development-related payments, we asked IBM to make its initial base-rental prepayment to our Putnik Russian bank account for two of their five apartment units.

Anticipating this income, we hired Tom Weber as our construction manager in January of 1992. Within a week, however, our Russian bank collapsed. Because our account was frozen, we were unable to pay him, but Tom continued working, unpaid, for more than three months. Using funds from a different account, we were eventually able to pay him at least in part, but he worked on nothing but good faith for many weeks.

Bolshaya Ordynka Building

Natalia Uvarova, who had been my Russian language teacher when I was Satra chief rep, told me about a dilapidated old building in a prime location on Bolshaya Ordynka Street. The small structure appeared to be an excellent candidate for office conversion. A Russian cooperative had the ten-year lease rights and wanted to sell them.

I couldn't buy the rights myself—at the time, I was overextended. Other than what I needed for living expenses, I was sending whatever I earned to Jill, both to support her and Sasha and to cover Chris's college tuition. A year earlier, we sold our house in Silver Spring to buy a more expensive home in Bethesda. The purchase and the ensuing renovations completely drained my reserves. Beyond my personal obligations, my company also took on debt from Michael Morgenstern's company.

I wasn't in a position to invest in the co-op, but Misha Pankin was. He and I agreed to reconstruct the building together on a 50/50 basis. In lieu of a cash investment from me, I was to be responsible for finding tenants and lining up financing by negotiating agreements that would include payment of rent in advance.

Even before I'd found a tenant, Misha had used his own funds to proceed with demolition and new basic construction. He then began to question why he should share the future profits of this project with me. Since Michael had returned from Siberia and was now back in Moscow working with Putnik, I agreed to give his company 20 percent interest in the Bolshaya Ordynka Building—retaining 30 percent for my company—in return for loans he would make to the project to help cover the costs of construction.

(With Misha Pankin)

In the wake of the German money scandal in October 1990, Michael, Misha and I were still in the position of having to convince both the authorities and any future tenants that Kanopa, our jointly-held Cyprus company, was in no way involved in this scandal. Nevertheless, we feared that Kanopa's name and reputation may have been irrevocably damaged and decided that we would not start any new projects under that banner.

Complications

There remained the matter of finding tenants for the Bolshaya Ordynka building, and it took me longer than I thought it would to do so. The French Banque Nationale de Paris (BNP) had been looking for offices and had intended to find a space jointly with Germany's Dresdner Bank AG. They would be desirable tenants, but we faced one potentially serious complication: the Putnik JV accounts that were at the heart of the German money transfer scandal had been opened at Dresdner Bank branches in Oslo and Amsterdam.

Because it took me until December of 1992 to conclude a lease agreement with these two banks, we financed the entire reconstruction of the Bolshaya Ordynka building ourselves. Throughout most of the construction period, we controlled the Bolshaya Ordynka site through the ten-year rental agreement between the city and the co-op, which was now owned by Misha and his friends and family.

In the aftermath of the dissolution of the Soviet Union in December of 1991, however, many property ownership laws changed—and kept changing. Dresdner Bank and BNP had officially moved into the Bolshaya Ordynka building on October 1, 1993, but in late January of 1994, the city property department informed us that only the city itself would be able to lease the building to the banks, and all rental income would go to the city.

I was initially shocked by this trend, but over time I realized that the Soviet people—who had been deprived of private property and the ability to make profits under communism for so many years—were somewhat resentful of the income and profits we Westerners were making as capitalism was reintroduced into what had been the USSR. I also came to understand that this resentment was widespread and was something I had to anticipate.

In an effort to show that this would discourage all further real estate investment in Moscow, if not in all of Russia, we held marathon negotiations with city officials and attorneys. Meanwhile, however, Dresdner and BNP paid rent to the joint stock company's account on a quarterly basis. Ultimately, we succeeded with the city property department and the law was changed again, but it was a while before Michael and Misha's companies were reimbursed for their investment and the project started to see a profit.

Sanctions Against Yugoslavia

As Jastrebac, our general contractor, was reconstructing the Putnik building, ethnic strife was raging in their home country of Yugoslavia, with insurgencies and conflict among Slovenes, Croats, Kosovar Albanians, Bosnians, and Macedonians. The government of Slobodan Milošević, a Serb, retaliated in brutal fashion. His actions led to charges of war crimes, a United Nations embargo, and the establishment of a UN International Criminal Tribunal. The United States and our Western allies imposed their own trade and travel sanctions, as well as a series of military actions that included naval blockades and the eventual bombing of Serbia by NATO forces.

The sanctions, fighting, and unrest had international repercussions, and Jastrebac's work in Moscow was caught up in it. The company had an exceptionally good reputation locally, and they continued working on the Putnik building throughout the German money scandal, even though we were unable to get them any hard-currency payments. Jastrebac understood all too well that walking off the job would have destroyed tenant confidence in the project, which would mean they'd never get paid for work they'd already completed.

Looming international sanctions against Yugoslavia meant we faced a hard deadline. On the date they went into effect, Putnik would no longer be able to do business with Jastrebac or import Yugoslavian materials. Jastrebac had to find alternative sources and vendors in other countries, which resulted in both higher costs overall and higher initial outlay. In some cases, we bought the same materials several times over, because what we'd already bought and paid for had been destroyed in the fighting in Yugoslavia.

Many of us had come to know Jastrebac personnel not just as clients but as friends. We greatly respected them, especially since they'd stuck with us and worked without pay during the worst of the PJV-Putnik conflict. Because we wanted to continue the construction of the Putnik building with this team of workers, and because Jastrebac wanted to finish the job, we cooperated with them in setting up a new legal entity called Contrex.

On paper at least, this new construction company would be headquartered on the island of Cyprus. Overseas corporate leadership for some of our tenants wanted assurances that our new general contractor was not a Yugoslavian company, so we provided a letter confirming that Contrex was based in Cyprus.

Our assistance to Jastrebac had a financial component as well. Putnik had wired a payment of several hundred thousand dollars to a Jastrebac account in Germany, but that account would be frozen when the sanctions took effect. To prevent those funds from getting stuck in Germany, I allowed Jastrebac to forward this money to one of our own Cyprus accounts and park it there temporarily, until they were able to establish their new Contrex financial relationships in Cyprus.

The change from Jastrebac to Contrex created additional delays for the Putnik project, including one very specific problem: we were no longer able to import the Yugoslavian bathroom fixtures needed to complete the otherwise finished mansard-level living spaces, including five apartments that IBM was anxious to occupy as soon as possible. The situation called for a creative solution. I had made friends with Paul Tatum, an American businessman whose company was a partner in the joint venture that had developed the Radisson Slavyanskaya Hotel in Moscow. When I learned that many Radisson hotel rooms were to be converted into the hotel's new business center, I negotiated with Paul for Contrex to purchase the hotel room bathroom fixtures—sinks, tubs, and toilets—that they no longer needed. These fixtures were then removed from the Radisson and reinstalled in IBM's Putnik apartments.

Mechnikova Lane 14

Periodically I was asked to speak at various Moscow business conferences about our commercial real estate success, and specifically how we had financed projects through advance rental payments, since commercial loans were unavailable in the Soviet Union and the early years of the Russian Republic. Other American businesspeople who came to Moscow to attend such conferences would often meet with me during conference breaks, and some were interested in doing business with me. With the financial difficulties I was facing due to delays in the receipt of advance rental payments for the Putnik project, I was ready to entertain offers. A prospective partnership with San Francisco investor and real estate broker George Tischer didn't pan out, but through it I was indirectly connected with a project controlled by Kruiz-Tourinterservis at Mechnikova Lane 14. Misha and I negotiated a development contract with them to organize the financing, handle the leasing, and manage the complete reconstruction of the building.

In December of 1992, I negotiated a build/lease agreement between Kruiz-Tourinterservis and Rank Xerox Limited which included the prepayment of three years of rent during construction in return for a discounted rental rate. Using Contrex as our general contractor and Tom Weber as our construction manager, we reconstructed the five-story, 1,400 square meter (15,070 square foot) building into prime office space. Xerox leased the five floors above ground, and Michael, Misha, and I set up our offices in the windowed basement level.

Divorce

My relationship with Vera had begun in October of 1990, but I did not tell Jill for almost two years. I continued making regular trips to Washington to see her and the boys. During winter holidays, when Chris was home from Boston University, we would take family trips together, including a trip to Hawaii. These were joyful excursions, but I knew that I was harboring a painful reality.

Jill's career was flourishing in DC, and she was as beautiful as ever. She had an influential social circle, and I did wonder whether she, too, was seeing someone else, just as I was. Early one Sunday morning in 1992, she called me in Moscow to say that she had been out to dinner with another couple. She talked wistfully about how romantic they were together, and how it reminded her of the closeness we had shared in the past. She said that she missed being with me like that, and then—unexpectedly—she asked me whether there was anyone else in my life.

Vera had just left after spending the weekend with me, and I realized that I could no longer continue being dishonest. I told her about Vera, and that was the start of our formal breakup. It took a long time to complete our divorce; it was another six years before it was finalized.

Children are collateral damage in a divorce, and I was concerned about how it would affect Chris and Sasha, especially Sasha. On my next trip to DC, I discovered that Sasha had written a poem expressing the pain he was experiencing as he tried to come to grips with a greatly changed relationship between his parents. As with any emotionally stressful event, it was helpful to confront those feelings directly and talk them through.

In terms of the paperwork for the divorce, Jill and I spoke with my old friend Gene Theroux in the law firm Baker & McKenzie in Washington. He advised us to each get our own attorney, but because he knew us both, he said it would not be proper for him to represent either of us. He connected Jill with one of the best divorce firms in Washington. The proceedings were not at all acrimonious, but there were still issues to resolve, including alimony. Alimony is tied to a determination of anticipated income, but with all the political and economic changes in Russia—changes that were still ongoing—it was exceedingly difficult to predict my future revenue stream. As a result, Jill and I postponed finalizing our divorce until we got a better idea of my business prospects.

CHAPTER 21

1993-1994

Project Gorky—Helping My Father Write His Second Memoir

In the 1970s, my father Victor had written a memoir called *The Brothers Reuther and the Story of the UAW*, which was published by Houghton Mifflin in 1976. In that book, Dad wrote briefly about the almost three-year period in the early 1930s when he and Uncle Walter had worked in the Soviet Union.

The Gorky auto plant had sprung from Ford's decision to phase out the Model A. Ford sold the Model A tools, dies, and production equipment right off the Detroit assembly lines for $13 million to the Soviet Union, and everything was shipped to Gorky. The GAZ (*Gorkovsky avtomobilny zavod*) auto plant went into production on January 1, 1932, and vehicles began rolling off the assembly line later that year.

(Dad – standing on the far right – and Uncle Walter – seated, bottom center – with other workers at the Gorky auto plant. Photo credit: Walter P. Reuther Library, Archives of Labor and Urban Affairs, Wayne State University)

The GAZ plant offered employment to thousands at a time when authoritarian regimes were on the rise and worldwide economic conditions were grim. The prospect of a paying job attracted people from many nations, but workers who trekked to Gorky in the 1930s found not just jobs but Stalinist oppression. The onset of World War II and the German invasion brought harsh wartime deprivation that included severe shortages of food and other basic necessities and extreme physical danger. Because the GAZ plant manufactured tanks for the Russian army, it became a prime target for the Luftwaffe. The plant was bombed forty-three times between October 1941 and June 1943, and workers died in the raids.

Too many of Gorky's foreign workers never made it home, and Dad wanted the world to know their story. He began to work on a second memoir he would call *Project Gorky—How Western Nations Deserted Their Own.* It was a detailed account about the foreigners who had come to the Soviet Union seeking work. In an initial draft of the foreword, Dad wrote:

For sixty years, the closed city of Gorky, now again known by its historic name of Nizhniy Novgorod, was off limits to all in the Western world. For all these years, it concealed a deadly secret. What happened to the hundreds of citizens of Western nations who had gone there, many with their families, either to help in one of the most impressive industrial projects of the Second of the Five-Year plans, the Gorky auto plant (GAZ), or as was the case with many others, were fleeing from Mussolini's fascist Italy, from Hitler's Nazi Germany, or the fascist Heimwehr in Austria... Historians estimate that between the late 1920s and the mid-1930s, approximately 80,000 workers from Western countries sought employment in the USSR. Only now are the shocking details of the methodical liquidation of many thousands of these foreign workers coming to light. In personal letters sent to me by survivors of the large international community of such foreign workers in Gorky, the magnitude of their Holocaust is revealed. Theirs is a story of dedication and sacrifice, of trust and betrayal. Their story must be told!

I believe that what triggered Dad's interest in writing *Project Gorky* was a section of the December 1990 issue of *Continuum Center*, a publication of Oakland University in Rochester, Michigan. A column by J. Dalley appeared in "Notes from the Editor's Desk," and Dad faxed me a copy.

Dalley and her husband had taken a Volga River cruise, and one of the stops was the newly reopened city of Gorky, which had been officially renamed Nizhniy Novgorod in October 1990. She wrote that she'd been walking around the city with a large group of tourists from the boat when a mustachioed Russian man approached her. "Hallo! Do you know Walter Reuther?" he asked in strongly accented English.

"My reaction was twofold," she wrote, "as I was both tickled and flabbergasted that, out of all the Americans that were wandering through his streets, he picked one from the Detroit environs to ask that question. How ironic, I thought. I'm sure I giggled, but I did manage to tell him that, although I hadn't known Walter personally, I certainly knew about Walter Reuther."

"Well, I knew Walter," the Russian man responded. "He came to Gorky to teach us to build automobile plant. I work with Walter then."

From Dalley's article, Dad realized that there were still people living in Gorky who had known the Reuther brothers in the early 1930s, and I did my best to help him connect with some of them. In the fall of 1992, I made the trip to Nizhniy Novgorod with author Peter Hauslohner, who was a special aide to Robert Strauss, then our US ambassador to Moscow.

Peter had many political contacts in Nizhniy Novgorod, including Boris Nemtsov, the young governor of the Nizhniy Novgorod region. At the time we met with him, Nemtsov had a promising political future, but he eventually became an outspoken critic of Vladimir Putin and paid dearly for his opposition. On February 27, 2015, four bullets were fired into Nemtsov's back as he was walking across a bridge near the Kremlin. He died at the scene.

While we were in Nizhniy Novgorod, Peter and I toured the GAZ auto plant where Dad and my uncle had worked. We visited the GAZ factory museum, which had a display that featured the Americans who helped set up and run the plant. I also met Jean Singer, one of the American women who had worked with them—she was still living in Nizhniy Novgorod. Jean had later taught English at the local Foreign Language Institute, where one of her former students was Yevgeniy Gorkov, the deputy governor of the Nizhniy Novgorod region, and a close friend of Peter's. Peter sent Dad contact information and phone numbers for both Governor Nemtsov and Deputy Governor Gorkov and suggested that they might be helpful in getting Dad's writings published in Russian.

Sometime later, a local Russian union newspaper ran an article about Walter and Dad having worked at the Gorky auto plant and mentioned Peter's and my visit to the GAZ plant. The article also mentioned Jean Singer, whose name in Russian was Evgenia, as the English translation of this article refers to her as E. Singer.

> *E. Singer was 19 years old when, together with her father, a specialist on machine-tool construction, she came to build the GAZ, dreamt of being instructed in the Soviet Union as an engineer and get higher education. Eventually her dream came true. She graduated from two university-level colleges, but there was a terrible tragedy. In 1938 she lost her father, who*

had worked at that time in Kuibyshev. He was executed by a firing squad as an enemy of the people. Before the war, the young woman came back to the Motor Works because, according to her, the best and splendid days of her youth were linked up precisely with GAZ. Incidentally, it was there that she got acquainted with the brothers Reuther.

Matrosov and Milchanov

On one of Vera's first-class flights from Paris to Moscow, she met Alexander Sergeyevich Matrosov, a vice minister of both the Russian Federation and the Moscow city government. Vera introduced me to him, and he apparently was impressed enough with our development work to consider setting up a new joint stock company to develop Moscow housing.

Matrosov was responsible for oversight of all infrastructure construction in Moscow, including roads and underground utilities. Andrei Stroyev reported to him but was several levels below him in the municipal pecking order. When Michael and I met with Matrosov and his deputies in mid-January of 1993, he proposed that we establish a new development company together—a cooperative effort between my company and the city of Moscow. I knew better than to get too far ahead of myself, but I did get a certain amount of anticipatory joy imagining the look on Andrei Stroyev's face when he learned I was now in business with his boss's boss's boss.

Nothing further came of the housing idea, but during one of our meetings with Matrosov, Vera recalled that a colleague of his was a highly respected Russian journalist named Aleksander Aleksandervich Milchanov. Milchanov had gained widespread attention for exposing the vast files that the KGB had kept on foreigners in the Soviet Union, including men and women who had disappeared during the Stalinist era. After those shocking revelations, an official committee was set up to investigate further, and Matrosov had been appointed to it.

Vera met with Matrosov and showed him a copy of *The Brothers Reuther*, then told him of Dad's need for a qualified research assistant to work with him on *Project Gorky*. He immediately picked up the phone and called Milchanov to set up a meeting. Two days later, Vera and I had dinner with Milchanov and his wife in their apartment. We learned that he had met his wife when they were both correspondents for the Soviet trade union newspaper *Trud,* and he remembered Harry Givorgian, the *Trud* journalist who had originally encouraged me to study in Moscow.

Milchanov expressed great enthusiasm about the possibility of working with my father on *Project Gorky*. He asked me to tell Dad that he was in a position to request information from various archives and have everything sent to DC. Vera and I offered to have the material translated into English. It was a service I was happy to pay for. I told Dad that after he and Mom had helped me financially for so many years, it was now time for me to return the favor. As the evening ended, I gave Aleksander and his wife a copy of *The Brothers Reuther.*

After he started working, we began faxing Milchanov's translated material to Dad on a regular basis. It was gratifying that he had taken an interest in my background and political experiences, and I was pleased with his request to share with him a copy of the photo of Dad, Mom, and me with Bobby Kennedy at the 1968 UAW convention in Atlantic City...

At least I was, until I found out why.

In April I opened the Russian language newspaper *Evening Moscow* and found a lengthy article by Milchanov entitled, "The Tragic Fate of Americans in Russia." It summarized all the work that he had been doing—ostensibly for Dad's book. It became quite clear, however, that he had been working only for himself.

It felt like a betrayal. My immediate reaction was that Milchanov had stolen something from my dad. *Project Gorky* had been my father's idea, and this was material he'd intended to use to attract a publisher. In the book, Dad would have revealed information and told stories that no one had heard before, but Milchanov ruined all that, and he had done so for his own personal aggrandizement. Not only did he reproduce the photo of Walter and Dad at Gorky from *The Brothers Reuther,* but he also added the photo he'd asked me for from the 1968 UAW convention, except that he'd cropped out my mother in order to show only Dad and me with Bobby Kennedy.

When I confronted Milchanov, he was unrepentant. He never apologized, and I don't believe he cared about ruining Dad's chance of publishing his book in Russia. It certainly ended whatever friendship we might have had. *Project Gorky* did get published in Germany. I am unclear on the details of how this came about, but I have to assume that there was interest there based on our family heritage, and perhaps also based on the number of Germans who fled east after Hitler came to power and found work in the auto plant.

CHAPTER 22

1993-1994

The 1993 Russian Constitutional Crisis

After the breakup of the Soviet Union, democracy in Russia proved to be a far more complex form of government than autocracy. Before the Bolshevik Revolution, Russia had been a monarchy for centuries. It had virtually no democratic tradition, and perhaps worse, everyone seemed to have a different understanding of what democracy should mean in a nation that was trying to reinvent itself after seventy years of communism and Stalinism and centuries of autocracy.

Some budding Russian capitalists defined democracy as their singular opportunity to amass great personal wealth, and they became adept at using government levers of power to do so. As the assets of the state were liquidated and redistributed, a new class of freewheeling Russian entrepreneurs emerged. With the political and socioeconomic situation in flux, there were few constraints on their behavior, and they knew it. Vast and pervasive corruption—both public and private—made regular headlines in Moscow.

Under the old Soviet regime, there had surely been fraud, greed, and exploitation, but without a free press, a lot of it remained under wraps. Now that it was blatant and out in the open, the public became increasingly cynical about those in power, and the economic situation didn't help. In the late 1980s, the ruble had been worth about $1.80. With the dissolution of the USSR, its value imploded. In 1993, it was worth roughly 0.00083 cents, or 1200 to the dollar. Everyone was scrambling to make ends meet.

With everything going on at Putnik and our other reconstruction projects, I struggled to keep abreast of the rapid political changes occurring in Russia, but by the fall of 1993, the standoff between President Boris Yeltsin and the Russian parliament became impossible to ignore. On September 21, 1993, Yeltsin attempted to dissolve the legislature, even though the constitution did not give him the right to do so. Parliament was having none of it. They declared Yeltsin's action invalid, then impeached him and proclaimed Vice President Aleksandr Rutskoi as acting president. In early October, the constitutional crisis spilled out into the streets.

On Sunday, October 3, I'd hunkered down in my apartment to accomplish a distasteful task I'd already put off for far too long: purging my files. With piles of papers arranged about me on every horizontal surface in the living room, I turned on my TV and found that CNN was carrying live coverage of a large anti-Yeltsin demonstration that had turned violent. Thousands of protestors had broken through barricades and police lines and swarmed the Russian White House, which housed the parliament. Gunfire was audible.

For the next three hours, I sorted papers and watched CNN report in real time on events taking place not far from my home. I kept switching channels, hoping to find local coverage, but there wasn't any. What Russian TV broadcast instead was in stark contrast to the gravity of events taking place and bordered on the absurd—American cartoons with Russian sub-titles, including *Casper the Friendly Ghost* and Walt Disney's *Winnie the Pooh*, a Mexican *telenovela* dubbed in Russian, and an episode of *Lassie*. Given what was on the air, I assumed that pro-Yeltsin forces still controlled the Ostankino broadcast center and had determined that a news blackout was the best way to starve Rutskoi of any latent public support.

At about 6:30 p.m., I heard rumbling sounds in front of my apart-ment building. The rumbling sounded like military equipment—tanks, heavy trucks, and armored personnel carriers, or APCs. During the August 1991 coup attempt, I'd been vacationing with Jill and the boys in California, and I'd always semi-regretted that I hadn't been a witness to those events. Now, history-in-the-making was rolling past my doorstep.

I loaded some low-light film into my very state-of-the-art, very auto-matic Minolta Maxxum 7xi camera, grabbed my camera bag and a dozen rolls of film, put on my coat, ski cap and gloves, and set off to document what I believed might become part of the battle for the future of Russia.

Within two blocks, I came to a building that had been commandeered as a military headquarters. I felt a rush of excitement. APC crews were sitting on their vehicles, automatic weapons at the ready. This was a shot I hoped to capture, but as I looked at the faces of these young men, I hesitated. It was not so long ago that foreign photographers had been forbidden to shoot pictures of Russian military equipment. Out of an abundance of caution, I kept walking.

I decided to see how close I could get to the White House. As I walked past the Foreign Ministry, I took a long look at the large, vacant lot across the street. It had been offered to me as a hotel site over a year earlier, and it was one of many locations fought over by ambitious city bureaucrats—men very much like Andrei Stroyev.

These newly minted Russian capitalists had been jostling one another—and then some—for the right to control these prime sites. They'd sought to control them in order to develop them as hotels in joint ventures with Western partners, and because the profits at stake were huge, the infighting among them was fierce. Their cage-match squabbling was ultimately self-defeating. The toxic political and economic climate had made American and Western European large investors so gun-shy that they were reluctant to commit to major projects in Moscow. Most of the old buildings had been razed, but not one of these hotels had been completed, or had even broken ground. Some sites had been cleared for five years or more—long enough to sprout not just weeds but sapling trees.

I kept walking and saw that Rutskoi's supporters controlled the mayor's building. The huge ground floor windows had been smashed, and I glimpsed several captured police shields propped up nearby. A command post was being set up in the foyer. Behind the badly mangled venetian blinds, furniture was being piled up to barricade against a potential counterattack by Yeltsin's forces. I could feel a rush of excitement, and I took my first pictures here.

I climbed the broad steps to the elevated entrance and found myself standing with about a hundred people at the shattered metal and glass doorway. An area about twenty-five feet deep and fifty feet wide had been cordoned off. This was where Rutskoi's shock troops stood guard with their Kalashnikovs. Emotions were running high. There was a great deal of nationalistic, pro-Communist talk, and an almost giddy anticipation of victory.

On both sides of the entrance, the massive, floor-to-ceiling window walls were riddled with pockmarks from automatic weapons fire. I initially assumed that the bullets had come from Yeltsin's forces, but I then realized that the bullet holes were clustered so close together that they must have come from automatic weapons fired at point blank range. This meant that the shots had come from Rutskoi's troops as they attacked the building.

I wanted to capture an image of the bullet-riddled glass, but in the darkness, I didn't want to startle anyone with the flash from my camera. I also didn't want to provoke the wrong reaction from Rutskoi's forces, who might still be stoked with adrenaline after successfully storming the building. Standing at the cordon next to an enthusiastic Rutskoi supporter and a guard with an automatic weapon, I overheard the two of them praising communism. "Now we only have one enemy," the supporter said to his armed comrade, "America!" I'd been about to ask whether they'd mind if I took a photo, but their conversation prompted me to reconsider.

I walked along the front of the building toward the White House and discovered the back half of a military truck still protruding from a smashed window-wall. At the rear bumper, two plain clothesmen were talking with a helmeted, armed guard. They gave me their permission to take a photo, but the flash on my super-sophisticated camera refused to cooperate. I feared for the fate of the driver of the truck, but I was even more concerned about how many others would be hurt in the violence that seemed sure to come.

I reached the rear of the White House, where red hammer and sickle flags were flying. From the balcony, Rutskoi was exhorting several thousand enthusiastic followers to wrest control of the Ostankino broadcast center from Yeltsin's forces. Military trucks and buses idled nearby; they were filling with armed Rutskoi supporters and were about to depart for that location. Seeing their weapons, I thought it unwise to take their picture, but I did get shots of the balcony and the crowds below.

With renewed faith in my camera, I returned to the truck wedged into the window, but once again, it wouldn't function. I then backtracked further to the entrance of the mayor's office. I tried to take a picture of the windows and their bullet holes, but three men were blocking my shot, and I asked them to briefly step aside. When Mikhail, one of the men, asked me where I was from, I told him that I was a businessman who had spent many years in Moscow. He persisted and asked again about my country of origin, so I smiled, put my hand on his shoulder, looked him in the eye and said, "The United States of America."

What a lecture I got, starting with what was wrong with President Clinton—"or is it really Mrs. Clinton behind US-Russian policy?" He intended it as an obvious slight, but I'd always thought Hillary Clinton was bright and impressive. Having just seen her on *Larry King Live*, I felt obliged to come to her defense.

Fortunately, Mikhail was a guy who really liked to talk. He spoke about his deep frustration with government corruption, then went on at some length about how Russian officials were enriching themselves at the expense of their countrymen, then transferring their ill-gotten wealth out of the country. Mikhail also denounced lawlessness in the streets, rising prices, and the abysmal value of the ruble. What he wanted was a restoration of his homeland's international prestige, but as he kept talking, he wistfully began describing his heart's true desire: a chance to see the United States. He'd always wanted to visit, he said, "but it's so expensive to travel these days." While he talked, I took photos of the bullet-riddled windows and got exactly the shot I wanted.

(Bullet-riddled windows at the mayor's office building)

(Shattered front entrance to the mayor's office building)

On my way back to the rear of the White House, I took more photos, including one of a young woman—a former youth Communist Komsomol leader from Ukraine—who was speaking from the balcony. My last shot on the roll was of CNN correspondent Claire Shipman standing on that same balcony with her camera crew. When I heard the film automatically rewinding inside the camera, I moved beneath a streetlight to read the speed on my next roll of film. I then did something no photographer should ever do. In the bright light of the streetlamp, I opened the back of the camera.

To my horror, I discovered that the film had only partially rewound. As I replayed the night's events—when the camera worked and when it didn't—I eventually realized that my problem was a weak battery. It explained why the camera wouldn't operate without at least some ambient light, and also why the film hadn't completely rewound. Anxious about my photos, I began the long walk home. I knew some of the shots were ruined; the question was how many.

As I tried to assess the political situation, I kept returning to one key difference between Rutskoi and Yeltsin. Rutskoi had fiercely devoted followers, many of whom sounded as if they were ready to kill or be killed for him. Yeltsin didn't command the same personal loyalty. When the time came to take back the White House, would Yeltsin's government troops put their lives on the line for him and for his troubled, sometimes-corrupt, still-evolving concept of democracy?

I soon got the answer to my question. When I first got home, it seemed that little had changed—only CNN was covering the standoff. Eventually, however, I was able to switch to TV Russia. In what had become a bloody confrontation, Yeltsin's troops had stood their ground, repelled Rutskoi's forces, and successfully defended the Ostankino broadcast center. The next day, government tanks fired on the White House from the bridge opposite the mayor's building. Rutskoi capitulated, and full government control returned to Yeltsin.

(The day after government tanks fired on the White House)

The day after the failed coup, my friend and potential business partner, Frank Brady of Shelter International, was flying back to Moscow from
a business trip to Kazakhstan. I sent Sayar, my driver, to the airport to pick
him up and bring him to my apartment, where he was to stay the night.
Traffic, however, was even more snarled than usual. Moscow residents
were determined to carry on with their daily routines, even though there
were still barricades at key intersections, even though there were soldiers
and armed vehicles in the streets. Getting from the airport into the heart
of the city was going to be a real challenge. I gave Sayar a sign to hold
up with Frank's name on it and the two successfully connected as Frank
emerged from customs and passport control. So far, so good, but because
Frank spoke no Russian and Sayar spoke no English, Sayar was unable to
tell him about the momentous events that had just taken place.

Tanks and APCs were still blocking many of the main thoroughfares
between the airport and my apartment, but Sayar had become particularly adept at navigating the streets of Moscow. Ever resourceful, he
took to driving on the sidewalks where necessary—to the great dismay
of his passenger.

When Frank arrived at my apartment, his knuckles were still white. He was sure that he'd survived Mr. Toad's Wild Ride with a lunatic behind the wheel. It wasn't until I explained what had been happening over the past few days that he had a context for Sayar's driving behavior and appreciated what he'd done to bring him safely to my home.

There had been casualties among both Yeltsin's troops and Rutskoi's forces, but there were serious injuries to innocent bystanders as well. During the fight to take back the White House, Julie Brooks, a twenty-three-year-old American paralegal who worked in the Putnik building at Baker & McKenzie, was badly wounded. She'd been standing on the roof of the apartment building where Bill, a Baker & McKenzie partner, lived and was hit in the midsection by two stray bullets. Bill's seventeen-year-old son carried the badly wounded young woman down the fire escape to his father's apartment. Bill and Paul Melling, my close friend and another Baker & McKenzie partner, quickly arranged for a staff driver to take Julie to the Botkin hospital. After that, relays of Baker lawyers and staff traveled to and from Botkin to donate blood. Once she was stabilized, Julie was Medevacked to Finland, where she eventually made a complete recovery.

The Expanding American Business Community in Moscow

While I was Satra's chief representative (1978-1981), we few Americans accredited to work in Moscow had access to the American Embassy cafeteria. We gathered there on Saturdays with our families for waffles and pancakes, and to share stories about our lives here. When the number of Americans doing business in the Soviet Union became so large that the embassy could no longer accommodate us, we found a new place to convene—Tren-Mos, a restaurant co-organized and run by my friend Jeffrey Zeiger.

Jeff was from Trenton, New Jersey—he was the "Tren." He had partnered with a local restaurant employees' union headed by Sergei Goryachev—Sergei was the "Mos." As mayor of Moscow's Lenin district,

Goryachev had signed a sister city agreement with Trenton, hence, Tren-Mos.

There were some comedic East-meets-West moments when the restaurant first opened. Because Sergei was a former city bureaucrat in a country where everything had always been done in lockstep with long-term plans, he asked Jeff how many pounds of beef he should order for their first six months in business. Sergei asked this question as if it were perfectly normal, but Jeff of course was astonished.

It didn't take long for the American business community to fall in love with Tren-Mos, and the restaurant became extremely popular with everyone. Not only did it offer an authentic American menu and dining experience, it accepted payment in a variety of currencies, including dollars, deutschmarks, pounds, Swiss francs and even rubles. This was a major draw for Russian patrons because at the time, it was illegal for them to possess hard currency. Because Jeff treated his customers like guests in his own home, many expats chose to celebrate Thanksgiving and other holidays at Tren-Mos. Eventually I brought Vera to the restaurant, and we remain friends with Jeff and his family to this day.

In a 1994 article in the English language newspaper the *Moscow Times,* Jeff spoke fondly of his Russian partner. "He was the tank," he told the reporter. "He dealt with the back, with the bureaucracy, while I dealt with the front, with the advertising, the look of the place, the tablecloths, the china." Sadly, it was a posthumous remembrance, because on July 31, 1993, an assassin lying in wait in Sergei's private garage shot him three times in the head and neck. The murder fit the classic description of a Mafia hit, but Jeff was sure it had nothing to do with Sergei's business life at Tren-Mos.

From the time I worked for Satra in the late 1970s, I was always aware that something like this might happen to me, but I didn't think about leaving. This was my life, the only way I knew how to support myself and my family. I also convinced myself that foreigners like me were unlikely to be the targets of this kind of violence.

Over time, our group of American expats outgrew even Tren-Mos, so we moved our periodic luncheon headquarters yet again, this time to the

Radisson Slavyanskaya Hotel, which was run by our friend Paul Tatum. Eventually we formalized ourselves into an organization we called the American Business Club, or ABC for short. In 1994, our ABC became the official Moscow chapter of the American Chamber of Commerce, or AmCham. I was a member of the Investment Committee, and one of the first co-chairs of the AmCham Committee on Real Estate and Construction. It was surely an ironic turn of events: this son of American labor had become a leader of the local Chamber of Commerce.

CHAPTER 23

October 1993-May 1994

The Battle for Putnik, Part I

It had been a long, hard struggle to get to this point, but by 1993, the Putnik office building was fully occupied. In December, Andrei Popov, once again chairman of the board and now executive director of Putnik JV, called a board meeting. Much to the surprise of everyone else on the board, he presented us with an official document issued by the city of Moscow. It was a certificate of privatization and was dated October 27, 1993. It declared that Popov's company, which had now been reregistered as PAIT, a Russian limited liability company, was the sole, 100 percent owner of the Putnik building.

(Putnik building completed)

According to the document, Putnik JV had reconstructed the building expressly for PAIT. In return, the JV had been granted twenty-five-year lease rights to the building, after which building ownership would revert exclusively to Popov's company.

The official city forms Popov showed us had been crudely amended. They contained an additional handwritten paragraph, which meant that Popov had one or more allies on the Moscow City Property Committee (*Moskomimushestvo*). I could only assume that he'd paid them to sign off on his hijacking of the building, because Moskomimushestvo had also become the registered city equity partner in our JV.

For the city of Moscow, this made no financial sense whatsoever. According to our initial agreement with the city, Putnik JV was to develop and reconstruct the building. In return, the JV was granted the right to receive rental payments for twenty-five years, but the city of Moscow retained complete ownership of the building and the land itself. Under Popov's 1993 privatization agreement, the city owned 17 percent of the JV, but nothing more—after 25 years, both the structure and the land would belong to Popov.

We were stunned. There was nothing whatsoever in our JV founding documents about the eventual ownership of the Putnik building. Why? Because the USSR was still in existence when we'd set up Putnik JV, and legally at that time, there was no such thing as private ownership of land or of an office building like this one.

We could not allow Popov's effort to "steal" the building to go unchallenged. We immediately expressed our complete disagreement and told him we would not accept it. Knowing we had a fight on our hands, the board voted in January of 1994 to appeal Popov's unilateral privatization of the building to the city. Popov, of course, was opposed. In a separate motion, we also voted to fire Popov as Putnik JV executive director.

As soon as we adjourned, I quickly informed our tenants that Popov had been relieved of his responsibilities and authority. This was essential, because in the wake of the vote to remove him, Popov's behavior did not change. Acting as if he were still in charge, he continued to sign documents on behalf of Putnik JV. He also notified our tenants that all rent, operating expenses, and management fees were to be paid into a new bank account under his sole control.

Kanopa and Unikombank filed our appeal with the city, asking that they reverse the decision to privatize the building in the name of PAIT. Within two months, the city ruled in our favor: the PAIT privatization was to be annulled. Moskomimushestvo also recommended that the building be privatized in the name of Putnik JV, so that all parties who had participated in building the project would benefit.

Popov then took the issue to arbitration court. He prevailed, but I found it strange that Moskomimushestvo sat out the entire process. They neither sent a representative to the court hearing nor did they furnish any documents in support of their decision to annul the PAIT privatization.

Meanwhile, Popov tried to tempt the other Russian partners on the board to vote against us as a block. To win them over, he offered to raise each Russian partner's equity to 25 percent, an increase that would come at the expense of Kanopa's equity. Under his version of the new Putnik JV, what had been a 50/50 Russian/foreign joint venture would instead become a 75/25 Russian/foreign stock company.

Because Popov refused to acknowledge that he was no longer in charge, his company associates, who still occupied some Putnik top management positions, continued to follow his orders. One evening, Misha, Michael, and I met with the attorney from Unikombank at the Putnik building. When it ended, one of the security guards asked Misha to show him his Putnik ID. The guard took it to his hut as if to examine it in the light, but confiscated it instead, saying he had done so on direct orders from Andrei Popov.

The next morning, my driver Sayar, a Putnik JV employee, called to say that he had been ordered not to drive me anymore, and that he was to report instead to Popov loyalists at Putnik management. For me, this was no small inconvenience—the car and Sayar's time were the only form of compensation I had been receiving from Putnik for the previous ten months, since spring of 1993.

There was also the matter of embezzlement. Six months earlier, Popov had started to siphon off Putnik funds for his own personal use. With Popov ostensibly representing Putnik JV and his wife, Tanya, signing on behalf of PAIT, the two had executed a clandestine husband-and-wife mutual cooperation contract.

The contract was little more than a legal fig leaf that gave Popov permission to take over Putnik funds and resources, which he used to benefit himself and his family. Over the six-month period, Popov had pulled several of our Yugoslavian workers off the Putnik building job site and reassigned them to work on the construction of his family home—*and* he'd paid them for their labor with Putnik JV money. One had received at least $12,000. We discovered that Popov had also sold him a Fiat worth roughly $7,000 for the heavily discounted price of $2,500. Of course, the car was not his to sell—it belonged to Putnik JV.

How did he get away with it? Putnik's top finance guy was a close associate of Popov. Michael Morgenstern knew a lot about finance, but in terms of the Putnik project, he was an investor, not a salaried employee. No one else was minding the store, which made it much easier for Popov to paper over his larceny.

With the formal support of Moskomimushestvo, we took Popov's company to court. Over the next eighteen months, we had no success whatsoever. We lost appeal after appeal, despite overwhelming evidence in our favor—including testimony from the handwriting expert from the Russian Ministry of Finance who confirmed that the handwritten paragraph declaring that the Putnik building had been constructed for PAIT had been added at least a year after the original certificates of occupancy had been issued.

Throughout the appeals process, we'd been represented by one of the best British law firms in Moscow, but after this string of losses, we consulted with a top Russian street attorney. He was not the least bit surprised at what had happened. "Of course you are losing," he told us. "Popov is meeting alone with each of the judges at every level of the appeal, and he's bringing bags of money with him. That's how the system works."

We were beginning to understand how extensive this backlash corruption was, and what it was doing to the political system. As the Soviet economy converted to capitalism and people who had eked out a living all their lives now saw an opportunity to generate income on a level similar to what Western businesspeople were making, ethics were set aside.

External Leverage

Since the fix was in within the Russian judicial system, I decided we could be most effective calling political attention to our plight. We realized that we'd have to create leverage elsewhere, and our political connections in the United States were the best place to start. Russia was still hungry for foreign capital, but the fact that we'd been cheated out of our investment would be a red flag for any potential investor.

To spread the word, we reached out to our elected officials in Washington. We wanted them to go on record to say that the investment climate in Russia had become precarious, and that they were prepared to strongly discourage Americans from participating in any future projects in Russia.

Over my years in Moscow, I'd kept in touch with Senator Ted Kennedy, and this seemed to be the right time to ask for his help. I told him that I'd been appointed by the American Chamber of Commerce in Moscow to a committee that would prepare a white paper on the problems of doing business in Russia, and that the most critical issue we intended to cover was breach of contract.

Too often, Russians did not abide by the terms and conditions of the agreements they had signed. Nothing was ever final. A deal was not a deal but was instead a point from which to begin renegotiating. Attempts to claw back percentages of successful projects were increasingly commonplace and were often carried out with the blessing and collusion of well-placed friends and family at all levels of Russian government. What we considered bad faith in the States had become business as usual in Moscow.

Our stalemate with Popov was the poster child for this problem. As we were dealing with Popov, various Moscow city employees made it clear that, as a quid pro quo, they expected us to increase the city's equity in the Putnik project. Their expectation was accompanied by a thinly veiled threat that the city would take away the building outright if we failed to agree.

I reached out to Senator Kennedy and received the following reply:

> *March 18, 1994*
>
> *Dear John,*
>
> *I understand that you have been appointed by the Moscow chapter of the American Chamber of Commerce to serve on the Chamber's advisory committee on "Problems of Investment in Russia," and that your committee has prepared a briefing report for Commerce Secretary Brown and his delegation, scheduled to arrive in Moscow at the end of this month.*
>
> *I congratulate you on this appointment, and I am confident that Secretary Brown will benefit from the advice of members of the American business community who have worked closely with their Russian colleagues in helping to develop the free market economy. When the report is released, I would appreciate it if you could send me a copy.*
>
> *I also recall hearing of your participation in the construction of the large Putnik office/apartment complex in Moscow, which I understand is now complete with a list of prestigious international tenants. I remember that this project and its partners faced unusual problems during its development and would appreciate it if you could give me an update on how these problems were resolved.*
>
> *With best regards,*
>
> *Sincerely,*
>
> *Edward M. Kennedy*

In addition to our efforts in Washington, we also reached out directly to Moscow's mayor, Yuri Luzhkov. We wanted to ensure that he was aware of our powerful, highly placed connections in DC. In my letter, I told him how honored I was to serve on the American Chamber of Commerce committee that was to advise Ronald Brown, our secretary of commerce, on the problems of doing business in Russia. I also attached a copy of a letter from my father's former aide, Representative Ed Torres of California. Torres served on the House Appropriations Committee, which reviewed American expenditures on foreign operations and export financing, and my brother Eric was on his staff.

I am aware of your interview and of the TV coverage of your apparently very successful Putnik office development project on NBC National News, as well as your interview in front of the impressive Putnik building on CBS's 60 Minutes. I trust that you will keep me posted of developments as this project comes to full completion.

You know, John, the American people have put a great deal of faith into their hopes that the relationship between our two great nations can be built upon peace and cooperative ventures. Our taxpayers have supported, so far, the Administration's and Congress' assistance to the economic development challenges in Russia.

We anxiously await reports from sources like yourself to assure our citizens that our assistance and willingness to join in equal partnerships with the Russian economic sector will be met with equal respect and fair play.

We had to convince Mayor Luzhkov that Congress would look carefully at our experience with the Putnik project, and at Russia's treatment of American businessmen working and investing in their country. After reviewing the difficulties we had overcome to bring the Putnik project to completion—including the German money transfer scandal—I then summarized the abnormal process by which full ownership of the building had been awarded to Popov's company. I asked the mayor for his support in having the building privatized in the name of Putnik JV, not PAIT, which would be a fair and equitable resolution of the problem.

I sent a similar letter to the Committee on Foreign Relations of the State Duma (Russia's Parliament). In addition to copies of the letters from Senator Kennedy and Congressman Torres, I attached supporting correspondence from Putnik tenant companies that emphasized the key roles that Michael Morgenstern and I had played in the launch of the project. I appealed to them to ensure that the dispute surrounding this important and highly visible project be resolved in a manner that was fair to all parties concerned. I asked this "in defense of all businesses in Russia who look for an atmosphere of stability and confidence to attract investments for their projects… so that together we can show other possible investors and important foreign interested organizations that the perception of unacceptable risk and instability in Russia is exaggerated."

Sergei and Vadim

In May of 1994, I wrote a long letter to Sasha, then seventeen, and tried to bring him up to date on the fight to regain our rightful share in ownership of the Putnik building. I told him that we were struggling daily "to maintain relations and agreements that were long ago agreed in writing and should not today be a subject for renegotiations." We were finding that there were "practically no business ethics here," and no matter what terms were agreed to at the start—when a project looked almost impossible to accomplish—now that it was completed, "everyone wants a bigger share."

I wrote that I felt that the government had been unable to generate necessary revenues because so much of the economy was under the table. Because of the experiences we'd had with partners trying to change the terms after a deal was done, we were completely discouraged from starting new projects.

I then told Sasha the story about how I'd reached out to Vadim Tumanov, a famous Russian businessman, about our Putnik problem. My friend Sergei had told me about Vadim, who was an almost legendary figure. He was in the gold business; he had started mining gold in Siberia after having been imprisoned for years in a gulag. Convicted for anti-Soviet propaganda and agitation, Vadim had apparently made a habit of reading forbidden literature and listening to banned songs. Initially sentenced to serve eight years, his sentence was bumped up to twenty-five years as punishment for his numerous escape attempts.

It was only after Stalin was dead that Vadim was released—this was in the mid-1950s. Over the next forty years or so, his reputation grew. Stories about him appeared in books and magazines, and he was often portrayed as a model of success and perseverance under all but impossible circumstances. By the mid-1990s, he'd become something of a folk hero.

Sergei described Vadim as someone who neither paid bribes nor dealt with the Mafia. I found that as refreshing as it was rare; at the time, the business climate in Moscow was pretty much a cross between the Wild West and the Roaring Twenties. I asked Sergei to introduce me to Vadim because I wanted to discuss the problems we were facing and ask his advice. As a side note, Sergei also thought Vadim might be interested in working with us to market prefab housing in Russia, something I was still pursuing with Frank Brady from Shelter International in New Jersey.

In mid-April of 1994, Sergei took me to meet with Tumanov, whose office was located in a prestigious old building near both the Russian White House and the US Embassy. After I gave him a brief history of our problems, Sergei mentioned that our antagonist, Andrei Popov, was known to use any means necessary to hold on to power. He also told Vadim that it was our understanding that Popov had threatened one of his business partners, and that the threats against the man and his family were severe enough—and credible enough—that he had resigned.

Vadim nodded as he listened to our story, then said our difficulties were common for foreigners who had made mistakes in selecting their Russian partners. He told me that he could tell from my eyes that I was being honest with him, and that I could be trusted. It was a shame, he added, that we hadn't met several years ago; he had real estate projects he would have been pleased to develop with me. Sadly, he was now on the verge of losing them for lack of financing. He then offered to use his connections within city government to help us.

If he were to succeed, this would be a huge win for Michael, Misha, and me. Putnik JV was to be restructured as a joint stock company, but Popov was still blocking legitimate board meetings and making important decisions unilaterally—or trying to. A city document was being circulated that would designate which Moscow agency was to represent city interests on the Putnik board of directors. To be valid, this declaration needed a slew of apparatchik approvals from many different departments, as well as the signature of the mayor himself. Vadim believed he could expedite that process, and that he would be able to secure Luzhkov's approval.

I met repeatedly with Vadim over the next two weeks. During one of these meetings, he brought in a man named Rashid and asked me to describe the Putnik situation to him. After listening to my story, Rashid said we would meet again after he'd discussed the situation with his colleagues. Vera came with me to this meeting, and as we left, she told me that Rashid made her extremely uncomfortable. From his appearance and from the men he came in with, she strongly suspected that Rashid was *bratva*—Russian Mafia.

I dismissed her fears and reminded her of what Sergei had said about Vadim, that he doesn't pay bribes and doesn't deal with the Mafia. Vera remained entirely unconvinced and reiterated that she was virtually certain of her assessment.

Rashid set up a lunchtime meeting at the Vavilon restaurant and casino. I had never been there, but it was near the White Russian train station, and I knew the address. When I was still at Perestroika, the building had been one of the structures that was under discussion for development as part of a new Hyatt Regency hotel.

After what Vera had said, I was concerned about going there, but I was also concerned about not going there. I didn't want to damage my relationship with Vadim, and I was afraid that refusing to go would insult him. I confirmed my attendance with Rashid, but because of Vera's misgivings, I let him know that I would bring Sergei and Misha with me.

That would be my second meeting with Sergei that day. We were already scheduled for a morning meeting at the Kazakhstan embassy about prefab housing. On the way to the embassy, we discussed the meeting at the Vavilon. Sergei said what I was already thinking—that it didn't make sense to go if Rashid was indeed Mafia. We decided to check in with Vadim to get a better idea of what—and who—we'd be dealing with.

Vadim indicated that he had known Rashid for many years, and that he and his people were trusted colleagues who had helped him in the past. He added that he thought it was important for us to review the situation with Rashid's group, since Sergei had mentioned that we had reason to believe Popov's people had used strongarm tactics in the past. He encouraged us to go through with the meeting, if only to get Rashid's advice.

Otari

At the time, I was perhaps especially sensitized to the burgeoning involvement of the various factions of the Russian Mafia in all aspects of Moscow life. Just a few weeks earlier, Otari Kvantrishvili, a man I'd known for some time, had been assassinated in a shocking, high profile killing.

Early in my work with Perestroika, I'd met Nona Fedortsova, who had been Paul Von Ward's translator and assistant. (Von Ward headed up Delphi Group, and had been Andrei Stroyev's first Perestroika JV partner, before Earl Worsham bought him out.) Nona and I got along well, and she introduced me to her circle of friends.

Mikhail Zvizdinskiy, her boyfriend, was an underground Russian songwriter and singer. Based on charges that may have stemmed from illegal clandestine nightclub performances, he had spent sixteen years in Soviet prisons. In 1988, he returned to Moscow and resumed his music career. We socialized often with him, and through him I was introduced to Otari Kvantrishvili.

All I knew about Otari was that he had some kind of vague, high-level, authority or prestige. Improbably enough, he operated out of a small house in the wooded hills on the grounds of Gorky amusement park. I saw Otari and his associates from time to time at evening get-togethers organized by Nona or by her boyfriend, Misha—Mikhail Zvizdinskiy.

I considered Otari a friend, but Otari was a man with friends in high places—and low ones, as well. Only later did I learn that he was a leading Georgian Mafia boss—what was called a "thief in law" in Moscow—and was one of the major organized crime leaders in the city. Apparently, he was also a master arbitrator. Otari was the middleman who facilitated interactions and mediated disagreements among government officials, newly established private businesses, and various Mafia factions—and that's probably what got him killed.

On April 5, 1994, Otari was leaving a bathhouse and was shot to death by a sniper who had concealed himself in the attic of a nearby kindergarten. This was big news in both Moscow and the United States. The *New York Times* described the memorial service:

> *The funeral three days later confirmed everything and nothing about Mr. Kvantrishvili's life and activities, but it provided a vivid insight into the way business, crime, sports and politics have become intertwined in the new Russia, where huge fortunes are made through connections, vice, and the sale of state property.*
>
> *Mr. Kvantrishvili's death, with its cinematic touches and abiding mysteries, has prompted an extraordinary emotional outpouring from his many influential friends in a bewildering variety of professions.*
>
> *The funeral last Friday, in one of Moscow's most famous cemeteries, Vagankovskoye, was packed with celebrities from entertainment, sports, and politics—and with police, secret and otherwise, aiming video cameras. There were famous actors, famous professional athletes, and Olympic champions in Greco-Roman wrestling, which Mr. Kvantrishvili coached for Dynamo, the club of the Moscow militia. There were also popular singers like Aleksandr Rozenbaum, and especially Iosif Kobzon, a friend to everyone, high and low, and rumored to have mob connections dating from Soviet times.*

In 2008, four men from the Orekhov-Medvedkov gang were convicted in connection with the assassination of Otari Kvantrishvili. The triggerman, who had received a Lada automobile as compensation for the killing, was sentenced to twenty-three years in prison.

Rashid

That memory of Otari and his violent end was still fresh in my mind as Sergei and I drove to the Vavilon for our appointment with Rashid. We arrived just in time to meet Misha as he parked his car. We filled him in on our apprehensions, and on what Vadim had said. We agreed to go ahead with the meeting, but all of us felt a little on edge. What followed was right out of *The Godfather*.

The Vavilon restaurant, bar and casino occupied the second floor of the building. Its casino tables had patrons even during the day, which was unusual in a city where gambling was known as a late-night activity. We were led into the restaurant dining room, where Rashid was sitting at a table in the corner with a couple of tough guys. These oversized men were bodyguards and then some—no-neck, thuggish types you'd expect to see as bouncers at a dive bar in a sketchy part of town. Although most of the dining tables were empty, a few were occupied by equally muscular men who looked like second cousins to the ones sitting with Rashid. I could see bulges in odd places under their jackets, and I had no doubt that they were armed.

Rashid greeted us and brought us to a larger table in the opposite corner, where he introduced us to his general director. Rashid surely told us this man's first and middle names, but whatever he said didn't register at all. I was too busy being taken aback by how much this man carried himself like an older, stouter, Slavic version of Don Corleone.

Sergei, Misha, and I introduced ourselves, and I gave Rashid's don a brief history of our problems with Popov. I told him that we were seeking a decision from the city about which committee would hold the government's equity in Putnik and would represent Moscow at our board meetings, a decision that would finally allow us to get on with the joint venture's business. When Rashid mentioned that the general director's particular specialty was enforcement, I felt compelled to reiterate that our interest was administrative, and decidedly nonphysical.

Rashid's general director boastfully informed us that his organization controlled about twenty of the top retail properties on Gorky Street. Gorky Street—now renamed Tverskaya Street—was Moscow's Fifth Avenue or Rodeo Drive, and it was located around the corner from the Vavilon. The general director claimed that his organization also owned banks and other legitimate establishments of all kinds. From the comments he made, it was clear that he had relationships with many key Moscow officials and bureaucrats—the same individuals whose signatures we needed.

There was no doubt that he could help us, the general director said, but he wanted to know what we were prepared to offer. After an uneasy lull in the conversation, Misha eventually spoke up to ask for clarification. He wasn't sure he understood what was meant by this. "You must know what you stand to lose," the general director replied, "so make us a business proposal that takes into consideration these possible losses."

We awkwardly said that this was unexpected, and that we were unprepared to respond immediately. We would not want to suggest any kind of business relationship, we said, by making a proposal off the top of our heads.

"Just make us an offer we can't refuse," the general director said.

Misha and I shot alarmed glances at one another across the table, our eyes were asking the same question: How do we get out of this movie—alive—without offending anyone?

I then asked the general director what he had in mind to deal with our situation. "We'll make Popov an offer he can't refuse," he replied.

We didn't stay for lunch.

After making excuses about why we had to leave, we quickly said our goodbyes and promised to get them an answer in a week's time. Sergei and I drove straight to Vadim's to recount the day's events and reiterate that we very much wanted to solve our problems without bringing in the muscle.

Later that night, Michael, Misha, and I met to assess the damage. Our fear was that we were now in an even more precarious position than we'd been in before. If we politely declined to deal with the general director, it was entirely possible that he would approach Popov instead—with the same offer. Either way, we were on his radar, and that was of concern. We'd brought the Putnik building to the attention of one of Moscow's strongest Mafia groups.

We were all concerned for our physical safety, but according to Vera, these guys were not that kind of Mafia. She believed that these men leveraged their high-level contacts in government and business and wouldn't necessarily need to get physical against us.

I still worried that we had inadvertently ended up on Rashid's ene-mies list, but that turned out not to be the case. When I met again with Vadim, he reassured me that no harm had been done, and that nothing would come of this. Thankfully, that was the end of it, and I had no further contact with Rashid or his organization.

It was not, however, the end of our problems with Popov, who found a way yet again to cut a deal with Moskomimushestvo, the city prop-erty organization. Under it, his company and the city of Moscow were to become the exclusive owners of the Putnik building—Kanopa and Unikombank would be cut out entirely. Under the initial privatization deal he'd arranged in October of 1993 and presented to us in December, the city would lose all ownership of the building. According to this new arrangement, the city would retain some percentage of ownership—and in a way, that made it even more worrisome.

CHAPTER 24

1994

The Battle for Putnik, Part II

As soon as I learned of Popov's back room deal with Moskomimushestvo, I began dreading our next Putnik board meeting. What I'd initially hoped would be a 3-1 vote against Popov was looking like it might end up in a 2-2 tie.

Popov apparently believed so as well. A few days before the board meeting, he sent our tenants a letter on Putnik JV letterhead—unauthorized, of course. In it, he gave them an ultimatum and a deadline: unless they made payments to his account at the European Trade Bank within the next five days, he would cut off their access to the parking garage and withdraw security from the surrounding streets. He signed the letter as Putnik general director, a title he did not have.

To counteract this attempted extortion, we rallied support from the tenants committee. They sent a letter to the chairman of Moskomimushestvo, and it was signed by Baker & McKenzie attorney William Atkin as committee chair, on behalf of IBM, British Gas, the British Chamber of Commerce, Morgan Grenfell & Co. Limited, Price Waterhouse, Fiat, Rockwell International, ICI–Zeneca, and the Embassy of the Republic of South Africa. Atkin emphasized that the innovative three-year prepayment of rent was accomplished in large measure because of my reputation and that of Michael Morgenstern and added that the Putnik tenants believed that this form of financing represented "a unique example of the successful attraction of foreign investment for the reconstruction of real estate in Moscow today."

It was not until the Putnik board met that we learned that our lobbying efforts had worked. The letter from our tenants' committee hit home with the mayor and the city; they didn't want to risk harming the climate for future foreign investment. Based on a decision from Mayor Luzhkov's office, Moskomimushestvo was officially designated to represent the city of Moscow on the Putnik board. The Moskomimushestvo representative must not have been one of Popov's cronies, because to his surprise, the board then voted 3-1 to confirm his removal as executive director—his was the only vote in opposition. It also barred Popov from acting on behalf of Putnik JV in any capacity. By the same 3-1 majority, Popov's nephew was removed as commercial director, and another member of his inner circle was removed as finance director.

As soon as we adjourned, I wrote to all Putnik tenants to inform them of these developments. I wanted to leave no doubt as to which bank account was the valid Putnik JV account and where they were to make payments—and do so in writing.

Although getting Popov removed as executive director was a huge step forward, the issue of who owned the Putnik building had yet to be resolved. While I was in DC in June of 1994, I thought it would be useful to build additional leverage from the other side of the Atlantic. I contacted First Secretary Vadim Udalov of the Russian embassy, filled him in on my background and the story of Putnik JV, then appealed to him to use his influence on behalf of a fair foreign investment climate in Russia.

I sent him copies of the letters from Senator Kennedy and Congressman Torres and told him that we had already acceded to an earlier request by Moskomimushestvo to increase the city's equity from 17 percent to 22 percent. In a spirit of compromise aimed at reaching a fair and timely solution, we had further agreed that this increase in Moscow's equity would come entirely out of our shares, even though this would change the nature of the joint company from a 50-50 Russian-foreign entity to a 55-45 Russian-foreign entity.

Apparently, however, the squeeze was ongoing, because the terms of the proposed settlement changed yet again. The solution advanced by the deputy directors of Moskomimushestvo now called for an increase not just in the city's equity but in that of the other two Russian partners as well—entirely at our expense. Under this scenario, our share of the building would shrivel from 50 percent to 32 percent. Perhaps not surprisingly, Popov was to be the major beneficiary of this reassigned equity, with PAIT's share increasing from 17.1 percent to 30 percent. There would be a tiny uptick in the equity of Unikombank from 15.9 percent to 16 percent, and as already agreed, the equity of the city of Moscow would rise from 17 percent to 22 percent.

I emphasized to First Secretary Udalov that a safe, secure investment climate was crucial to the success of economic reform and economic development in Russia. I also conveyed our hope that the Russian embassy and foreign ministry would be willing to lend their gravitas and prestige to the effort to convince other stakeholders of the need for an unbiased, evenhanded settlement. "This is important not only to us," I wrote, "but to all enterprises in Moscow and Russia who hope to attract foreign investment for their projects, and who look for an atmosphere of stability and confidence to maximize this possibility… and to avoid… the inevitable negative press coverage which would result from a less than equitable solution."

I returned from DC in time to hear Mayor Luzhkov speak to the American Chamber of Commerce, now three hundred members strong, at the Radisson Slavyanskaya Hotel. His address was a newsworthy event that attracted an A-list audience. Beyond AmCham members and Ambassador Thomas Pickering, Leslie Brown, who headed our embassy's commercial office, and many members of the press were in attendance. In words that seemed to be playing to the media, Luzhkov criticized American companies for making what he called limited investments in Moscow and compared our efforts unfavorably to companies from much smaller countries.

I had arranged in advance to be one of the first called upon during the Q&A session that followed Luzhkov's speech. Amped up by a microphone to ensure that my question would be heard by everyone in the room, I related the story of how the Putnik building—originally an apartment building in grave disrepair—had been successfully and painstakingly reconstructed over a four-year period. I then described how, despite contract terms that had been agreed upon in advance among all partners, it had now been suddenly and surreptitiously privatized in the name of just one Russian minority partner. I then warned that if this was not corrected, foreign investment in Moscow would suffer greatly. In his response, Mayor Luzhkov confirmed that initial contracts such as ours were to be respected.

Luzhkov's remarks and his interchange with the audience garnered a lot of press coverage, especially his one-word response to a question about allegations of corruption within city agencies: *Absurd!*

The answer was more than a little disingenuous, since at the time, various arms of the city government were believed to be equity partners in no less than 168 enterprises similar to Putnik JV. In addition to stories in the local press, Fred Hiatt covered the mayor's address in the *Washington Post*. In his article, Hiatt described Luzhkov as the undisputed capo of Moscow.

Luzhkov is a despot ruling over a corrupt administration who stymies entrepreneurship and investment by keeping his hand in every possible venture. He controls everything from the sale of valuable land to the appearance of neighborhood shopfronts and has launched plans for grand skyscrapers and amusement parks while potholes make many city streets practically impassable.

… John S. Reuther, an American real estate developer here, described what many said was a typical case. Reuther and his partners owned 50 percent of a modern office building, occupied by prestigious foreign tenants. Three Russian partners—including a city agency—owned the other 50 percent.

Late last year, when the building had paid off its initial debts and was about to move into profitability, the city 'privatized' the building to the Russian side, cutting out the American partners. Now, Reuther said, the city agency said it will rectify that action, but only if the American side agrees to give up more than one-third of its equity—with the city agency, among others, picking up the difference.

'There's absolutely no logic to why [the Russian partners] should go up this much, and why it should all be at our expense,' Reuther said. 'That's one of the problems with the city still being part of what has essentially become a commercial business.'

About a week later, Michael Morgenstern and I attended a meeting at the office of Oleg Michailovich Tolkachyov, the chairman of Moskomimushestvo. At this meeting, Tolkachyov informed us that the city would not permit Kanopa to own more than 32 percent of the Putnik building. A joint stock company would become the building owner, and when that occurred, that 18 percent of our interest was to be taken from us and redistributed to the three Russian partners—PAIT, Unikombank, and Moskomimushestvo.

This was pretty much the same deal that the Moskomimushestvo deputy directors had already put forth. Tolkachyov's ostensible objection was that Kanopa was "foreign," but of course, that had been the original point of all the JVs that the Russians had encouraged. It seemed to me that Tolkachyov was using this as a pretext—but if he hadn't used this, he would have invented something else.

Even at the time, it was no secret that the single greatest inhibitor to investment in Russia was the perception of risk due to instability, specifically with regard to taxes on foreign profits and constantly changing laws affecting the rights of investors. With the Putnik building, the city of Moscow had an excellent, high visibility opportunity to show investors—both foreign and domestic—that this perception of unacceptable risk and instability was false. At the moment, however, the city was showing exactly the opposite.

The attempted seizure of our equity by Moskomimushestvo was totally without foundation. Going forward in discussions with the city and in court, we stated repeatedly that the precise division of ownership share and profit distribution rights among Putnik JV partners had been set forth in the official founding documents. Because these apportionments equated with our contributions to the Putnik JV capital fund, Kanopa's share of both ownership and profit distribution had been pegged at 50 percent. Our founding documents also stipulated that upon the successful reconstruction and leasing of the building, Kanopa was entitled to 50 percent of the profits for as long as Putnik JV had contractual rights to the property.

We pointed out that any organization that would be granted ownership of the Putnik building would be legally required to respect, honor and fulfill any contract obligations that the previous owner and tenants had concluded with Putnik JV. That would include distribution of profits according to equity ownership percentages of the JV partners.

One allegation that Moskomimushestvo put forward to justify their intention to appropriate a portion of our ownership share was that Putnik JV had not secured all necessary approvals to increase the square footage of the building to the extent that we had. This was not only false but a source of potential city embarrassment. We'd been meticulous throughout the construction period and could easily demonstrate that the city had issued us all the requisite architectural, engineering, fire, and safety permits. Our final, unassailable piece of evidence was our occupancy certificate, proof that the city had signed off on the building and had officially designated it as complete and fully in compliance with all requirements.

To counter fears of possible foreign ownership of the property, we noted that any new joint stock company owning the building would be a Russian legal entity, regardless of the percentage of ownership that a foreign partner might have. We also pointed out how "foreign" the building already was. In addition to being financed by a JV with 50 percent foreign ownership, funds for reconstruction had been prepaid by foreign tenants; the general contractor was a foreign entity; and most of the equipment, engineering systems, and finishing materials were of foreign origin. We then asked the key question: If it was legal for a foreign company to contribute 50 percent of the equity to the capital fund of a Russian joint venture to reconstruct a building, why would it not be permissible for that entity to have a similar share in the Russian company that would own the building after completion? At the time, we got no response to our objections—everything was being kicked upstairs to more senior government officials.

Not long after Mayor Luzhkov addressed the AmCham luncheon, I spoke with Leslie Brown, head of the commercial office at the embassy, to discuss whether Ambassador Pickering would be willing to meet personally with Mayor Luzhkov on our behalf. I was hopeful that the ambassador might convince him to intercede and right the wrong that had been done.

In a further communication with the ambassador, I told him that a compromise proposal from city representatives was already circulating that would increase the city's equity from 17 percent in the current joint venture to 22 percent in the joint stock company that would assume ownership of the building. To accommodate this increase, Kanopa was prepared to reduce its equity by the full 5 percent. Beyond that, however, we saw no justification for a further 13 percent reduction of our share, a decrease that would benefit PAIT and raise their equity from 17.1 percent to 30 percent, as reflected in a protocol signed by all three Russian partners on June 3, 1994.

Ambassador Pickering was most cooperative and held a personal meeting with the mayor to discuss our case, as well as others where American investor rights were being threatened. On August 12, 1994, Mayor Luzhkov wrote to Ambassador Pickering. Leslie Brown faxed me a copy of the Embassy's English translation.

Dear Ambassador Pickering:

On your request, the Government of Moscow have considered the situation with the Putnik Joint Venture founded by a number of companies, including the company Kanopa Holdings Ltd. headed by Mr. John Reuther.

It should be admitted that a number of mistakes, caused by the imperfection of the legislative basis, were made by some officials of Moskomimushchestvo (the Moscow Committee on Property) during the determination of the right of ownership of the building located at 22/25 Bolshoy Strochenovsky Pereulok.

After a thorough consideration of the problem by the experts of the Moscow Government, I gave a respective order to the management of Moskomimushchestvo, which will meet with the conflicting parties in the nearest future and make proposals concerning the settlement of the problem. I would like to point out that these proposals will be aimed at the restoration of rights of the company headed by Mr. Reuther.

Sincerely,

Yuri Luzhkov

Mayor of Moscow

Mayor Luzhkov appointed one of his top aides, Andrei Borodin, to investigate and meet with all parties, then get back to the mayor with a full report. Borodin found that PAIT's Ownership Certificate had been illegally issued and called for it to be recalled. He recommended to the mayor that JV Putnik be declared the one true investor, but that, since the Putnik building reconstruction was "an investment project located in the Central Administrative District, the city was entitled to 50 percent ownership." He then recommended that the other 50 percent be distributed among the Putnik JV partners, with 30.1 percent to Kanopa, 10.3 percent to PAIT, and 9.6 percent to Unikombank.

At some point after Popov had illicitly taken control of the Putnik bank accounts, it became clear that he was in cahoots with Unikombank and the city. All three claimed that our role was merely to finance the project, with no—or very greatly reduced—right to residual ownership. In one pivotal meeting orchestrated by Misha, he and Michael met privately with Popov and the representatives of Unikombank and the city. Misha made it look like we would give into their demands if they and we all signed a document that Misha had prepared. This document essentially admitted that the three had colluded at our expense. Misha passed around copies for the others to sign, which they did. When it came to our turn, Misha put the documents they had all signed into his briefcase. He and Michael then abruptly left. Popov and the other two then realized they had been played.

This was a pivotal moment. In the court hearings that followed, Popov was admonished by the judges for the forged documents and lost his case. After that, Unikombank and the city distanced themselves from Popov.

Popov tried to continue to fight us in court, but he eventually realized that if we didn't come to an agreement among ourselves to privatize the building in a way that reflected our existing equity in Putnik JV, Borodin's recommendations to the mayor would prevail. With the understanding that 17.1 percent for PAIT was better than 10.3 percent, Popov agreed to a truce and a joint management agreement. Ownership of the building was transferred to the Putnik Limited Liability Company according to our original equity percentages, and we worked in partnership with him from then on. The city of Moscow ended up with 17 percent of the building, which reflected its original ownership share in Putnik JV.

Aftermath

Kanopa and PAIT eventually bought out the equity of both Unikombank and the city of Moscow. As a result, Kanopa owned 72.4 percent of both Putnik Limited and the building, and PAIT owned the rest. In 2013, Andrei Popov was diagnosed with an advanced case of stomach cancer and passed away on October 28 of that year.

Andrei Borodin became CEO and co-owner of the Bank of Moscow. In April of 2011, having fallen out of favor with Vladimir Putin, he fled to London to avoid prosecution. In February of 2013, despite being accused of committing massive fraud through his position at the bank and being placed on an Interpol Red Notice, he was granted political asylum by David Cameron's government in the UK. Perhaps not surprisingly, he has since been the target of multiple assassination plots. In addition, as noted in the UK *Telegraph* newspaper article of March 1, 2013, soon after Borodin fled to London, he bought Britain's most expensive home, Park Place Estate, near Henley-on-Thames in Oxfordshire. The sales price was £140 million ($219 million at that time).

The fraud that Borodin was alleged to have committed is intriguing. He was accused of making $440 million worth of improper loans to shell companies. The money from those companies was then transferred to a female construction mogul—Mrs. Yuri Luzhkov, the wife of the mayor of Moscow.

CHAPTER 25

1994-1996

Adventures in Housing

My relationship with Vera grew deeper and more loving by the day. After she had a talk with Valery, her ex, he agreed to move out until she could find a place of her own. She eventually found an apartment and signed a renovation contract with a company run by Dragan Stoyanovic—chief architect of Jastrebac, later Contrex—but it would take some time to get it ready. Meanwhile, Vera and her daughter Anya spent most weekends with me. They were a source of love and strength in what had become frustrating times.

(With Vera and Anya in Moscow)

Vera provided so much more than emotional support. She also helped me connect with potential business clients and partners. In 1994, she introduced me to Oleg Pogrebniak, president of the East European Association of Business Cooperation. Pogrebniak wanted to explore possible development of American style single family homes in the Moscow area and was particularly interested in manufactured housing made of light gauge steel framing. I knew that this was a product that my friend Frank Brady could provide. Several years earlier, I'd met Frank, whose company, Shelter International, manufactured modular housing and was headquartered in Morristown, New Jersey.

Other than dachas—the weekend retreats and summer houses that were perks for high-ranking party and government officials—very few single-family homes had been built during the Soviet era. Many Moscow residents lived in co-op apartments. Built in the 1950s and 1960s, these drab, cookie-cutter, five-story walk-up "Khrushchev buildings" had gone up all over the city. Occupants had their own separate living and sleeping quarters but shared both kitchen and bathroom facilities with other units on their floor. The disputes and clashes created by this arrangement were as acrimonious as they were predictable.

The demise of the Soviet Union and the rise of the wild and woolly Russian free market economy created a nouveau riche business class, and with it a fierce demand for quality housing. For these newly flush entrepreneurs, a single-family home was a prized status symbol, but what they coveted was almost nonexistent—which meant that building them now presented a great business opportunity.

That opportunity was not without challenges. Building almost anything took more time in Russia than it did in the United States, and the problems weren't all due to the massive amounts of red tape generated at both the local and national level. Severe Russian winters meant that the ground in the Moscow area was likely to heave as it froze and settle as it thawed, so new single-family construction required an extra deep foundation to ensure that the home retained its structural integrity.

In September of 1994, Oleg Pogrebniak asked me to work with him to build developments of steel and/or wood-frame single-family homes in and around Moscow. His company was engaged in real estate development, and I suggested we conclude a development and project management agreement that would cover not just single-family housing but also offices, apartments, hotels and other commercial development.

We expected to import most of what we needed from the States, specifically from Shelter International, at least at the outset. As soon as possible, we planned to switch over to locally available materials and components instead. Our goal was to maximize use of Russian-made building components and materials which would be manufactured to Shelter International specifications.

The participants on my company's side would be Vera and me in Moscow, and Tom Weber in the States. Tom would assist with coordination and scheduling for the ten-person Russian delegation Oleg wanted to bring to the States to see how manufactured single-family homes were produced. At the time, Oleg was president of the Western Division of the Russian Chamber of Commerce, so we concluded a services agreement between JSR Holdings (my Cyprus company), and the Russian Chamber of Commerce.

I prepared a preliminary budget of $31,000, expedited the US visa application process, and organized the two-week program, including hotel reservations, a 15-passenger minibus, and meal arrangements. I also set up entertainment, business, and social arrangements, including tickets to a Broadway musical. The trip was paid for by the Russian Chamber of Commerce. Because Vera and I were members of the delegation, our travel costs were included in the budget, as was a modest retainer for my company.

With Shelter International as the US sponsoring organization, I extended the invitation for members of the delegation to come to New York and New Jersey. During their time in the States, they would explore a possible contract with Shelter International for approximately fifty prefab units for the Uspenskoe housing complex in the Moscow suburbs.

After commercial and technical meetings at Shelter International offices in Morristown, we toured several sites where Shelter International components were being used in construction, then spent our last two days in Washington, sightseeing and shopping. We also enjoyed a cocktail reception at my parents' home. The large, brick home I grew up in came with two full lots. When Mom and Dad sold the house—to a member of Congress—they retained ownership of the side lot and constructed a prefab wooden home for themselves there.

On the eve of the delegation's return to Moscow, we attended a farewell cocktail gathering in an elegant two-story townhouse in Georgetown. This event was especially meaningful to me, because it was hosted by my wife, Jill. We had a wonderful evening and it was the start of a warm and enduring friendship between Vera and Jill.

Although we had a productive experience with this visit to the States, and we continued for some time to study possible business relationships between the parties, no serious work came out of this for me down the road.

Mom's Diagnosis

Vera and I began making periodic trips to the States. We often stayed in Washington with my parents, but at the end of 1994, we flew to Florida with Anya to spend the holidays with them. For many years, Mom and Dad kept a winter home in Fort Myers on the banks of the Orange River. The house originally belonged to Uncle Walter and Aunt May—it was to be their retirement home. Their daughters, Linda and Elizabeth, inherited it after the fatal plane crash, and eventually sold it to my parents.

(With Vera, Anya and Dad)

(Anya with Mom)

By this time, Mom's health was in decline. She was already suffering from Parkinson's disease when she was diagnosed with stomach cancer. Her doctor indicated that this was a localized tumor and scheduled her for surgery to remove it.

Mom was always very organized. Before we brought her to the hospital in Washington, she went through her files and documents to "put her affairs in order" in case she never came home. On the night before her operation, she sat me down in the living room and produced two slips of paper: a grocery store coupon from a local newspaper and a store receipt. "Two weeks ago," she began, "I sent your father to shop for groceries, and I gave him this discount coupon for frozen orange juice. John, your father didn't use this coupon. He paid... full price."

Mom had always been extremely frugal and uttered the words "full price" with great distaste. In our family, buying everything at a discount was a way of life—I was the kid who'd gone to a black-tie function at the White House in a bargain basement dinner jacket and pair of home-made tuxedo pants Mom had created by sewing satin ribbon over the side seam on a pair of black trousers. Handing me both the coupon and the receipt, she assigned me an errand: I was to go to the store and demand that they honor the coupon and refund the difference.

In the morning, Vera and I drove my parents to the hospital and helped Mom check in for her surgery. Dad stayed with her while Vera and I went to the grocery store, coupon and receipt in hand. The store manager readily issued the refund, but to make sure that Mom didn't think I'd covered the small sum out of my own pocket, he put an official store stamp on the receipt, together with an explanatory note bearing his title and signature.

Soon after the operation began, Mom's surgeons discovered that her malignancy had already metastasized. Her condition was terminal. They closed the incision, then broke the sad news to my father. When Mom came out of anesthesia, he couldn't bear to tell her the truth—in part, I think, because he couldn't bear accepting it himself. He led her to believe that the surgery had gone well but neglected to tell me that's what he'd done. I visited with her assuming she already knew her prognosis, and inadvertently became the one who told her she was dying.

I realized that sometimes I could be an honest fool, but true to her no-nonsense nature, Mom thanked me for being straightforward. "Your father is a coward and didn't have the nerve to give me the bad news," she declared.

Anya

As Russia emerged from communism, it had to grapple with its Soviet-era school system and doctrinaire curriculum. There was much to be undone; virtually every textbook had to be rewritten. Vera and Valery wanted the best education possible for Anya, then twelve, but had no confidence she'd be able to get it in Moscow because the pace of improving and updating their schools was far too slow.

In September 1995, Vera and Valery got Anya enrolled at Clayesmore Preparatory School in Dorset in southwest England. A Russian classmate, Dima Adamovsky, had been admitted at the same time, and Vera and I flew to England with Dima and his parents to get the children settled in for the start of the school year.

The head of school did his best to help Anya adjust, but her initial months at Clayesmore were nevertheless difficult. As her English improved, however, she rose to the challenge and began to make new friends. Vera and I saw her on school breaks and holidays. For winter break in 1995, we flew with her to DC, then drove south to see my parents in Fort Myers.

By this time, my father had become Mom's full-time caregiver. She could no longer walk. The cancer had spread to her esophagus, and she was having trouble swallowing. Despite her weakened condition, she was clearly thrilled with the lovely vest that Anya had made for her for Christmas. It was to be the last time we saw her.

In the summer of 1996, Vera and Valery had to pull Anya out of Clayesmore. For financial reasons, it had become necessary for Anya to continue her studies in the UK through another education consulting organization, which arranged for her to study at Leighton Park School in Reading. The problem was not the tuition at Clayesmore, but the fee charged by the previous consulting company, with whom Vera and Valery had severed ties.

Vera's Fashion Business

During the Soviet era, Vera had made a living purchasing high end women's clothing in Paris and reselling it to clients in Moscow. Her business was very successful, but it was entirely under the table. Once the USSR dissolved, however, she was left with a sterling reputation as an excellent businesswoman—a Russian TV station even included a segment on her success in a national broadcast.

Vera was hired to manage Danata, an upscale fashion boutique. The boutique was under the control of Umar Dzhabrailov, a wealthy and influential Chechen businessman who had named the shop after his daughter. In time, he opened a second boutique, which he called Danata II. In early 1996, he made Vera that store manager.

Danata was located in the Radisson Slavyanskaya Hotel. Although the hotel itself was quite new, it had undergone substantial remodeling in 1992 to make room for a business center. Umar represented the Moscow City Property Committee's interest in the hotel and the key American partner in the business center joint venture was my colleague, and fellow American Chamber of Commerce member, Paul Tatum. When they gutted a number of the Radisson's guest rooms to create the business center, Paul had been the man who facilitated our purchase of the hotel bathroom fixtures that were no longer needed. This arrangement proved to be essential for the timely completion of the IBM apartments in the Putnik building.

I often visited Vera at the boutique, and sometimes dropped in to see Umar, her boss. I also got together with Paul Tatum; the two of us would commiserate over lunch about the difficulties we faced with our Russian business partners.

I went out of my way not to see Tatum and Dzhabrailov on the same visit as it was an understatement to say that the business partners did not get along. A piece in *Fortune* described why:

In the spring of 1994, Tatum accused the joint venture's general director, a man named Vladimir Draitser (whom Tatum himself had recruited), of embezzling funds. Tatum cut Draitser's phone lines and access to bank accounts, barred him from the hotel, and declared his contract expired. Draitser posted a brigade of guards at the Slavyanskaya entrance to keep Tatum out... Tatum won a court order allowing him back into the hotel. He returned with a battalion of bodyguards and refused to leave, camping out in his office...

On Valentine's Day 1995, one of Tatum's bodyguards... was stabbed in the chest with a penknife. His assailant said, "Tell Paul it's high time he left for home." Tatum hired a 24-hour brigade of guards, started wearing a bulletproof vest, and began using a cellular phone exclusively, contending his phone lines were bugged...

That April, Tatum decided to pitch what he hoped would be a decisive battle, filing a $35 million lawsuit against the Moscow City Property Committee for discriminating against foreign investors. The case would be heard in Stockholm at an international arbitration court, which increasingly had been sought out by embittered Westerners seeking an escape route from deteriorating joint ventures. But Tatum needed $150,000 to pay court costs. So, he took out full-page ads in Moscow newspapers offering to sell investors "Freedom bonds," promissory notes that would pay back a 100 percent return in six months, when he expected to be flush with court-awarded winnings. The bonds were to mature on April 2, 1997, his 42nd birthday...

In fall of 1996, Vera and I were in the Radisson coffee shop when I saw Paul walk by and asked him to join us. Twenty feet away, his two bodyguards stood alert and vigilant as we talked. When I introduced Paul to Vera and told him she ran Dzhabrailov's Danata II boutique, he asked, "Is your shop also selling narcotics, like Dzhabrailov?"

Vera denied it, of course, but we both knew that Paul could be abrasive. Not surprisingly, he was involved in numerous acrimonious disputes—not just with Dzhabrailov, but with his American partners as well. Seeing him with his bodyguards, it occurred to me how vulnerable he was when he was out in public. Despite his protection, anyone could open fire and gun him down.

Several months later, that's exactly what happened. On the evening of November 3, Paul left the Radisson Center on foot and headed for the metro at the adjacent Kiev train station. He had two bodyguards with him, one on each side, but it didn't help. As he descended the outdoor stairs to enter the metro, a gunman with an assault rifle opened fire from the railing overhanging the stairwell. He died instantly.

The way *Fortune* described the assassination left no doubt that it was a contract hit:

> *The 5.45-caliber Kalashnikov assault rifle was fired so expertly as to rule out a nonprofessional. Five of the twelve bullets entered at the neck, indicating the killer knew Tatum might be wearing his bulletproof vest. Whoever fired was well trained in preventing the weapon's powerful kick from spraying passersby. Both Tatum's bodyguards were unharmed.*

Just a few days after the murder and Paul's memorial service, Vera and I went to see Umar Dzhabrailov. He knew that I had been a colleague of Paul's, and he adamantly insisted that he was not responsible for Paul's killing. He then played a message—in American-accented English—on his office answering machine. "We know you did this, Umar, and we're going to make you pay."

During their long-running dispute, Paul had publicly accused Dzhabrailov of planning to kill him, but I never believed that Umar had anything to do with it. It seemed to me that their clash was too public, and Dzhabrailov was too smart to believe he could rid himself of his problems by killing Paul. I think it is more likely that Paul got into money difficulties with someone else—someone who finally came to collect when Paul couldn't or wouldn't deliver.

Did it affect Umar's reputation? It did not. He ran for president of Russia in 2000, the year that Vladimir Putin was first elected. He was later elected to the Federation Council, the upper house of the Russian parliament, serving from 2004 to 2009.

The Death of Sophie Reuther

By early 1996, Mom needed more care than Dad could give her at home. She was transferred to a hospice in Florida, and I knew that her life was nearing its end. After not taking nourishment for three days, she started slipping in and out of consciousness. The cancer had taken over her body; there was not much left of her except her lucid mind and strong heart. I called daily, and Dad always answered—he never left her side. He would then hold the phone to her cheek so she and I could talk.

We had planned a family celebration in her honor in DC that would be held on April 13, four days after her eighty-third birthday. She already understood that it would take place without her, but as happy as she was about the gathering, she worried that Dad would be lonely. Dad told me that she took his hand and gave him his marching orders: "Go out and find a new lover!" she said.

On February 19, Dad let me know that her death was imminent. When I called, he held the phone to her ear. He'd already warned me that although she could hear me, she could no longer speak. It was all I could do not to cry, but I needed to tell my mother how much I loved her and how much she'd shaped the man I'd become. I told her that throughout my life, whenever I had done something right, it was because I had listened to her and to Dad, and whenever I had done something wrong, it was because I had not. Mom passed away hours later, very early on February 20.

I had the sad task of writing to Anya to let her know that the woman she knew and loved as Nana had passed away.

Although she was almost 83 years old and had been very sick with cancer for three years, it's so difficult to accept that she is gone. I spoke with her for the last time on Tuesday, and I gave her all of our love, from you and Vera, too!

You only came to know Nana during the last years of her life, when she was already quite ill and weak. But I will always remember with such pride how you brought love and happiness to her with your genuine and open affection. She loved you very much, Anya, and I am so pleased that you and she were able to spend the time that you did together. It makes me feel much better just thinking about that.

With much love,

John

In an era when women were expected to take a back seat to their husbands, my mother never did. She was always so much more than Mrs. Victor Reuther—and Dad loved that about her. Her *New York Times* obituary acknowledged her accomplishments, her wit, her compassion, and her willingness to speak truth to power.

In April 1938, two gun-wielding anti-union thugs forced their way into Sophie Reuther's 25th birthday party at Walter Reuther's Detroit apartment (a delivery of Chinese food had been expected), and began pistol whipping her brother-in-law until a guest scrambled out a second-story window and began shouting for the police.

When the police, widely assumed to be in the pay of the automakers, began a perfunctory investigation and asked Mrs. Reuther to describe the thugs, she did not miss a beat. "They looked very much like you," she said...

Known as a woman who recognized no limitations on what she could do, Mrs. Reuther obtained a fine arts degree from George Washington University at the age of 55 in 1968, and was a Robert F. Kennedy delegate to the Democratic National Convention that year.

It was during an official union visit to India that year that Mrs. Reuther left her husband with the enduring image of her humanity. At a mine near Calcutta, he recalled, a miner's widow, an untouchable, approached his wife, bent down, and kissed her shoe.

Then, in a breach of caste protocol, "my Sophie reached down and lifted the woman up and embraced her." Mr. Reuther recalled. "The women were shocked. The men were shocked."

"That was my Sophie," he said. "She felt a kinship with the suffering of all people."

In mid-April, just as planned, my father hosted a very special gathering of family and friends in Washington to celebrate Mother's extraordinary life. Vera, Anya and I flew to Washington to be there. We wouldn't have missed it for anything.

(One of my favorite portraits of Mom)

CHAPTER 26

1995-1998

Housing for Embassy Employees

In early March of 1995, our embassy in Moscow sought bids from developers and site owners to build apartments for embassy personnel. The Notice of Bid Solicitation stated that the embassy was interested in "up to eighty housing units… suitable for single employees, couples, and families with up to three children." The residences were to be ready for occupancy within two years, by sometime in 1997. This would be a turnkey operation, and it was emphasized that "no funding would be provided by the United States government for the design or construction required for these residences."

Expressions of interest in this project were due by March 21. After paying the $25 fee to register as an interested party, I was handed the official submission requirements, but I was unable to identify an appropriate site and chose not to respond.

I assumed that was the end of it, but five months later, Vera introduced me to Gregory Katsev. Vera and Gregory had been friends for many years. Like Valery, Vera's ex-husband, Katsev had had a successful career in the music business but had since moved on. He was now engaged in residential and commercial real estate development and had financed several small projects in Moscow with the help of some of his prosperous former associates from the entertainment world.

When we first met, Gregory told me he had a site on Trubnikovsky Pereulok that was located a block from the American embassy. At the time, he knew nothing of the embassy's need for housing, but wanted my advice on how to secure construction financing for the nine-story apartment/office complex he intended to build. I realized immediately that his site would be ideal for the embassy project. Located on a quiet street a block south of the main embassy entrance and a block east of one of Moscow's major shopping and commercial streets, it was not just close to the embassy, but also convenient to entertainment and recreation amenities.

Gregory's original plans called for a structure of approximately 15,000 square meters (about 162,000 square feet), and a two-level subterranean garage for 54 cars. To meet embassy specifications, the project would require some redesign to maximize apartments rather than office and commercial space, but we knew what they were asking for was feasible.

(Trubnikovski Pereulok No. 13 construction)

When I told the embassy housing office about Gregory's site, they were immediately interested. Days later, he and I escorted their team to see it firsthand. Proximity to the embassy was a huge plus, but the team also liked the preliminary plans and the fact that Gregory had a Slovenian contractor who was already committed to the project and was scheduled to begin work within the month.

The embassy housing office then confirmed that although they were interested in a proposal from us, they feared they might not be able to afford it. In a way, the site was too good. The location was so close to the embassy and to shopping areas that it might be too convenient, and therefore more expensive than they could afford.

They let it slip that they could not accept proposals in the $800 to $900 per square meter range, which at the time was the market rate for office space in that area. Gregory really wanted to make this project work and was prepared to come in lower. We came up with an offer of a fixed rental rate of less than $550 per square meter per year for an initial six-year term.

Prior to meeting with the embassy representatives, Gregory had prepared a preliminary cost estimate of $18 million, but we knew there were several factors that could increase the cost. The city of Moscow owned 40 percent of the project with Gregory's company, and if we were going to conclude an agreement with the embassy, it would make sense for the developer to buy out the city's interest, which would add another $2 million. Other add-ons would come from revisions to technical specifications and apartment layouts to meet embassy requirements, as well as from the purchase and installation of built-ins such as appliances.

A line item for project management would also be over and above the $18 million estimate. This would essentially cover my involvement, and that of Tom Weber. Tom's wife Lydia, who was of Ukrainian heritage and spoke fluent Russian, was open to the prospect of returning to Moscow and working with Tom for several years on the construction management phase of this project, even though she had just given birth to their second child.

I prepared a proposal for Gregory regarding participation costs for Tom and me. This included fees for handling bid preparation and lease negotiations, and for organizing the financing. It also covered compensation for construction management, which would involve liaison with the embassy, the developer, and the contractors.

Our first priority, of course, was to secure financing. Gregory had already received a commitment of $5 million from local investors, including a Russian bank that wanted offices in the complex. I was hopeful that Tom would be able to raise enough from alternative sources that we could avoid having the bank as a tenant, because it was already clear that the embassy was looking for exclusive use of the entire building.

If the embassy carried through on this intention, that bank would not be the only disappointed prospective tenant. When Vera had introduced me to Gregory, she let me know that she looked forward to purchasing an apartment in the building. For his part, Gregory was quite willing to make that happen, and not just out of friendship. Vera had made valuable introductions for him to city officials controlling the site. Offering her an apartment at a considerable discount was an acknowledgment of how much he valued what she'd already done for him.

Tom and I would work with Gregory to prepare the leasing bid package, so I expected to agree on a separate fee for this phase of the work, and it was clear that this fee would not be paid if we failed to organize the financing. While Tom worked on that aspect of the project with his contacts in the States, I planned to approach international banks in Moscow.

Beyond our involvement in finding financing, I had to convince Gregory and his contractor that they needed Tom and me for construction management. In addition, we had to come to terms on a fee that would cover compensation for Tom and Lydia, including their travel expenses, housing, and health insurance. I then had to have a conversation with Tom about the need to downsize his compensation expectations. A few years earlier with Perestroika and Putnik, I'd received $150,000 a year, and he'd received $100,000, but since then, it had become far more difficult to get Russian organizations to pay anything near that much. At Putnik, I was now receiving the same salary as the Russian directors—$600/month in rubles, minus Russian taxes. Nevertheless, I promised Tom that I would try to set up a fee structure with Gregory that would be in the range of what he had received from Putnik. This would be essential if we were to lure Tom and Lydia back to Moscow.

Of course, everything depended on getting the deal with the embassy and securing our financing, and speed was essential for several reasons. If the embassy turned this project down, Gregory intended to press forward with his original plan. He wanted to begin selling office and apartment suites as currently designed because he had to generate the advance of $2.2 million that he would need to pay the general contractor to begin work.

Another reason we needed to move quickly was that Tom had received a fax from our friend Dragan Stoyanovich, the lead architect of Contrex, our Putnik contractor, telling him that Searle— a major pharmaceutical company—was putting up a plant near Moscow, and Dragan's company was building it. Searle needed a site manager to represent Searle's interests, and Dragan thought Tom would be ideal for the job.

I sent Tom an email with additional information on Gregory's project, but I also let him know that I was aware that Dragan had reached out to him, and that I had no intention of holding him back. I advised him to keep his options open since we didn't know whether we would get the lease and financing on the embassy project.

On September 7, 1995, Gregory and I submitted our formal proposal. We supported it with a mountain of documents, including the project plans and renditions, a copy of all Moscow government-issued project rights and approvals in Russian and English, a list with photographs of Moscow real estate projects and buildings then currently under the management of Gregory's and my related companies, a list of developer references, and full information on the project general contractor, E. E. Engineering.

We offered them two rental options, including one that was substantially lower than the going market rate in this prime location. On

September 21, Gregory received a formal letter of intent from the embassy, and we were told to plan for meetings in Rosslyn, Virginia in early October with the head of the realty office review team at the State Department office of Foreign Building Operations (FBO). We understood these would be both technical and commercial negotiations, and that this department had already met with all the other bidders.

From the beginning, we'd been upfront about the fact that Gregory's project as initially envisioned did not fully comply with embassy specifications. That said, we were equally forthcoming about his being willing to make the design changes they wanted, provided that they accepted the commercial terms we had proposed. Reasonably enough, of course, Gregory refused to make those revisions unless and until he received their commitment to lease the units.

And this is where the project sat—in limbo—for more than three years.

(Trubnikovski Pereulok No. 13 building)

In March of 1998, Vera and I flew to Washington, then set off on a long road trip to Arkansas to visit Carole, my sister. Carole had been battling the little-known and still incurable autoimmune disorder called scleroderma, which affects skin, joints, and internal organs. I had heard that scleroderma may be triggered by stress, and I think this had been the case with Carole. When our mother Sophie was struggling through her last days of life, Carole and her husband Jim were in the process of moving from Illinois to Arkansas. As a result, Carole had been unable to come to Fort Myers and say her last goodbyes. We enjoyed our visit with Carole and her family, but this turned out to be the last time I saw her. She passed away from scleroderma the following year.

Our embassy housing negotiations resumed soon after Vera and I returned. In April of 1998, we confirmed a build-lease agreement with the embassy for forty-three apartments, after which they invoked their option to purchase the premises outright. There was one condition, however: we had to secure the approval of the Russian Foreign Ministry.

Our embassy had been pursuing this approval since August 1997, but on January 23, 1998, their request to purchase the Trubnikovsky apartments had been officially denied. One possible reason was that this was a case of tit for tat that involved alleged bad behavior by Russians in Manhattan. New York's then-mayor Rudy Giuliani alleged—with some justification—that Russians attached to their UN delegation were flagrantly abusing their diplomatic privilege. During the first six months of 1996, the 122 vehicles of the Russian UN mission racked up 14,437 parking and traffic citations in the city. The number of tickets, along with the fact that none of them had been paid, really angered New Yorkers—so much so that Giuliani asked that the worst repeat offenders be expelled from the mission and sent home.

Another reason was financial. Most of the housing where our embassy employees resided was leased to the embassy by UPDKh, a division of the Russian Foreign Ministry. During the Soviet period, UPDKh had a lock on leasing office and housing facilities to diplomats, foreign correspondents, and foreign businesspeople working in Moscow. Now, however, their units faced stiff competition from more modern apartments built by free market commercial developers. It was highly likely that our embassy would cancel any remaining rental agreements with UPDKh as soon as the Trubnikovsky units were ready for occupancy, and I suspected that the Foreign Ministry was reluctant to lose that revenue stream.

UPDKh already had a history of trying to control the market to their advantage. When Perestroika JV offered office premises to foreign companies in the late 1980s, UPDKh had tried to prevent it. They told several foreign businesses, including ABC News, that they were required to lease premises exclusively from UPDKh and no one else. This wasn't true, but only after our lawyers furnished UPDKh with copies of Soviet legislation allowing joint ventures like Perestroika to offer both housing and office space to foreign entities—including corporations, journalists, and diplomatic missions—did they back off.

As soon as they conceded that ABC had the right to lease space from us, however, they tried a different strongarm tactic. They threatened ABC News with the loss of all their Russian employees, who at the time were required to be hired through UPDKh. Perestroika lost ABC News as a prospective client, but several years later they contracted with another developer for their own building.

Even though we had been turned down by UPDKh, Gregory and I never imagined that *nyet* would be the final answer. The city of Moscow was our partner in the project, and we were meeting with highly placed individuals in city government. We anticipated that the city would use its clout to pressure the Foreign Ministry to reconsider in our favor.

At the same time, Gregory was approaching the problem from another direction. He began negotiating with the quasi-commercial department of UPDKh to come in as an equity partner in Respect-R LLC. Respect-R LLC was the Russian investment and development company that Gregory had created with two co-investors, both successful Russian joint stock companies, specifically for this project.

We knew that UPDKh had already partnered with a number of Western developers on several projects in Moscow, including housing developments and a golf club. Since learning of the rejection in January,

Respect-R had met twice with top-level UPDKh representatives. The tacit understanding was that as soon as UPDKh confirmed its participation in Respect-R LLC, our embassy would get the green light from the Russian Foreign Ministry.

As we sought to understand the basis for the ministry's objections, we were told that the *lease* of the units would have been less problematic than the *sale*. If Foreign Ministry approval was not granted within a reasonable time, we understood that this might have to become our fallback option. With that in mind, we negotiated a revision to our agreement with the embassy in April of 1998. It stated that if the Russian Foreign Ministry prohibited selling the units to the US government, our agreement would revert to a leasehold basis, pursuant to the original terms dating from September of 1996.

At the time, we saw this as a safety precaution. Based on information from our sources inside UPDKh, we believed that everything had been resolved, and that Foreign Ministry approval would soon follow.

We believed wrong.

On July 6, 1998, our embassy made another appeal to the Russian Foreign Ministry for reconsideration of their denial. A month later, the answer was still no.

This put us in a bind. Although we had a sales agreement with the US government and over $15.5 million of US government funds had been allocated and transferred by cable to the US Embassy Moscow account, we could not secure financing and begin construction while there was still a good chance that the Russian government would put a stop to the project. The embassy continued appealing to the Foreign Ministry on a regular basis, asking that they reconsider, but no one could predict how they would respond—or when.

Accordingly, we realized that we had to set a deadline for ourselves. We suggested that if the embassy had not received a final, positive response from the ministry by September 28, the parties would agree that the terms of the agreement would revert to a leasehold situation.

On August 12, the embassy request was again denied, which meant that we would go forward with the units on a leasehold rather than sales basis. Meanwhile, however, the economic climate in Russia went south. A major Russian banking crisis prevented us from pivoting to the lease alternative. This abject collapse of the Russian banking system was accompanied by an enormous jump in inflation. The value of the ruble cratered. As a result, we were never able to make this project work for the embassy. Respect-R had to revert to marketing office space and apartments to local Russian clients. In time, Gregory Katsev was able to do exactly that.

Given these deplorable economic conditions, Yeltsin's government lost public support. He tried to rectify the situation by firing Prime Minister Kiriyenko and reappointing former Prime Minister Chernomyrdin, but the Duma refused to consent. Yeltsin then nominated Yevgeny Primakov, the very popular foreign minister, as prime minister. I knew Primakov personally. In April 1988, he'd been the Soviet leader of our joint US-Soviet delegation to Afghanistan. With strong support in the Duma, he was confirmed in September of 1998.

CHAPTER 27

1998-2003

Moving On with Our Lives

It was a time of both endings and new beginnings. In 1998, Michael Morgenstern decided to stop working in Russia and return to the United States. Through our respective companies, Misha Pankin and I bought out Michael's interests in our joint projects on a 50/50 basis. As a result, my company received 40 percent of the profits from our B. Ordynka project and held an equal 50/50 ownership with Misha's company of the foreign equity in Putnik Joint Venture.

Meanwhile, back in the States, my brother Eric and his fiancée Deborah had moved into our DC family home with Dad. Vera and I then rented a two-bedroom apartment in Chevy Chase, Maryland, a short drive from there.

We bought our furniture for the apartment from Scan, a nearby Scandinavian store. Vera and I developed a friendly relationship with James, the African American salesman who sold us our couches, chairs and bedroom set. When he met Anya on one of her visits to DC, he told us that he, too, had a daughter. James was very proud that she sang in their church choir and invited us to come hear her sing.

The church was located in Southeast Washington, and as soon as we arrived with Anya on Sunday morning, we realized that we would be the only Caucasians in the congregation. During his sermon, the pastor asked everyone who was attending services there for the first time to please stand. I felt a little self-conscious as I rose to my feet, but in seconds, all that awkwardness disappeared. A substantial portion of the congregation walked over to where we were standing and greeted us warmly. "Welcome! We're so glad you're here," they said. Their greetings were accompanied by eye contact, warm smiles, and a hug or a firm handshake; there was no doubt that each member of the welcoming committee was absolutely genuine and sincere. It was a wonderful, unforgettable experience for all of us.

With all the time Vera and I were now spending in the States, we decided to enroll Anya in a boarding school in the DC area rather than in England. Our family had kept in close touch all these years with Toni House, my brother Eric's first wife. After a long stint as a reporter for *The Washington Star*, Toni became the public information officer for the US Supreme Court, a position roughly analogous to being White House press secretary.

Toni recommended that Anya apply to the Madeira School. Madeira is a highly regarded girls prep school in McLean, Virginia, with both boarding and day students on its 373-acre campus. The school counts Brooke Astor, Katharine Graham, Mika Brzezinski, and Stockard Channing among its distinguished alumnae. Although it was too late in the application period for Anya to take entrance exams, they nevertheless agreed to interview her on the strength of Toni's recommendation.

Madeira also asked Anya to submit an original essay for their review. Her assignment was to write about a valuable and meaningful experience in her life, one that had influenced her outlook and values. Anya chose to write about attending services at the African American church, an experience that had affected her profoundly. Her writing impressed me, and it must have impressed the Madeira admissions office as well because Anya matriculated there as a ninth-grade boarding student in September of 1997.

Jill was gracious enough to host Anya at her Georgetown condo during school breaks at Madeira when Vera and I were in Moscow, and my old friend Barbara Salkin, with whom I'd worked on the Birch Bayh presidential campaign in 1970-71 and who had helped in my own congressional campaign of 1974, also welcomed Anya into her Gaithersburg, Maryland home. Barbara at the time ran a nonprofit exchange organization that brought Russian high school sports teams to the US and sent US teams to Russia. By pure coincidence, Galina Brakina, Vera's sister, worked for the Russian side of this program.

In early 1998, Jill and I finally completed our divorce. Vera and I were married on May 29, 1998, in Rockville, Maryland, in the backyard of the home of my cousin, Theo Reuther, and his wife Patty. Theo's father was Uncle Ted—the oldest son who'd stayed behind in Wheeling, West Virginia to support Grandpa Val and Grandma Anna when Walter, Roy, and Victor left for Detroit to get jobs in the auto industry. Anya, of course, was present at the wedding, as were my father and my brother Eric.

Soon thereafter, Vera, Anya, and I were driving around Bethesda and saw a house for sale. When we called the broker to get more information, she told us that it was already in escrow, but she had another in mind that she thought we might like. She was right. We loved it instantly and quickly signed a purchase agreement. Our two-story home had a master bedroom on the ground floor, three bedrooms on the second floor, and another two in the finished basement—plenty of room for Anya, Sasha, and Chris, and for other visitors as well. There was also a home theater, with a fireplace in the basement and steps that led up to the pool in the large backyard.

We had wonderful neighbors in Bethesda, one of whom had a pleasant, responsible young Lithuanian woman named Gintare who worked part-time for them. We soon offered her one of the spare bedrooms as a place to live in exchange for forwarding our mail to us in Moscow and taking care of Anya during school breaks.

Unfortunately, there was some very sad personal news about this time. On September 29, 1998, Toni House passed away from lung cancer at the age of fifty-five. All nine Supreme Court justices attended her memorial service.

Meanwhile, back in Moscow, Vera undertook a major step up from managing other people's fashion shops. In November, 1998, she bought her own retail shop located on one of the busiest commuting avenues in Moscow leading to one of the wealthiest suburban areas of the city. Her shop, Sunduchok, which means treasure chest in Russian, was a great success and was patronized by many famous Russian actors, singers and dancers.

After Anya graduated from Madeira, she enrolled at Drew University in Madison, New Jersey. Assuming that Anya would spend four years at Drew, Vera and I sold the house in Bethesda and bought a home in Cedar Grove, New Jersey, a residential area halfway between Madison and New York City. Vera went into the city often to meet with fashion designers and place orders for clothing and accessories that would then be shipped to Sunduchok. Vera didn't drive, however, so while we lived in New Jersey, she was completely dependent on me for transportation. This was not very convenient for Vera—she'd had a full-time driver in Moscow for many years.

It was less than convenient for me as well, but it turned out to be a short-lived obligation. During her freshman year at Drew, Anya became fascinated with the arts. To pursue this interest, she transferred to the School of Visual Arts in Manhattan. At that point it made sense for Vera and me to move into the city. We'd not only be close to Anya, but to Chris and Sasha as well. In 2003, we purchased and renovated a two-story co-op penthouse. The building was located on Broadway in the financial district, a block from Ground Zero, an area soon to be completely reconstructed. Since an automobile in Manhattan is a liability, not a convenience, even I decided not to drive. We sold Anya's car, gave mine to my brother, and then enjoyed getting around by subway.

CHAPTER 28

2004

My Father's Passing

My father, then ninety-two, was feeling his age. No longer up to maintaining the DC home he'd lived in for so long, he sold it and moved into an assisted living facility in Georgetown.

Vera and I were still working full time in Moscow, but we visited him as often as we could. On one of these visits, he asked me a question that made it apparent that he was losing his memory. As Vera and I were about to say our farewells for the evening, he paused for a moment, then said, "What is our background, you and me?" Thinking he might have forgotten the details about how his parents had immigrated to the States, I began reminding him, but he soon waved me off. "No," he said. "I mean, how do I know you?"

We talked a bit longer, and as we were leaving for the night, Vera gave him her usual warm smile. "I don't remember her name," Dad whispered to me, "but I will always remember her smile!"

We returned the next morning to say goodbye before heading to Dulles for our flight back to Moscow. This time, he was Dad again, absolutely lucid. He recognized me as his son and Vera as my wife and even said that he'd like to come visit us in Russia.

In June of 2004, Vera and I had just returned to New York, where the renovation of our Broadway co-op apartment was nearing completion. The phone rang; it was my cousin Theo. He and his wife Patty had always been close to my parents. Living in Maryland, where Vera and I were married in their backyard, they visited Dad often at the assisted living facility. On June 3, Theo was calling with sad news. Dad had passed away earlier that day.

My brother Eric, my cousin Alan, and other members of our extended Reuther family joined me in planning a memorial service for Dad at the National Cathedral. It was attended by union and civil rights activists, and by present and former elected officials, including Maryland senator Paul Sarbanes. Many spoke—and some sang—to pay our respects and express our love for my father, the last of that generation of Reuther brothers. When it was my turn to speak, I said:

> *I have now spent half of my life studying, working, and living in Russia. I know Dad was pleased that I had followed in his footsteps in this respect, even though my work in Russia was commercial real estate development, not trade unionism. I think he understood that the philosophy of life taught to him and his three brothers and sister by their father and their mother had been passed on to the next generation of Reuthers, and I know that it is just as important to treasure and maintain these values no matter what your calling is in life. As we say farewell to our father today, I want to reassure him that we will!"*

(One of my favorite photos of Dad. Photo credit: Walter P. Reuther Library, Archives of Labor and Urban Affairs, Wayne State University)

My son Sasha found a way to use his own particular talents to honor his grandfather. While studying film at Tisch at NYU, he' d become fascinated with the life story of his grandfather and his great-uncles and had conducted over ten hours of filmed interviews with Dad. Sasha incorporated parts of those interviews into the highly praised documentary that he wrote, directed, and co-produced. Called *Brothers on the Line*, it was narrated by Martin Sheen. Following its release in 2012, it was shown at film festivals all over the country and received a glowing review in the *New York Times* from award-winning journalist Steven Greenhouse.

(With Sasha during the recording of my interview for his documentary)

CHAPTER 29

2004-2025

Florida

Once we settled into our lower Manhattan co-op, Vera and I often made trips to Fort Myers, Florida to visit my brother Eric and his wife, Deborah. They were living in the home where Mom and Dad had lived during the winter, the one that Uncle Walter and Aunt May had originally purchased as their planned retirement home. We still went back and forth between Moscow and New York, but as we spent more time in the States, Vera and I began thinking about relocating our US residence to Florida.

(With Vera in NYC)

While in New York, Vera was having some dental work done, and she told the dentist about pain she was experiencing in and around her jawline. X-rays taken to pinpoint the source of the problem revealed something significant: she had multiple, deep-seated skull base tumors under her brain. They were removed by one of the city's top surgeons, and we were greatly relieved when the lab confirmed that all of them were benign.

Health experiences like this often give one time to reflect on the bigger questions of life, and when we returned to Moscow, Vera realized that she no longer wished to continue running her boutique. She retained ownership of the shop but leased it out and began to enjoy the rental income it brought, as well as her newfound free time.

When we returned to the States, we again went to Fort Myers to visit Eric and Deborah, but this time we also had the pleasure of linking up with our close Russian friends, Igor Bobrin and Natalia Bestemianova, his wife. Both are internationally acclaimed figure skaters. Natalia and Andrei Bukin, her skating partner, were gold medalists in ice dance at the 1988 Winter Olympics in Calgary. Igor, a four-time Soviet men's figure skating champion, was the 1981 European Men's Champion and World Bronze Medalist.

We first met Igor and Natalia in 1995 at a dinner at the Moscow apartment of Gregory Katsev, my partner in the US Embassy housing project. When Natalia and Igor finished their competitive careers, Gregory helped them organize and manage a touring skating show similar to Ice Capades or Stars on Ice. They toured the world, with great success. They had just returned to Moscow from their shows in India when Gregory and his former wife had them over to dinner and invited Vera and me to join them. Since then, we have become close friends, and our friendship has persisted in multiple locations. When we were in Moscow, we got together all the time. The same was true when we were all in New York and New Jersey. We now have our condo in Naples, Florida, where they also rent a house, as does Gregory with his wife, Natasha.

Igor and Natalia, whom we call Natasha, divide their time between Russia and the United States, and on one of our trips to Fort Myers, they were coaching their clients—young Japanese figure skaters—at the Hertz Arena in Estero, just outside Fort Myers. As soon as we told Igor and Natasha about our interest in exploring a move from New York to Florida, they immediately suggested that while we were nearby, we should take a look at Naples.

Naples is about forty-five minutes south of Fort Myers. Its main commercial thoroughfare, Fifth Avenue South, runs east from the Gulf of Mexico beach for about nine blocks and is full of shops and restaurants. The town won us over instantly. As we were exploring, Vera and I were both able to picture ourselves living here. We were so taken with the community that we walked into a realtor's office and asked her to find us a condo. When she showed us a three-bedroom unit six blocks from the beach and a block off Fifth Avenue South, we purchased it.

In the summer of 2015, we sold our New York duplex penthouse and moved to Naples. Vera had often told me how much she enjoyed living in New York, but now she loves Naples even more. We can walk anywhere—and we do. We share long morning walks to our favorite park, and in the evening along the avenue.

(With Vera and Sasha in Naples)

Misha

After Andrey Popov died in 2013, the remaining owners of the Putnik building started to think about selling it. At the time, Misha and I owned 73 percent, split evenly between us. Six surviving members of Popov's family owned the rest.

As we considered our options, tax accountants told us that it would be in our best financial interest if our respective LLCs, which at the time were the official owners of record, were to sell their interests to us as individuals. Once a buyer for the building had been located, each of us would then sell our personal share to the purchaser. In April 2017, after prolonged negotiations with a Turkish company, we sold the Putnik building to its Russian subsidiary, one piece at a time. The sales price in rubles was over US $14.5 million.

Until the Putnik sale was completed, my Cyprus company continued to receive quarterly profit distributions from Misha's Cyprus company—compensation for my work on the Bolshaya Ordynka Street building. This was the project for which I'd negotiated leases with two banks: Dresdner Bank and the French BNP.

Misha's co-op still owned the building itself. In appreciation for the contributions that Michael and I had made to the success of this project, Misha had authorized quarterly payments from his Cyprus company to our Cyprus companies. Those payments reflected the equity share we'd agreed upon among the three of us when the project began: Misha would keep 50 percent and I'd share the other 50 percent with Michael, keeping 30 percent for myself and giving him the rest. When Michael returned to the States, Misha and I had bought out his equity and split it between us, 10 percent to Misha and 10 percent to me. Once we bought Michael out, Misha's Cyprus company was paying my Cyprus company 40 percent of the quarterly profits.

That was about to change. After we closed the sale of the Putnik building, Misha asked to meet with me, away from the office. He had something he wanted to tell me, and he clearly did not want our staff to be present when he said it. He suggested meeting at a nearby McDonald's, where he casually told me that he would no longer recognize that I had any interest whatsoever in the income generated by the Bolshaya Ordynka building. Going forward, my 40 percent of the revenue stream would shrink to zero.

Misha told me that he had always been offended by the great disparity in our salaries. Apparently, he'd resented me for this for a long time—seemingly for decades. He'd never considered it fair or equitable that as an American, my paycheck was so much larger than his—and that I'd been paid primarily in dollars, not in rubles.

Misha was an attorney who drafted and put together contracts with our construction contractors. He would also negotiate the deals we made with city organizations for our participation in a project. His contribution was valuable, and I understood how the disparity in our compensation might rankle. At the same time, it also seemed to me that Misha wasn't giving me nearly enough credit for the role I'd played in making these projects financially feasible. Upfront payment of three to five years of rent—in hard currency—was an innovative approach to funding new construction, and I was the person who devised and implemented it. I was the one who secured top-of-market lease agreements with major international corporations as tenants. I was the one who convinced them to pay in advance, which was the only way these buildings got built at all. To my knowledge, it was not being done anywhere else in the world, but in the sunset years of the Soviet Union, it was essential.

Equity partners and staff at both PJV and Putnik were aware that I wasn't using my salary to live it up in Moscow. I sent much of it home to support Chris and Sasha, and later Anya, and to pay for their education. Without the equivalent of an American income—paid in dollars, not in rubles—I would have had to seek work elsewhere to support my family.

All that aside, Misha's co-op company had legal ownership rights to the Bolshaya Ordynka building, and I had little or no recourse to contest his decision to cut me off. I was going to take the hit, and it was going to be quite a blow. I estimated that my interest in the building was valued at about $1.5 million, if the building had been sold at that time.

Since my paycheck had obviously been bothering him for a long time, why did he wait until the Putnik building was sold? I can only guess that he wanted to be sure that I had adequate funds to survive without income from the Bolshaya Ordynka building. Whatever his rationale, I told him I didn't think he was being at all fair to me, but he was adamant. I met with Gregory and his key real estate attorney, and they confirmed what I already knew: I had no legal grounds on which to contest this.

It saddens me to this day that this was the end of a long friendship. We had an understanding—if I was in the States and he was in Russia at the time of his birthday or mine, we would connect by phone. No more. That conversation in McDonald's was our last; I've not spoken with him since.

Stranded, Part I

Vera and I still had our large home in the Moscow suburbs, where we lived with Anna Andreyevna, Vera's mother, now in her nineties, her nurse/caregiver, and our four dogs and numerous cats. This was where I had my home office, where I kept all of my files—including the documents I drew on for reference while I was writing this memoir.

As long as I was still earning income in Moscow and we spent more time in Russia than we did outside it, I was required to pay Russian income tax on any worldwide income I earned, including income paid to me in the States by my Cyprus company, which I had now closed. Since I no longer had Russian income, Vera and I made the decision to spend less than half of each year in Russia. This meant that the revenue I was now generating in US financial markets from investing my share of the proceeds from the sale of the Putnik building would not be subject to any Russian tax obligation.

How would the Russians know how much I earned outside Russia? Ever since I met Boris while working for Satra in Moscow in 1978, I had a feeling that "the boys" were following everything I did, anywhere in the world. As a result, it never occurred to me to try to hide any financial or tax information. I have no reason to believe that anything has changed.

For years while working in the USSR/Russia, I used the financial auditing firm Price Waterhouse to draw up and file both my Russian and US tax declarations. My company also paid income tax in Cyprus. Now, Michael Morgenstern, my former business partner and still close friend, handles my finances, even though he won't accept a penny for it.

Vera and I continued to divide our time between Russia and the US and traveled to the States about three times a year. We spent most of that time in Naples, but also visited New York to spend time with

Sasha, with Chris and his husband, Al, and their twin sons Tommy and Luca, and with Anya and her husband, John, and their son Avery and daughter Hunter.

(Front row: Vera's sister Galina, Anya with Avery, and Vera. Back row: Chris with Luca, me, Al with Tommy, and John)

In all our visits to New York and Florida, we'd never been able to be here long enough at a stretch for Vera to apply for a green card. To preserve her ability to travel back and forth, she applied for and received three-year multiple-entry visas from our embassy in Moscow.

This didn't become a problem until 2020, when COVID changed how and where we traveled. Vera and I left the States for Russia on February 5, intending to stay just a few months. While there, we planned to renew Vera's multiple-entry visa, which would expire that April. Shortly after we arrived in Moscow, however, the pandemic shut down almost all international travel, and the US Embassy stopped issuing or renewing entry visas.

We were stuck there for more than eight months. We finally solved the problem because of my long-standing friendship with British attorney Paul Melling, who was still practicing law in the Moscow offices of Baker & McKenzie. I'd known him for decades—in 1989, I had negotiated his firm's Moscow office lease when I was at Perestroika. In 2020, in addition to his ongoing responsibilities at Baker & McKenzie, Paul was serving as the chief legal advisor to the British Ambassador in Moscow. This was a post he'd held for some time, and he was able to use his close contacts in the American Embassy on our behalf to persuade them to issue Vera a new visa. On November 11, we finally returned to the States.

Eric

One of the benefits of spending so much time in Naples was that we were able to see my brother Eric and his wife Deborah frequently. Sadly, however, Eric's health began to decline. He suffered from bleeding aneurysms in his stomach and leg, and despite several rounds of surgery, the bleeding continued. Since post-op recovery was both painful and debilitating, Eric refused to have any more operations and instead chose to receive hospice care at home.

Vera and I always spent the winter holidays in the United States. We usually flew back to Moscow in mid-February, after watching the Super Bowl with family and friends. Eric's birthday was February 1, so we often had the chance to help him blow out the candles before we left. In 2022, Sasha flew in for Eric's birthday. I picked him up at the airport, and although Vera was unable to join us, we drove to Eric's home for his eightieth birthday. We had a wonderful time celebrating this milestone with Eric and Deborah and her brother, Eric Ward, and several other close friends, but it turned out to be the last time I saw my brother. He succumbed to a fatal heart attack on February 22.

*(One of my favorite pictures and memories with brother
Eric, on a family holiday in 2013)*

Stranded, Part II

Vera and I were in Moscow when he died, but we had already planned out our next trip to Florida. I had booked and paid for our nonstop flights—Moscow-Miami-Moscow—on Aeroflot, the Russian airline, but we now wanted to move up the trip and come back as soon as possible to help organize a memorial service for Eric.

That simple plan fell victim to world events. On February 24, two days after Eric passed away, Russia invaded Ukraine. Aeroflot was immediately placed under international sanction. Their flights were not only banned from US airspace but from the airspace of many Western European countries as well.

With Aeroflot grounded indefinitely, I was about to find out the hard way that the war in Ukraine had other far-reaching ramifications as well.

I had booked our tickets through Expedia, and when I contacted them to reschedule, I expected to be able to pay for them with credit from our canceled Aeroflot reservations.

I was quickly informed that was not an option. There would be no refund, and the only way I could use the credit was to fly somewhere else on Aeroflot. One of the few airlines still flying to and from Russia and also to the US was Turkish Airlines, and I was able to get reservations for Vera and me on one of their flights from Moscow to Istanbul, and then on a connecting flight to Miami. So far, so good, but when I tried to pay for the tickets with a credit card, none of them would work. My credit cards had been issued by American banks, but it was clear that I was booking our flights from a location inside Russia. It was a *Catch-22* situation: since Russia was under sanction, I essentially had no credit whatsoever until I left the country, but as long as my credit cards were useless, I had no way of paying to get out.

To break the impasse, I reached out to my cousin Mark Richey, and he was able to help. Mark is the son of my father's sister, my late Aunt Christine, and runs Mark Richey Woodworking, a high-end architectural woodworking firm that designs and installs large-scale finished carpentry projects for museums, corporate headquarters, and academic institutions across the country. After a few emails back and forth, Mark's wife Teresa booked and paid for our tickets. I reimbursed them as soon as Vera and I returned to Naples. We were finally able to return to the States on March 22, 2022, and we were soon joined by extended family members and close family friends for a memorial celebration of Eric's life.

I've not been back to Russia since. Vera has returned several times, primarily to see her mother, but also to try to access some of her investment funds. When Vera sold her shop in 2018, she invested most of the proceeds through Russian banks. Those banks had reinvested her money through Western European investment firms. With the war in Ukraine, however, those investment firms refused to deal with the now-sanctioned Russian banks. This meant that Vera was frozen out of access to most of her money, other than rubles earning interest in Moscow.

It was important for Vera to free up whatever she could. We needed the funds to cover the cost of maintaining our home outside Moscow and to pay her mother's caregiver. Sadly, soon after Vera returned to Naples from Russia in late June 2023, her mother passed away. She was just three months shy of her hundredth birthday.

Both of us now spend the bulk of our time in the United States, and hope that the war in Ukraine ends as soon as possible. Vera was finally able to apply for her green card, which she received in April of 2025.

Epilogue

During the dispute with Popov over the Putnik project in the early 1990s, I got to know a gentleman by the name of Yevgeny Monakhov, whom we hired as our new executive director after the leadership shakeup. Yevgeny and I began to spend considerable time together and, when we were out walking one day, we got to talking about educational backgrounds. Though Yevgeny was younger than I was, I learned that he had graduated from the physics department of Moscow State University. He not only knew my friend Kolya—the commander of the student construction detachment from my summer of 1969 in Kazakhstan—but had worked with him on similar student brigades.

Learning of that happy coincidence, I told Yevgeny that I would love to link up with my old friend again. He then shared some upsetting news: Kolya had died about a year and half earlier. Apparently, he had been drinking heavily on a fishing trip and had drowned while swimming. I was shocked and deeply saddened to hear this. I mourned his passing, and I mourned the loss of the friendship we had shared.

Many years later, I met up with Kolya's daughter and son at our home outside of Moscow. We exchanged photos, and I played a few audio recordings for them from my student construction brigade days. Kolya can be heard on the tapes. Hearing their father's voice was surely an emotional moment for his now adult children, and it was emotional for me as well. They presented me with something just as precious and just as personal: a handwritten letter from me to Kolya that they had discovered in a small collection of his personal files.

I recognized the envelope as soon as I saw it. I had picked it up from the American embassy; it bore a postage stamp commemorating the historic Apollo 11 moon landing. Dated September 9, 1969, and written in Russian, the letter inside read: "Kolya, let's get together at my place at

6 o'clock Friday. At first, we will go out to drink some cocktails and then meet with the ambassador."

That night and surrounding events suddenly came rushing back to me. I had invited Kolya to join me at a farewell dinner for an embassy staffer who had been so kind and helpful during my time in Moscow. Ambassador Jacob D. Beam and his wife were at our table that evening. The letter in my hands was short and simple, but seeing it again was a powerful reminder of how close Kolya and I had become.

Our friendship undoubtedly raised our profile with "the boys" of the clandestine services—on both sides. I know that they monitored my comings and goings, as well as those of my friends. Kolya came with me to events that were supposedly for Americans only, including that farewell embassy dinner and a meeting with Senator Eugene McCarthy during his visit to Moscow in January of 1970.

Without question, our friendship made Kolya's life more difficult with Soviet authorities, and I am responsible for some of that. After he had offered me access to unauthorized travel, I had foolishly spoken openly and excitedly about my trip to Kuybyshev and Tolyatti, an area foreigners were strictly forbidden to enter. Kolya lost most of his potential for leadership at Moscow State University and with the construction detachments. He was removed as commander of the brigade. I can only imagine how such demotions affected his ability to get work after he graduated. One can't help but wonder if a troubled life led to his untimely death.

As I look back at my life in the former Soviet Union, especially during those early years, I regret some of my actions and the unintended consequences they may have had. I was by nature open and straightforward with all my contacts, whether Russian, American, or otherwise, but I didn't always take the long-term effects of this honesty into account. My youthful naivete and my genuine desire to bridge a cultural divide through shared experiences—an intention which is with me still—overrode what should have been commonsense caution about what to say, and to whom. Although I understood the value of talking to "the boys" on both sides in diplomacy and in business, I should have been more careful, especially during those particularly sensitive and dangerous times of the Cold War.

In the process of assembling stories for this memoir, I became more aware of a running theme: I am a community organizer, as were my parents. I did so in a somewhat different form and under different conditions, but the roots of my approach would appear to be genetic. As I pointed out in the Prologue, my father believed in talking to everybody, which is why Russian trade union representatives were at our home on that fateful evening when Harry Givorgian offered to arrange a year of study in Moscow for me.

Talk to everybody... No matter the stage in my career—politics, real estate development, or international relations—I prioritized person-to-person connections and sought ways to unite opposing sides for a common purpose. It's because I cared so deeply for the American and Russian people that I felt compelled to bring those communities together as often as possible and to talk, a lot.

Recently I came across a Facebook post of mine from March 4, 2014, written shortly after Russia occupied and annexed Crimea, which had been part of the nation of Ukraine. It was an emotional time. As I look back on my life more than a decade later, the war between Russia and Ukraine is ongoing, and I believe my writing has even greater urgency and relevance now than it did then. The post I wrote at the time provides a good summary of my life, my cultural bonds, and my dedication to finding that common purpose that ties us all together. It was originally accompanied by a photo, but the actual image is not the point.

Why am I posting a photo of this beautiful child? She could be an American child, or French, or British, German, Canadian, Italian, or Ukrainian, just to name a few countries where I have close friends. But this child happens to be Russian, from where I am writing this post today, a country where I have spent 75 percent of my life, over the last 41 years. We all have such photos of our children, whom we love and whom we will protect with any means from harm. But I am posting this photo not to show a Russian child, but to show the face of what we all can understand is the future of humanity on this planet!

In the late 1960s, I was a graduate language student at Moscow State University (MSU), arriving in the USSR only days after the 1968 Soviet incursion into Czechoslovakia. I spent two years at MSU during the height of the Vietnam war, when the largest contingent of foreign students at the University were Vietnamese (and not those supporting the USA). During this period, you can understand that I had many opportunities for political disagreement with my fellow students in Moscow, and we did disagree. During the summer of 1969, I went to the steppes of Kazakhstan with a group of physics students from MSU, where we worked together in a student volunteer construction brigade, building a hospital and farm-related structures. We worked, not just as close friends, but as brothers and sisters, and we did not always agree. But in our disagreements, we did not question each other's moral character and values. We recognized that we each viewed the world around us from the perspective of our own personal experiences, family values, educational background and history of each of our countries.

In 1978, I returned to Moscow as an American businessman, working for three more years during the height of the Cold war, during a time when the Soviets took forces into Afghanistan, and the US and other countries fought back with military aid to the mujahideen and with economic and political sanctions, even an Olympic boycott against the USSR. I was fortunate to have close friends among the Russian staff who worked at our American trading company those three years, and I am proud to have some of them as Facebook friends today. Did we agree with each other politically then and now? No, and on some issues, we still openly disagree today, but so do I disagree with my American Republican friends. But once again, we are all shaped by our upbringing, history, and personal and social background and experiences.

During the 1980s, I worked with a Washington institute that brought together Soviet and American specialists on regional conflicts, in an effort to understand our differences in developing countries with internal conflicts, where the Soviets were militarily supporting one side and the

US the other. We even traveled together to Afghanistan with a high-level joint delegation while the Soviet forces were still there. Who knows if we had any impact? Certainly, we cannot take credit for the Soviets leaving Afghanistan in the late 1980s, and I don't think anyone will blame us for the US actions in Afghanistan since 2001. But the point is that we brought together like-minded people to talk and try to understand our differences, in the hope that peaceful means of resolution would prevail.

Since 1988, I have been developing and managing commercial real estate in Moscow, and during this period of what we all felt was a gradual ending of the Cold War and period of increasing cooperation between countries, most of the disagreements I have had with my Russian colleagues have been business related, not political. That doesn't mean that I found much support here for US foreign policy, some of which I questioned myself, (i.e., the war in Iraq), but over the years, I have developed close friendships in Russia as strong as close friendships I have with my friends and family in the US. I also have family in Russia, as my wife, Vera, is Russian, and we live here with her daughter Anya and Vera's 90-year-old mother, who lost most of her family during World War II, and whose favorite toast to this day is still "Let there not be war!"

So why am I posting a photo of a child that I call the face of the future of humanity on our planet? Because we are going through a political crisis in the world today arising from events in Ukraine. I have close Russian friends, and I have close Ukrainian friends, and we all have children and grandchildren for whom we want to make the world a safer place. Let us all take this opportunity to think and not just act! Let us show the strength that comes from understanding our differences and working with each other to understand each other and each other's history and try to quiet the fears that come from a lack of feeling for the differences that we all have. This is a time for strength of character and moral strength, which is much more powerful than any strength of arms. We owe this to all children and to ourselves.

I am an American who loves his country for all that is good about it. I was raised in the United States during the Cold War and saw everything that happened from the American perspective. I fell in love with a Russian woman, who also loves her country and was also raised during the Cold War. We lived through the same events, the same history, but she saw it all from the opposite perspective. And what have I learned all these years since I first set foot in Russia? As people, we want the same things for ourselves and our families. We want to believe in our countries and our systems of government, but we each see problems that need to be fixed. I have tried to live my life in a way that helps us understand each other, in a way that helps bring our two countries together, based on mutual understanding, mutual interests, and mutual respect. The world will be a much safer and much more livable place when we do.

Acknowledgments

First and foremost, I am deeply grateful to my son, Sasha, whose unwavering support and insight were instrumental at every stage of this memoir. In the early days of writing in my home office outside Moscow, I was able to find so much helpful information looking through the faxes I'd sent Sasha—and other family members—relating events as they transpired in Russia. Sasha's experience as a documentary producer—especially his work on *Brothers on the Line*—and his deep knowledge of our family's history brought invaluable depth and clarity to this project.

I also wish to thank my son Chris, my daughter Anya, my brother Eric, my former wife Jill, and my dear friend Michael Morgenstern. Each offered essential memories and details that helped shape the narrative with authenticity and heart.

To my editor, Kay Diehl, thank you for transforming a sprawling first draft into a cohesive and thoughtful manuscript. Your global perspective and editorial precision were a true gift. I'm also grateful to Alison Schwartz, Nate Roberson, and the team at Gotham Ghostwriters for connecting us, and to Mona Houck at Miller Korzenik Rayman LLP for her legal guidance.

My sincere thanks to Gordon McClellan and the team at DartFrog Books for believing in this collection of memories and for your steadfast support throughout the publishing process.

I am especially thankful to Yevgeny Monakhov, whose connection to my 1969 summer in Kazakhstan led me to Slava Matveyev. Slava's photos and recollections brought those experiences vividly back to life.

Finally, to my wife Vera, thank you for your love, patience, and perspective. Your understanding of history and the Russian spirit enriched this memoir in countless ways. I hope these pages reflect the partnership we share and our enduring belief in unity and peace.

About the Author

John Reuther was born in Detroit, MI to a family of trailblazing labor organizers and political activists. From the 1930s through the '70s, his father Victor and uncles Walter and Roy led the United Auto Workers (UAW), transforming the fledgling union into a powerful force for social and economic justice in America and abroad. Raised in Washington, DC, John majored in US-Soviet Relations at American University while working in LBJ's War on Poverty program and on Bobby Kennedy's primary campaign in California. Disillusioned by the war in Vietnam and death of RFK, John enrolled in a study-abroad program in the late 1960s. He spent two years learning Russian and conducting research at Moscow State University. It was a profound experience that shaped the trajectory of his life.

After resuming his political work in the US for a few years, John returned to Russia, where he would spend almost forty years. There he worked with non-profit organizations and in business development. John directed the first US-Soviet commercial real estate joint venture, Perestroika JV, and became Chairman & CEO of JSR Holdings Limited, a Moscow-based real estate development, finance, marketing and building management company.

With a deep understanding of the language, culture, and business climate in Russia, John Reuther shares his unique experiences as the son of one of American labor's preeminent families turned capitalist adventurer abroad.

www.ingramcontent.com/pod-product-compliance
Lightning Source LLC
Chambersburg PA
CBHW020903060726
47591CB00004B/1062